# REFLECTIONS IN A
# MALE EYE

# REFLECTIONS IN A
# MALE EYE

## JOHN HUSTON AND THE
## AMERICAN EXPERIENCE

**EDITED BY
GAYLYN STUDLAR AND DAVID DESSER**

**SMITHSONIAN INSTITUTION PRESS
WASHINGTON AND LONDON**

Editor: Tom Ireland
Production Editor: Jack Kirshbaum
Designer: Kathleen Sims


Library of Congress Cataloging-in-Publication Data

Reflections in a male eye: John Huston and the American experience /
edited by Gaylyn Studlar and David Desser.
p. cm.
Includes an interview with, and short stories by Huston.
Includes bibliographical references and index.
**ISBN 1-56098-194-6 (cloth); 1-56098-292-6 (paper)**
1. Huston, John, 1906–1987—Criticism and interpretation. 2. Men
in motion pictures. I. Huston, John, 1906–1987 Selections. 1993.
II. Studlar, Gaylyn. III. Desser, David.
PN1998.3.H87R44 1993
791.43'0233'092—dc20     92-43059

British Library Cataloging-in-Publication data available

Manufactured in the United States of America
96 95 94 93          5 4 3 2 1

∞ The paper used in this publication meets the minimum requirements
of the American National Standard for Permanence of Paper for Printed
Library Materials Z39.48-1984.

Cover illustration: John Huston. Photo by Irving Penn. Courtesy Vanity
Fair. Copyright © 1983 by the Condé Nast Publications Inc.

For permission to reproduce any of the illustrations, please correspond
directly with the sources. The Smithsonian Institution Press does not
retain reproduction rights for these illustrations individually or maintain a
file of addresses for photo sources.

FOR OUR DADS

# Contents

# Foreword

J ohn Huston belonged to a generation of Hollywood filmmakers
whose most successful mem-
bers—such as Orson Welles, Preston Sturges, and Billy Wilder—typically
not only directed but wrote and even acted in their films. Of this elite,
Huston enjoyed the longest career. He began to direct in 1941 with *The
Maltese Falcon* and died in 1987 while working on the production of *The
Dead*. His remarkable career spanned the studio system at its peak, the
breakup of that system, World War II, blacklisting, the rise of television,
the Civil Rights movement, and Vietnam. This longevity, the critical
praise garnered by much of his later work, and his daughter Anjelica's
successful if somewhat offbeat acting career (which extended the family
dynasty begun by his father, Walter Huston) assured John Huston of extensive media attention in recent years, with commercial presses publishing
several biographies and family portraits.

Yet, as Gaylyn Studlar and David Desser point out, Huston has not been a darling of the academy. When auteur criticism was at its height, the movie critic Andrew Sarris damned him as a once-competent craftsman who had suffered a dismaying decline—a nowhere man who did not believe in the action ethos yet staged intimate scenes as if playing croquet with a sledgehammer. Huston's successful work was often attributed to casting coups; they were "Bogart pictures" more than "Huston pictures" (six films written or directed by Huston starred Bogart). Then in the late 1960s and 1970s, with the rise of militantly leftist critiques that often were informed by the work of Louis Althusser, Huston's films were typically seen as too complicit with the ideological apparatus of Hollywood, particularly in comparison to those of Welles and Sturges, whose Hollywood careers were relatively stormy and brief. And in an era that has been profoundly influenced by feminist theory, Huston's preoccupation with the male psyche and homosocial world made him appear hopelessly retrograde. Barely a decade ago, a film such as *Reflections in a Golden Eye* (1967) was easily dismissed as a reactionary picture of the worst kind.

Today new concerns and perspectives make Huston a figure that cultural historians are able to engage with greater sympathy and understanding. In recent years, the rise of poststructuralist theory and a renewed emphasis on history have transformed film studies; consistency and coherence—trademarks of an outmoded auteurist approach—have ceased to be simple, absolute criteria for value. Scholars have become more accepting of—and intrigued by—gaps, lacunae, and disturbances in the careers of filmmakers. They are more interested in the larger industrial and social framework of filmmaking practices. Moreover, the issue of masculinity and male identity has again become a serious topic for discussion, not only as a response to and extension of feminist theory and criticism but in relation to the new problematic of sexual identity posed by gay theory. It can provide a necessary perspective on films such as *Reflection in a Golden Eye*, which offers a superficially banal but finally painful and damning portrait of military life during peacetime: An army captain (Marlon Brando) cannot cope with his own homosexual longings and so ultimately kills the enlisted man to whom he finds himself attracted. This disturbing film of the Vietnam era, which seems to favor a psychoanalytic rather than a Marxist insight into American involvement in Southeast Asia, inspired the title for this book, *Reflections in a Male Eye: John Huston and the American Experience*. The editor's choice for a title was particularly astute, for the film itself has a synechdochal relationship to the problematic of Huston as director, writer, and author.

The ways in which Huston could be used to explore issues of authorship and sexual identity—and vice versa—were not at all obvious three years ago when Studlar and Desser began to create this book. I came to appreciate their perspicacity, and that of their essayists, while reading many of these articles in manuscript. I found myself thinking about Huston differently and going back to many of his films—and seeing others for the first time. This book should stimulate readers in a similar fashion and make Huston an object of more serious intellectual discussion and inquiry. Studlar and Desser have gathered together a group of provocative articles—many published for the first time, others revised or now republished in a fresh context. They have reprinted two of Huston's early short stories, an interview with the writer-director previously available only in French, and short essays by James Agee and Andrew Sarris that have tended to frame previous discussions about Huston. Not only a timely intervention, this book exemplifies the multivocal employment of written materials that will keep film and television studies a vital discourse.

Charles Musser
Yale University

# Acknowledgments

**T**his book has its roots in a film studies class we both took as graduate students at the University of Southern California with Professor Drew Casper. We wish to thank Drew for giving us an enthusiastic introduction to Huston's films. David's panel for the joint conference of the Society for Cinema Studies and the University Film and Video Association in 1988 also contributed to our decision to put together a book on Huston. Our thanks to those who participated in that panel and to all who submitted manuscripts in response to our call for articles for this book. Thanks go also to David Cook, who first told us of Smithsonian's interest in publishing works on American directors and who helped initiate our contact with Martin Williams at the press. We thank Martin for his wonderfully encouraging response to our project. Charlie Musser and Mark Hirsch continued our author-editor relationship at Smithsonian with a spirit of generous cooperation and kind concern. We also appreciate the comments for revision provided by

William Luhr and our other manuscript reviewer, which were indispensable to the completion of the book. Also indispensable were Judy Kallman and JoAnn Carrier, who worked tirelessly in word processing this manuscript through the steamy Atlanta summer, and Annie Hall, who kept it all running smoothly. We are also indebted to our authors, who were flexible, understanding, and inexplicably patient with us. We appreciate their unwavering commitment to this project from beginning to end. Finally, thanks go to our spouses, Thomas Haslett and Cathy Desser, for always being there.

A number of the articles and documents in this volume have been published previously. Minor changes have been made in some of them for stylistic consistency. The editors and Smithsonian Institution Press gratefully acknowledge the following for permission to reprint these materials:

Gary Edgerton. "Revisiting the Recording of Wars Past: Remembering the Documentary Trilogy of John Huston," *Journal of Popular Film and Television* 15, no. 1 (Spring 1987): 27–41. Reprinted with permission of the Helen Dwight Reid Educational Foundation. Published by Heldref Publications, 4000 Albermarle St. N.W., Washington, D.C. 20016. Copyright © 1987.

James Naremore. "John Huston and *The Maltese Falcon*," *Literature/Film Quarterly* 1, no. 3 (1973): 239–49. Reprinted by permission.

The interview with John Huston originally appeared as "Recontre avec Rui Nogueira et Bertrand Tavernier," *Positif* 116 (May 1970).

"Undirectable Director" reprinted by permission of Grosset & Dunlap from *Agee on Film,* vol. 1, by James Agee. Copyright © 1958 by the James Agee Trust; copyright © renewed 1986 by Teresa, Andrea, and John Agee.

Andrew Sarris. "John Huston." From *The American Cinema* (New York: Dutton, 1968), 156–58. Use by permission of the publisher, Dutton, an imprint of New American Library, a division of Penguin Books USA, Inc.

Andrew Sarris. "Johnny, We Finally Knew Ye." *Village Voice,* May 19, 1980, 49. Reprinted by permission of the author and the *Village Voice.*

# Introduction

GAYLYN STUDLAR

T he thirty-seven narrative films and three major wartime documentaries directed by John Huston constitute a paradoxical and somewhat perplexing oeuvre. From the time he emerged as a promising director-screenwriter during the heyday of the Hollywood studio system, to the posthumous release of his last feature film, *The Dead,* in 1987, Huston directed films encompassing almost every genre and including such indisputable classics as *The Maltese Falcon* (1941), *The Treasure of the Sierra Madre* (1948), *The African Queen* (1951), *Beat the Devil* (1954), *The Misfits* (1961), *The Asphalt Jungle* (1950), *Fat City* (1972), and *The Man Who Would Be King* (1975), as well as the controversial documentaries of World War II: *Report from the Aleutians* (1943), *The Battle of San Pietro* (1945), and *Let There Be Light* (1946/1981). Nevertheless, in spite of some dozen Academy Award nominations, Oscars for writing and directing, Directors Guild honors, and the American Film Institute Life Achievement Award, Huston was alternately

1

praised and vilified by critics throughout much of his six-decade career as a director, screenwriter, and actor.

The extreme terms of this paradoxical pattern of response to Huston's filmmaking career were perhaps first established in 1950, when James Agee wrote of the man who would later become his collaborator: "The most inventive director of his generation, Huston has done more to extend, invigorate and purify the essential idiom of American movies, the truly visual telling of stories, than anyone since the prime of D. W. Griffith."[1] The critical and popular success of *The Asphalt Jungle* and *The African Queen* appeared to confirm Agee's early "canonization" of Huston,[2] but this high praise would seem embarrassingly premature by the end of the decade, when *The Barbarian and the Geisha* (1958) and *The Roots of Heaven* (1958) suggested that Huston's talent was in decline or had been something of a mirage to begin with. Huston's directorial efforts in the 1960s often appeared ambitious but consistently flawed, with *The Misfits, Freud* (1962), *The Night of the Iguana* (1964), and *Reflections in a Golden Eye* (1967) each receiving (at best) a mixed critical reception.

The reception of these films, however, seemed generous when compared to the critical disdain that generally greeted other Huston projects of the same decade, including *The Unforgiven* (1960), *The List of Adrian Messenger* (1963), *The Bible* (1966), *Casino Royale* (1967), *Sinful Davey* (1969), and *A Walk with Love and Death* (1969). In the 1970s, after the release of the startlingly cynical *Kremlin Letter* (1970),[3] a Huston comeback was announced with the release of *Fat City* and then again with *The Man Who Would Be King*. In spite of the notable success of these films, the uneven pattern of his most recent work raised doubt that Huston could repeat either the critical success of *Fat City* or the combined critical and box-office success that greeted *The Man Who Would Be King*. His career appeared to be dogged by an inability (willful or inadvertent) to recognize poor scripts, including that for *The Life and Times of Judge Roy Bean* (1972). In a characteristic comment, combining candor with ironic defensiveness, Huston once defended the patchwork of his career by saying: "I thought it was better to do a picture than rob a bank."[4] But he was obviously aware that his output, as varied as it always was in terms of genre, also varied widely in quality. His direction of *The Mackintosh Man* (1973) supposedly spurred his renewed interest in filming Kipling's "The Man Who Would Be King" because he so desperately wanted a project that "would be something we could hold our heads up about afterward."[5]

Huston was able to hold up his head after the release of *The Man Who Would Be King*, but his career was interrupted by open-heart surgery. He returned to film with another critical (though not box-office) success, an adaptation of Flannery O'Connor's grimly funny *Wise Blood* (1979), which Huston turned into an equally grim and funny film. The 1980s were marked by an uneven beginning redeemed by *Prizzi's Honor* (1985) and *The Dead*, films that evoked the kind of critical praise usually reserved for the work of "old masters." Even this praise, with its predictable rhetorical hyperbole, could be considered a kind of curious and paradoxical return to the beginning of Huston's directorial career—to the praise that had washed over him and many of his film efforts of the early years. Yet, this phenomenon raises a question: Was the praise forthcoming because the last films were so very good or because Huston was so very old (or so very dead when his last film was released)? This is exactly the kind of irreverent question that Huston might have chortled over—or dealt with in his films in his characteristically ironic way.

The ironies regarding the critical reception of Huston's work persist, for in spite of the ultimate rehabilitation of Huston's reputation in the popular press, his films continue to suffer from scholarly neglect. The notable exceptions to this occur when films such as *The Maltese Falcon* and *The Asphalt Jungle* are discussed as part of a larger category (in this case, *film noir*) that is of ongoing interest to the film studies field. One of the few serious attempts to deal with the director's career acknowledges "the widely held assumption that John Huston's life is more interesting than his films."[6] John Huston's biography may be a more popular subject than his films because, as David Desser relates in the "Biographical Sketch" in part 3 of this volume, Huston's life was an unusually colorful one for a director; his various exploits, both behind the camera and apart from it, often made deliciously juicy copy for those interested in excess (gambling, womanizing, etc.). Huston's autobiography, *An Open Book*, capitalized on the interest in the "adventure" that was his life, as do numerous other articles, interviews, and books, including William F. Nolan's *John Huston: King Rebel* and Peter Viertel's fictionalized account of the making of *The African Queen, White Hunter, Black Heart.*[7]

The seemingly unabated trend to ignore Huston's films and instead dwell on his life, on the lives of members of his family, or on the production histories of his films, nevertheless, by itself cannot fully explain the long-standing tendency of film scholarship to ignore his films. This tendency is attributable, in part, to a precedent set in the mid-1960s by the "auteur theory" and critics such as Andrew Sarris, who helped make up the first wave of director-centered, "serious" American film studies. In pursuing the noteworthy goal of resurrecting Hollywood film and American directors from critical condescension, Sarris proceeded to bury Huston. In his 1968 book, *The American Cinema: Directors and Directions, 1929–1968,* he dismissed Huston as one of those directors "with reputations in excess of inspirations."[8] Huston could not be an *auteur,* Sarris concluded, because his films lacked the stamp of his personality as well as a unique personal vision. Along with Elia Kazan and William Wyler, Huston was relegated to directorial purgatory, to a category of directors whose work was described as "Less than Meets the Eye." Sarris went on to attribute much of the success of Huston's films to "casting coups" rather than to "directorial acumen."[9] In the same year as Sarris's devastating assessment of his work, Huston, possibly in response, dismissed American film criticism as "about the worst in the world."[10]

In taking Huston's films as the subject of our interest rather than his life, our anthology has two primary purposes. First, we do not think it is necessary to reconsider Huston's films because of some nostalgic wish to elevate the director to a pantheon of auteurs from which he was formerly excluded. Although any director-centered anthology, by its very nature, inescapably implies the importance of the director as a figure participating in making the meaning produced by his or her films, the articles in this anthology do not collectively attempt to sustain the view that John Huston is the sole source of meaning and the sole interpretative key to "his" films. On the contrary, our first goal is to demonstrate that a director-centered anthology, while "auteurist" in some sense of the word, need not perpetuate some idealistic notion of personalized cinematic authorship transcending the boundaries of either institutional or ideological constraints. As Robert Sklar notes in his contribution to this volume, "Huston's role as author is inseparable from industrial and ideological contexts." His remark could be taken as the fundamental starting point for many of the articles in this collection. We hope to show, through a plurality of critical approaches to a number of different films, that the meaning of the films directed by John Huston is not unproblematically reducible to directorial personality (if that is possible to precisely locate), but neither is it reducible to historical or political context or to industrial constraints. We wish to keep the notion of multiple determinants in mind, even as we build on the primary assumption that certain directors—in this instance, John Huston—provide an important mediation point for various influences on the film text and do, in spite of the complex collaborative nature of most filmmaking practice, deserve investigation in terms of their role in that creative process.

Our second intention is to reconsider Huston as a distinctly American filmmaker who is widely regarded, as Martin Rubin notes in his article, as a "quintessentially male director." On one level, certain Huston films such as *The Red Badge of Courage* (1951), *The Misfits,* and *Wise Blood* depict characters, settings, experiences, or systems of belief that may appear to be uniquely (or in the case of *Wise Blood,* perversely) American. Nevertheless, the "Americanness" of Huston's films resides also in their discursive strategies and in the dynamics created between film, filmmaker, production system, and the historically specific cultural context. Although our anthology includes discussion of many films in the Huston canon that are overtly American in subject matter or point of view, it also includes analyses of films that speak to other aspects of the issue as we define it more broadly: to film as a discourse of national values and beliefs, to the changing Hollywood production system, and to the storytelling codes of Hollywood film as a product to be consumed and a text to be understood and experienced by an audience.

Our anthology is divided into three sections. Part 1 concentrates on the relationship between ideology and Huston's films as interpretations of American experience. Part 2 explores the representation of masculinity in his films. Part 3 consists of a biographical sketch, an interview with Huston, examples of Huston's own published writing, and seminal contributions to the critical debate surrounding him. A complete filmography and a selected bibliography follow.

The essays in part 1 go beyond the boundaries of any one film to analyze contexts and intertexts, both pervasive and specific, and their influence on Huston's films. These contexts range from the original source material that provides the basis of the film script to the historically and nationally specific conditions of production, from the film's place within a generic category, to its place within a changing cultural and political climate in the United States.

The Hollywood production system, a key contextual determinant of filmic meaning throughout the anthology, is emphasized in part 1. Excluding any critical argument over the "quality" of his films, the sheer longevity of Huston's career should attract attention from scholars. His work as a director and as a screenwriter merits attention in its revelation of the historically and economically determined conditions of American cinema's production and reception. The films Huston directed are exceptional as a body of work in that they span the studio system of the 1940s, the wartime government production of information and propaganda, and the emergence of independent international filmmaking in the 1950s; they even extend into the conglomerate-ruled domain of Hollywood in the 1980s.

In different ways, the essays by David Desser, Gary Edgerton, Robert Sklar, John Engell, and Stephen Cooper address some or all of these related questions: How does ideologically inflected meaning arise from a given Huston film taken to be a point of conjunction for various contexts? What were the historically and ideologically determined constraints on various Huston films? How did these constraints affect how his films appear to affirm or question dominant American values of the time? Can some of his films be seen as critical of American society or specific aspects of that society? Are there linkages between his films in their treatment of ideologically infused issues?

Part 1 begins with David Desser's response to critics who deny that Huston's films reflect a cohesive worldview. Taking an auteur-influenced stance toward filmic authorship, Desser examines the bipolar *"noir"* and "therapeutic" dimensions of Huston's wartime films, both the fiction and nonfiction ones. By exploring a formative period in Huston's filmmaking career, Desser shows how Huston's three wartime documentaries follow these two "significant strands" of vision, which continue to be played upon throughout Huston's postwar narrative films. These strands, argues Desser, grow out of the context of Huston's own combat experience and his exposure to psychoanalytic theory and practice during the 1940s. It is in *Key Largo* (1948), Desser shows, that these strands are most memorably played out as a related pair. His article also raises the question of whether later Huston films demand analysis in terms of these elements.

Also refocusing critical attention on Huston's wartime documentaries, Gary Edgerton provides a different contextualizing approach to these three films in his article, "Revisiting the Recordings of Wars Past: Remembering the Documentary Trilogy of John Huston." Edgerton suggests that these controversial films "afford a privileged view of a wider spectrum of feelings, insights, and attitudes about living through and fighting the 'good war' than those provided by any other American documentaries produced in this period." Edgerton argues that these films may ulti-

6

mately be less subversive of dominant ideology than has been suggested by critics who label them "antiwar." He shows how the documentaries include clearly established "authoritarian aspects" that serve a "propaganda imperative," while at the same time they anticipate cinema vérité, with that nonfiction film style's presumably different ideological implications. Although the films' hybrid of documentary styles might seem of limited subversive value to modern-day viewers, Edgerton demonstrates why Huston's documentaries were remarkable achievements for their time, both for ideological and stylistic reasons. Edgerton's article also serves to anticipate some of the concerns of the articles in part 2, for he shows that not only did these documentaries predate cinema vérité experiments by a number of years, but from film to film they increasingly worked to demystify the "myth of the invincible warrior" when valorization of that male myth appeared to be culturally and politically indispensable to American thinking.

Robert Sklar's article, "Havana Situation: The Revolutionary Situation of *We Were Strangers*," addresses the ideological contradictions raised by Huston's 1949 film about political terrorists in Cuba. The film is an early example of a subgenre of Hollywood films about Third World revolutionary situations that has become more prevalent in recent years with the release of films such as *The Year of Living Dangerously, Salvador,* and *Havana.* That Huston's film would anticipate by many years a group of films whose appearance seems tied to a specific historical moment becomes even more significant in light of Sklar's uncovering of a curious (and curiously ignored) historical fact: This film project was chosen by Huston as the basis of his first independent film production at a very unlikely point in time, one marked by "escalating anti-Communist repression." Sklar demonstrates how a study of the conditions of production and those of reception can be used to account for the film's apparently ambiguous ideological perspective. By comparing the film to *The Battle of Algiers,* Sklar shows why *We Were Strangers* must be examined as a discourse of history shaped by factors that extend beyond directorial psychology or even the most influential political mind-set of the times.

Although Sklar shows the value of returning to historical discourse and social myth in the analysis of Hollywood film, any collection proposing even a modestly comprehensive examination of Huston's work requires a return to the issue of adaptation. It should not be forgotten that it was Huston's penchant for literary adaptation that helped relegate him to auteur oblivion as a dreaded *metteur en scène,* and the majority of Huston's most famous films are adaptations of texts produced by a wide variety of American novelists and playwrights, including Dashiell Hammett, Carson McCullers, Stephen Crane, Herman Melville, Maxwell Anderson, Arthur Miller, Tennessee Williams, and Flannery O'Connor. Other significant Huston films have been drawn from no less luminary foreign writers, including C. S. Forester, Rudyard Kipling, and James Joyce. By auteur standards, Huston's supposed literary pretensions were evidence of a lack of original personal vision and a derivative style, with little if any guiding visual distinctiveness to anchor his films and identify them as his. However, current interest in authorship and signification suggests that the films of *metteurs en scène* such as director-screenwriter John Huston can tell us much about the ideological power of film's discursive and narrative strategies vis-à-vis those of the purely written word.

The articles by John Engell and Stephen Cooper provide a critical perspective on the process of adaptation. In spite of using very different models of analysis and applying them to what would seem to be two radically different films (*The Treasure of the Sierra Madre* and *Reflections in a Golden Eye*), both authors create a useful clarifying distinction between the production of meaning as negotiated through literary discourse and the ideological and textual functions that may be assumed by various cinematic strategies and patterns. Such analyses help us understand the shifting negotiations of Hollywood film style within the context of generic and historical change.

Like Sklar, John Engell argues for the ideological complexity of a specific Huston film; unlike Sklar, he concentrates on questions of ideological transformation raised by Huston's "Hollywoodization" and "Americanization" of the politically radical material that became the basis of his acclaimed film, *The Treasure of the Sierra Madre.* Engell's study shows that in spite of what might first appear to be Huston's faithful translation of B. Traven's novel to the screen, the film version of *The Treasure of the Sierra Madre* takes a story originally intended to promote a radical European philosophy of "individualistic anarchism" and transforms it into a "traditional moral fable" that sentimentally affirms American liberalism and "rugged male individualism." Engell delves into the probable sources of this discursively based ideological transformation to account for the textual production of ideologically inflected meaning in this important Huston film.

In "The Undeclared War: Political *Reflections in a Golden Eye,*"

Stephen Cooper offers what might be regarded as a methodological extension of Engell's discussion by combining an analysis of textual transformation with an exploration of the extratextual fields of politics, military
theory, and national experience. Cooper investigates how Huston's 1967
cinematic adaptation of Carson McCullers's 1941 novella creates a "counterpart" to the original literary text. Huston's film, he argues, demonstrates
the creation of a complex nexus of contextual relations that complicates
McCullers's dissection of what Cooper names as her subject, the "interper-
sonal wars of attrition in the peacetime army." By examining Huston's
film in direct contrast to its literary source, Cooper gathers the critical-in-
terpretive evidence to challenge the commonly held view that Huston's
*Reflections in a Golden Eye* is absent of any political implications, especially in connection to the historical crisis that marked the period in which
the film was produced—the United States' involvement in Vietnam. Inte-
grating references to fictional and historically real contextual worlds,
Cooper explores the possible subversive effects of the film's experiments
in the desaturation of color in what emerges upon analysis, he argues, as a
"deeply political" film.

The articles of part 1 demonstrate that Huston's films offer a lesson in
the economic, ideological, and historically specific contexts that shaped
American filmmaking practice. These articles show also that the films directed by Huston merit attention from anyone interested in the evolution
of Hollywood film as a mode of representation emanating from an institution. They also show the necessity of recognizing the complex relationship
of individuals (such as Huston) to that institution.

The articles in part 2 demonstrate how Huston's films yield unexpected insights into specific representational and narrational dimensions of
classical Hollywood cinema. In particular, part 2 refines the discussion in
part 1 by concentrating on the representation of masculinity and the male
body in Huston's films. While treatment of the female body and female
representation in classical Hollywood cinema has been much discussed in
contemporary film studies, the representation of masculinity and the male
body has, until very recently, been marginalized. This marginalization has
serious implications for any study of gender difference and film. As Peter
Lehman suggests:

> Masculinity is not simply a position of power that puts men in comfortable
> positions of control. If we ignore studying images of the male body, we are
> likely to think of masculinity as an ahistoric, powerfully secure, monolithic

ɛr than one riddled with cracks. If we understand masculinity
_ ∪nstant contradictory struggle rather than just the privileged position
within a power disequilibrium, we come closer to a full definition of
gender studies.[11]

Huston's films seem to be ideal material for a study of American cinema's
construction of masculinity as a dynamic process rather than as a stable
and unified representational system. The director obviously favored so-
called male genres, and, as James Naremore states, his films "have also
shown his admiration for a male world." In this world (or, if we prefer,
"worlds") of men, even compulsory Hollywood heterosexuality frequently
takes a back seat to the bonding between male buddies who share toughness rather than sex. "Women," Virginia Wright Wexman says in her article, are "rendered irrelevant" in Huston's filmic world because his concerns are expressed through and for an "American male-centered ethic." In
spite of this, Huston's films should not be dismissed as unworthy of study.
On the contrary, they should be regarded as an important site of inquiry
into American film's often troubled—even anxious—construction of masculinity.

Of course, not all of Huston's films are populated only by male characters (a fact to which *The African Queen* and *The Dead* most clearly at-
test), but the male-centered aspect of Huston's films has long been noted
(see Agee article in this volume). While it is inarguable that Huston's films
are primarily male-centered and at times overtly misogynistic, it by no
means follows that they represent men in ways that always affirm male
power and authority. Nevertheless, the films' variety of genre and source
material, and their spanning of many decades, increase their appropriate-
ness as a site of investigation into Hollywood's construction of masculinity. As the articles by David Desser and Gary Edgerton in part 1 suggest,
even Huston's documentaries merit attention as demonstrations of how
American masculinity was thrown into crisis by the horror of war.

Ironically, it is Andrew Sarris, who once condemned Huston, who offers insight into this aspect of the director's work in his retrospective article of 1980, "Johnny, We Finally Knew Ye" (reprinted in part 3). In this
revision of his earlier critical assessment of Huston, Sarris suggests that
Huston's films do have value as expressions of "the universal experience
of pointlessness and failure." Although Sarris bypasses the gender implications of Huston's films, his allusion to "pointlessness and failure" is

more than a little interesting, for these are not the qualities scholars have often come to expect of Hollywood's classical paradigm of American masculinity. The nature of this paradigm was suggested by Laura Mulvey's influential analysis of the construction of sexual difference in Hollywood cinema:

> While mainstream cinema, in its assumption of a male norm, perspective and look, can constantly take women and the female image as its object of investigation, it has rarely investigated men and the male image in the same kind of way: women are a problem, a source of anxiety, of obsessive enquiry; men are not. Where women are investigated, men are tested. Masculinity, as an ideal, at least, is implicitly known. Femininity is, by contrast, a mystery.[12]

Mulvey's statement should not be completely rejected, but it requires qualification, especially as it applies to Huston's films. At the very least, the director seems to have pursued the problems of American masculinity more persistently and more thoroughly than most of his contemporaries. Many of his films can be seen as complicating or destabilizing conventionalized norms associated with classical Hollywood heroes.

James Naremore's article, reprinted here for the first time, was originally published in 1973, long before the current critical interest the filmic representation of gender and sexuality was extended to a consideration of masculinity. Naremore addresses the textual construction of the "male world" of *The Maltese Falcon* by means of a broadly based approach that considers casting and performance, *mise en scène,* and camera setups to show that the 1941 film presents its private-eye tale "as a male myth rather than as a slice of life." This distinction is an important one, for Naremore proceeds to call attention to the differences between the novel by Dashiell Hammett and Huston's film adaptation, which offers a "near allegorical world" full of visual symbolism. This symbolism, Naremore argues, is often directed toward stressing the normative maleness of Sam Spade and "the femininity of the other characters." All operate, says Naremore, within a stylized world of criminality that registers a certain ambivalence toward the male world, created through a deliberately caricatured rhetoric.

The relationship between male representation and stylistic elements is analyzed in further detail and with application to a larger group of films by Martin Rubin in "Heroic, Antiheroic, Aheroic: John Huston and the Problematical Protagonist." Rubin pursues the assumption that Hollywood cinema is fundamentally a heroic mode that Huston investigated and structurally altered in his pursuit of a more complicated depiction of masculinity and heroism. Although Rubin refers to a number of Huston films, he focuses his discussion on the treatment of the heroic in *The Red Badge of Courage* and *The Treasure of the Sierra Madre*. He is interested in revealing how these two films construct a male "hero" that is a significant innovation on the classical norms of Hollywood film practice and the construction of protagonists. Rubin argues that not only does Huston make problematic and call into question "the very institution of heroism" within the narratives, but the presentation of male characters is conceived in his films so as to undermine expected point-of-view configurations. These configurations typically are used to create a male "vision" of the world, but even as Huston reconstitutes them, he also reconstitutes elements of *mise en scène* "commonly used in mainstream cinema to reinforce a sliding collusion between audience identification, character subjectivity and the fictional universe." Rubin argues that what frequently have been considered limitations in Huston's visual style must be reexamined. That reexamination must take place in the light of what Rubin regards as the director's attempt to reconceptualize male heroism as "no longer a given but a problem, which has to be continually defined and redefined, and which is liable to vanish or transform itself at any moment." Thus Rubin's article suggests the complexity and significance of Huston's construction of ideals of masculine behavior.

In an anthology with seven male contributors and incessant talk of men and masculinity, it is somehow appropriate that two women have the last word in the discussion of Huston and his male world. Virginia Wright Wexman's and Gaylyn Studlar's articles demonstrate the methodologies and concerns of feminist film studies. Reflecting the variety of positions available to feminist approaches and, perhaps, the complexity of Huston's work, these two authors put forward very different arguments regarding his films' treatment of masculinity and their representation of the male body.

Drawing on a wide range of historical and theoretical sources, Virginia Wright Wexman's "Mastery through Masterpieces: American Culture, the Male Body, and Huston's *Moulin Rouge*" examines the aesthetic strategies of Huston's 1952 film, which takes as its basis the life of painter Henri de la Toulouse-Lautrec. Wexman is interested in the relationship of the film's narrative and Huston's act of filmmaking to the myth of male prowess. Following this line, Wexman links Huston's representation of masculinity in *Moulin Rouge* to a preoccupation with an American-identified myth of male prowess and power, also found in canonical American writers and artists such as Herman Melville, James Fenimore Cooper, and Charles Remington. She argues that Huston's decision to make a movie about Toulouse-Lautrec might seem incongruous within the context of that myth, but the subject of the disabled painter, she says, presented the director with "the opportunity to extend his analysis of the theme of male heroism by freeing it from its association with the superiority of the masculine body." For director Huston, as for artist Toulouse-Lautrec, Wexman argues, mastery comes through masculine prowess defined in the professional realm rather than through physical prowess, so that Huston's film itself becomes the locus of a complex stylistic and narrational strategy involving creative appropriation and cultural usurpation. American cinematic technology allows Huston to appropriate European cultural tradition and force it to submit to his national and patriarchal domination. Even as Toulouse-Lautrec attains an "unassailable dominance over his world . . . through aesthetic mastery," Wexman suggests, Huston's male mastery is achieved through an ideology of cultural and cinematic mastery that transcends the physically compromised body of the male.

In my article on Huston's representation of male failure and male violence in *Fat City,* I look at questions that Huston's films both answer and generate in relation to contemporary theoretical assumptions about gender-differentiated spectatorship. I start with the assumption that Huston's films often reflect a troubled and unresolved fascination with masculine failure. Although many critics have alluded to this phenomenon in Huston's work, they have not explored its more subtle ideological implications nor its role in generating the pleasures enjoyed by male spectators, the "ideal" viewers often thought to be anticipated textually by male genre films such as the boxing film—a genre of films with roots in the very beginnings of American cinema.[13] I argue that *Fat City* does not valorize male authority but "exposes the ideological contradictions in an American ideal of masculinity defined through competitive violence and commodity fetishism." Viewed from this perspective, *Fat City* is a boxing film that may lead the spectator to realize the "impossibility of the body as a site of male power in the twentieth century." In this process, the film's representation of masculinity is inscribed within carefully delineated structures of race and class. As a result of these strategies, *Fat City* deviates in important ways from the classical Hollywood boxing film typified by *Body and Soul* (1947) and more recent boxing films such as *Raging Bull* (1980) and the *Rocky* saga (1976–). I employ these crucial differences in the textual inscription of masculinity to question contemporary theories on the relationship between cinematic violence and spectatorial pleasure, as well as certain notions of how the male body is represented in Hollywood cinema for the gaze of male viewers.[14]

Finally, to clarify the critical issues advanced in parts 1 and 2 and to offer an overarching perspective on the work of John Huston, we offer a "Documents" section, which begins with a biographical sketch of Huston by David Desser. Included also in this section are "Fool" and "Figures of Fighting Men," two short stories on boxing that were published early in Huston's writing career in the *American Mercury;* seminal critical commentary on the director by James Agee and Andrew Sarris; and an interview with Huston conducted by Rui Nogueira and Bertrand Tavernier, translated into English by Ruth Hottell, which may provide unexpected insights through Huston's response to his own films. The short stories offer a historical dimension to Huston's much later exploration into the world of boxing in *Fat City* and a cross reference to his filmmaking. The article by Agee and the two by Sarris represent important (and obviously much-cited) interventions in the critical debate over Huston's work.

The essays collected for our anthology are arranged in an order that should help the reader achieve a progressive understanding of the films of John Huston. It will be obvious that many of the authors have differing opinions regarding the social, political, and stylistic implications of Huston's films, but in assembling these selections, we have made an effort to suggest a range of critical approaches that might be applied to his films. Although we do not presume to offer a completely comprehensive view of Huston's canon, we do hope that our book will help bring his work into the field of vision of contemporary film studies and begin the pleasant task of correcting the scholarly neglect of an important American filmmaker.

## NOTES

1. James Agee, "Undirectable Director," in *Agee on Film* (New York: McDowell Obolensky, 1958), 330. Reprinted in this volume.

2. Andrew Sarris coined this phrase in his famous commentary on Huston: "The

late James Agee canonized Huston prematurely in a *Life*-magazine auteur piece circa *Treasure of the Sierra Madre*. Agee was as wrong about Huston as Bazin was about Wyler, but Huston is still coasting on his reputation as a wronged individualist with an alibi for every bad movie." Andrew Sarris, *The American Cinema: Directors and Directions 1929–1968* (New York: E. P. Dutton, 1968), 156. Sarris's commentary on Huston is reprinted in this volume.

3. *The Kremlin Letter* is yet another Huston film that begs for a critical reassessment. It seems less a bad film than merely one with a post-Watergate sensibility, marking it as ahead of its time.

4. Quoted in Gaylyn Studlar, "Life Achievement Award: John Huston," *Magill's Cinema Annual 1984* (Englewood Cliffs, N.J.: Salem Press, 1984), 9.

5. John Huston, *An Open Book* (New York: Knopf, 1980), 351.

6. Scott Hammen, *John Huston* (Boston: Twayne, 1985), x.

7. See William F. Nolan, *John Huston: King Rebel* (Los Angeles: Sherbourne Press, 1965); Peter Viertel, *White Hunter, Black Heart* (Garden City, N.Y.: Doubleday, 1953); Axel Madsen, *John Huston* (Garden City, N. Y.: Doubleday, 1978); and Gerald Pratley, *The Cinema of John Huston* (New York: Barnes, 1977).

8. Sarris, *The American Cinema,* 155.

9. Ibid., 156.

10. Quoted in Studlar, "Life Achievement Award." Unfortunately, I have not been able to find my original source for this quote.

11. Peter Lehman, "*In the Realm of the Senses:* Desire, Power, and the Representation of the Male Body," *Genders* 2 (Summer 1988): 108.

12. Laura Mulvey, "Visual Pleasure and Narrative Cinema," *Screen* 16, no. 3 (Autumn 1975): 11.

13. Discussions of the earliest cycle of boxing films include Charles Musser's in "Full-Length Programs: Fights, Passion Plays, and Travel," a chapter in his *The Emergence of Cinema: The American Screen to 1907* (New York: C. Scribner's, 1990), 193–208; and Dan Streible, "A History of the Boxing Film, 1894–1915," *Film History* 3 (1989): 235–57.

14. The theoretical basis of the current discussions of masculinity is derived in part from the work of Steven Neale, "Screening the Male," *Screen* 24 (Nov.–Dec. 1983): 2–16. Other notable early contributions are offered by Ian Green, "Malefunction," *Screen* 25 (July–Oct. 1984): 36–46; as well as Paul Willemen's succinct though influential "Anthony Mann Looking at the Male," *Framework* (Summer 1981); Pam Cook, "Masculinity in Crisis," *Screen* 23 (Sept.–Oct. 1982): 39–46; and Richard Dyer, "Don't Look Now: The Male Pin-up," *Screen* 23 (Sept.–Oct. 1982): 47–53. The theoretical marginalization of masculinity's representation in film should be corrected by a number of forthcoming volumes including Steven Cohan and Ina Rae Hark's anthology, *Screening the Male* (Routledge), and Peter Lehman's *Running Scared* (Temple University Press, 1993).

# Part One

HUSTON, HISTORY, AND IDEOLOGY

# The Wartime Films of John Huston: *Film Noir* and the Emergence of the Therapeutic

DAVID DESSER

I n thinking about the wartime films of John Huston one first considers his famous series of documentaries—*Report from the Aleutians, San Pietro* (also known as *The Battle of San Pietro*), and *Let There Be Light*—made between 1942 and 1945. But I would like to reconsider the question of "wartime films" by extending the discussion forward and backward, framing the documentaries with Huston's films that preceded and followed them. Specifically, *The Maltese Falcon* (1941), *Across the Pacific* (1942), and *Key Largo* (1948) all somehow qualify as wartime films. The concept of wartime films can also be extended to include a number of Huston's later efforts, films not simply about war, or wartime, although I do significantly find *The Red Badge of Courage* (1951, starring World War II hero Audie Murphy) in this category, but films that grew out of Huston's personal experience of the Second World War, and the culture's experience of it as well. I will merely for now suggest that in thinking about Huston's wartime films, war documen-

19

taries, and war experiences, later films such as *The Treasure of the Sierra Madre* (1948), *We Were Strangers* (1949), *The African Queen* (1951), *Moby Dick* (1956), *Heaven Knows, Mr. Allison* (1957), *The Unforgiven* (1960), *Freud* (1962), *Reflections in a Golden Eye* (1967), *A Walk with Love and Death* (1969), *The Mackintosh Man* (1973), *The Man Who Would Be King* (1975), *Phobia* (1980), and *Victory* (1981) may also be placed within this context. Now obviously many of these films have a life outside this war-film environment—I am not claiming that the wartime films totally determined Huston's later career or these particular films, which make up the bulk of it—rather, that significant strands within the wartime films, originating in Huston's combat experiences and his exposure to psychoanalytic theory and practice, play a role in fully appreciating the later films within the context of Huston's canon.

The significant strands within these films can be put within a binary opposition, or at least a related pair, which arises quite clearly in the wartime films, that is, within the films of the 1940s that I have named above. This binary set I would like to call the *noir* vision and the *therapeutic* vision. These visions are oppositional but not so much in competition with each other, as they are mirror images. The *noir* vision is somehow always prevalent within the context of the wartime films and their extensions throughout Huston's career, but the therapeutic vision may be absent or present. The therapeutic vision lightens the *noir* vision; in its absence all remains dark.

I take the concepts of the *noir* vision, of course, from *film noir,* the French term for a cycle of Hollywood detective and crime thrillers originating with *The Maltese Falcon* (with its roots in Dashiell Hammett's novel and the Black Mask literary group, German Expressionism, French Poetic Realism, and Warner's house style of the 1930s). Obviously, I need not demonstrate that Huston's directorial debut, *The Maltese Falcon,* qualifies as *film noir,* especially in its inauguration of the Hollywood version of the femme fatale. Rather, I place this film within the wartime context, at least as I am defining it here, to see how it looks forward to elements within the films to come that specify them as wartime films.

Stuart Kaminsky finds that *The Maltese Falcon* contains "the image of the ill-fated group," which characterizes a number of Huston's films, and "that such groups are doomed families."[1] The idea of "the group" is crucial to Huston's cinema in general, especially to the numerous wartime films named above. The group turns out to be the protagonist, if you will, of war—modern warfare (at least until the advent of total technologized weaponry) is fought by groups, ranging from the small patrol, to the platoon (and a memorable recent film of that name), to a company, a battalion, a division. What we find in Huston's fiction films of the 1940s is still the Hollywood individualist: Sam Spade vs. the corrupt group in *The Maltese Falcon;* Rick opposing the spy ring in *Across the Pacific* (although now he has help from the femme fatale, Mary Astor, again); Frank McCloud single-handedly taking on Rocco's gang in *Key Largo.* But in between these fiction films, in the distance between *Across the Pacific* and *Key Largo,* Huston experienced the group in all its glory, although it was a glory tinged by injury and death.

*The Maltese Falcon* can be seen as a precursor to *Casablanca* or a retrospective justification for American isolationism. *Falcon's* links to *Casablanca* are obvious from the presence in both of Humphrey Bogart, Sidney Greenstreet, and Peter Lorre. More subtly we find the figure of the loner, the alienated outsider portrayed by Bogey—Sam Spade and Rick Blaine—and in both films he is surrounded by Europeans engaged in their unsavory business (the black bird, the war). And Bogey must intervene, or is drawn into, the respective conflicts; in both, he is faced with an ethical/moral dilemma revolving around finding and sticking to the proper code of conduct. On the other hand, we may find in *Falcon* a vision of European decadence strong enough to require isolationism. Kasper Gutman and Joel Cairo are clearly European (Cairo is also "Levantine," as Hammett describes him, appropriate to his name—he is also oriental by this standard). Even Brigid O'Shaughnessy is a name just foreign enough. More significantly, they all chase after the dingus, the black bird, a falcon created by medieval knights. Thus an outmoded European code of conduct continues to exert unwanted, unclean influence on American life.

Now we wouldn't want to push this allegorical connection to World War II too far. After all, Hammett's original novel, to which the film sticks quite closely, was "written and set in 1928–9." However, as Kaminsky notes, "The Huston script is clearly updated to 1940."[2] Nevertheless, I am less interested in this wartime connection than in the origination of the *noir* vision, which appears quite clearly in *Across the Pacific,* where it runs directly into the Second World War. This film was definitely conceived as a follow-up to *The Maltese Falcon,* reteaming Bogart, Astor, and Greenstreet. The characterization of the three stars is virtually identical, and even bits of dialogue from the earlier film return. The world of *noir* is

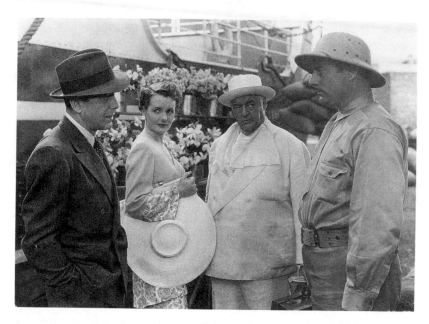

*Across the Pacific* was something of a remake of *The Maltese Falcon* in the wartime context.

invoked by Astor's presence and the ambiguity of her character throughout much of the film. We again find "the fragmenting group," one whose characteristics help create the *noir* atmosphere. Kaminsky writes that the film "deals with a group of people, all of whom are hiding behind masks, pretending to be what they are not."[3] However, in contrast to the loner standing up to the corrupt group, Huston allows Bogart's Rick to have help from the femme fatale, who is not in this case corrupt or fatal. (*Across the Pacific* is in more ways than this also a *Casablanca* precursor.)

Similarly, the atmosphere of the film evokes *noir* in its use of night, shadows, and fog—obvious, but useful, visual correlatives for *noir* paranoid vision, for its recognition of the dark side or underside of people, for precisely the lack of clarity that pervades the *noir* universe. That Warner Brothers was a studio that typically shunned lavish productions due to budgetary constraints only aided the developing stylistic of *noir*. The suggestiveness of the major set (the Japanese tramp steamer) and the use of low-key lighting to hide its limitations further create, happily, the *noir* atmosphere. We should not underestimate Warner's house style as a crucial component in the developing *film noir* cycle, just as we would not overlook the Second World War and its aftermath as contributing to the growth and development of *noir*.

As it turns out, however, the world of *noir* was curiously appropriate to the Second World War—curious precisely because *noir*'s origins in the Black Mask school of hard-boiled writing (Hammett, Raymond Chandler, and James M. Cain) and German Expressionist cinema of the immediate post–World War I era seem to have little connection to World War II. On the other hand, a third crucial forebear of *noir,* French poetic realism, *is* intimately connected to World War II. Marcel Carné's poetic realist classics were made virtually on the eve of and during World War II and the Nazi occupation: *Quai des brumes* (1938), *Le jour se leve* (1939), *Les visiteurs du soir* (1942), and *Les enfants du paradis* (1943–45). Similarly, American proto-*noir* such as *The Maltese Falcon, Across the Pacific,* and *Casablanca* arise in the initial American forays into the war. *Noir* and the war meet explicitly in Howard Hawks's *To Have and Have Not* (also from Warner's), while *noir* in its perfect form also arises during the war with no overt references to it in Billy Wilder's adaptation of Cain's *Double Indemnity* (1944). While *noir* would reach its apotheosis after the war, from 1946 to 1952 (including Huston's own *The Asphalt Jungle* [1950]), one is intrigued, if still somewhat puzzled, about *noir*'s origins during the war.

There is in *Across the Pacific* both an unfortunate racism and an unambiguous optimism that would disappear in most of Huston's later films. The spy ring that Bogart's Rick defeats has more in common with the world of Charlie Chan than with the well-armed, intelligent Japanese enemy America would face. (Although the critical works on Huston mention that the Japanese Americans in the cast were temporarily reprieved from going to the internment camps, the lead Japanese villain is played by a Chinese American, as are many other Japanese characters.) Similarly, when the Westerner who professes admiration for the Japanese reveals himself as unable to commit hara-kiri (*seppuku* in Japanese, the ritual suicide of the warrior), we might take it that his cowardice extends to the Japanese themselves—a propaganda ploy that would similarly prove untrue and tragic for both American and Japanese soldiers.

Racism, intended or not, was a typical strategy of American World War II films. So too, was optimism. It shines through in this film, which might be considered a spoof of *film noir* before *noir* was coded. To anyone familiar with *The Maltese Falcon,* the characterizations in *Across the Pacific* of Bogart, Greenstreet, and Astor seem parodies of their earlier efforts. More significantly, the film loses whatever tension it earlier sustained by Rick's unbelievable heroics and derring-do in escaping from his captors late in the film. This slackening was a function of Huston's own irreverent attitude. He had enlisted in the Signal Corps some few weeks before shooting this film and was called up for service before completing it. Right before he left, Huston claims, "I spent the . . . day making it utterly impossible for Bogart to make a false move without getting shot. Well, I saw the picture some time after the war and it lost credibility from that moment on."[4] Why Huston expresses some surprise at this, considering he left director Vincent Sherman, who took over for Huston, no choice in the matter, is puzzling. Perhaps he simply forgot, in light of his own war experiences, that he once possessed a certain irreverence, a misguided optimism, about our coming combat experiences. Such comic, good-natured optimism would disappear in a little town in Italy called San Pietro.

Huston's wartime documentaries are often conceived of as a trilogy, although there were efforts to make more films than the three that eventually emerged. As John McCarty notes, the films follow a progression: *Report from the Aleutians* focuses on the preparations for battle, *San Pietro* on battle itself, and *Let There Be Light* on war's aftermath.[5] The troubled post-production history of virtually all of these films, especially *Let There Be Light,* meant that these intensely creative documentaries, short of influencing emerging documentary styles of the postwar era, tended merely to look forward to them. But their effect on Huston, thematically and technically, cannot be overestimated.

One might claim *The Battle of San Pietro* marked a turning point for Huston, considering that of the three films he made during his army service, only this one features his own voice-over narration. The battle of San Pietro took place between December 8 and December 15, 1943, just a small part of the Italian campaign, which Huston subtly reminds us to powerful effect. Perhaps the most powerful and certainly the most daring stylistic feature of the film was never allowed to remain in it—voice-over discussions with American soldiers as we see corpses stuffed into body bags and loaded onto trucks, and later discussions with survivors of this battle about their hopes for the future, the film then revealing that these men perished in later battles.

*San Pietro* relies on a deceptive simplicity in its basic structure, a

In *Across the Pacific*, Bogart learns that the femme fatale is not always fatal.

chronological approach in which voice-over narration and shots of maps provide information. The voice-over situates us in space and time, and relates a little of the history of the small town and the valley in which it rests. The battle scenes are thus framed by images of peace: what the town was like up until the war and what it will return to after the victorious American troops depart. The battle scenes are, on one hand, curiously dispassionate. Shot on the spot in the midst of actual combat, the film is not able to rely on standard Hollywood techniques to communicate the feel of battle: multiple angles, point-of-view shots, and dynamic montage are almost impossible. (One exception comes late in the film, when enemy counterattacks against the summit of Mt. Lungo are cut to the rhythm of artillery bursts.) A real battle does not feel as energetic and exciting as a staged battle. The long takes, hand-held mobile-camera shots, are both grainy and unsteady. (*San Pietro* clearly had an influence on Stanley Kubrick's *Dr. Strangelove* in the scene where the army attacks Burpleson Air Force Base.) On the other hand, their very documentary nature makes them gripping. Dispassionate single-take long shots of men falling from machine-gun fire or being struck by a burst of artillery show the dispassionate horror of war. As Gary Edgerton notes, *"The Battle of San Pietro* was not the only WW II nonfiction film to employ hand-held combat footage. . . . What is significant, though, is that John Huston at times strikes the pose of an observer rather than a propagandist, and lets these pictures stand on their own without interpretation."[6] The necessarily distanced (although not too distanced) camera work combines effectively with the voice-over narration, which is quietly passionate, but for the most part objectively informational about the toll of casualties, both enemy and allied. We learn, for instance, that volunteer patrols attempted to reduce enemy strongholds: "Not a single member of any such patrol ever came back alive." We see and learn about U.S. tanks that attempted to take the town under direct enemy observation. Of the sixteen tanks, only four return. Five tanks are immobilized, five others hit mines, two were destroyed outright. The cost of taking Mt. Summocro is one man per yard. We see shots of wounded soldiers, of body bags and dog tags, of men digging grave markers. One hundred decorations for acts of valor do not seem enough to counteract the incredible human loss.

But then there is the other side, the quiet aftermath, the town people appearing to the strains of choir music. We learn that while "liberation of people is of an incidental nature, people look upon us as their deliverers."

This is quiet irony, but irony that would deeply affect Huston in years to come. It is an irony that, along with the dispassionate shots of wounded and dead soldiers, the U.S. Army would not appreciate. The film was not released to the general public until May 21, 1945, when the European war was already won.

On June 25, 1945, "Major John Huston was assigned to produce 'The Returning Psychoneurotics,'" a perhaps not very catchy title for the film that was later to be called *Let There Be Light*. Narrated by Walter Huston from son John's script, it is a deeply moving film that honestly shows war's aftermath. The naive optimism and brightness of *Across the Pacific* is replaced by a darkened vision, but one that finds reason to hope for renewed light. Although the film was not released commercially when completed in 1946 (the first unofficial public exhibition was in Los Angeles, on November 8, 1980; the first commercial opening on January 16, 1981), it was seen by army groups and psychiatrists. But its importance for John Huston is what concerns us here.

Huston wrote that "the time at Mason General [the hospital where the film was made] affected me almost like a religious experience. It made me begin to realize that the primary ingredient in psychological health is love: the ability to give and receive it."[7] Although his interest in psychiatry in general and Freud in particular is credited to this period, it is interesting that "love" turns out to be what Huston takes away from the experience. At that time, the interest in psychological health for the returning veteran, that is, the growing awareness of "shell shock" (today's post-traumatic stress disorder, PTSD), was widespread in the country. Gary Edgerton perceptively notes Dory Schary's RKO and United Artists productions about this topic, films such as *The Enchanted Cottage* (1945), where a slight physical injury has severe psychological repercussions; *I'll Be Seeing You* (1944); *They Dream of Home* (1945); and *Till the End of Time* (1946). And one might as well mention in this context *The Best Years of Our Lives* (1946). Returning home, or finding a home once one has returned, is the key to these theatrical films and to Huston's documentary. But returning home is difficult for some men: "For some the moment is very different from the dream." And this is tragically so because of what these men experienced away from home, at war, and how they have dealt with these experiences.

The film's voice-over narration insists on seeing these men as war casualties and mental trauma as every bit as seriously damaging as physical trauma. The men are called "human salvage" who have experienced "casualties of the spirit." There is constant comparison to physical wounds: Psychiatry is likened to surgery. Individual soldiers are singled out via their initial psychiatric interviews, and the film follows chronologically their entrance, treatment, and release. The success rate with these patients seems unrealistically high, the length of treatment too short. Moreover, many discussions in the film between psychiatrists and patients relate the childhood theory of neurosis, thus undermining the basic premise that it was the war, as such, that transformed these young men into "psychoneurotic soldiers." Nevertheless, we do see results. A patient psychosomatically unable to walk is returned to the use of his legs; another possessed of a debilitating stutter is relieved of his symptom. And we are inescapably moved by the soldiers' experiences in this hospital. The use of close-ups particularly enables us to feel for individual soldiers in a manner denied us in *The Battle of San Pietro.*

Of particular interest for our purposes here is the way in which the soldiers are said to share similar dark feelings—"unceasing fear and apprehension"; "a sense of impending disaster"; "a feeling of hopelessness and utter isolation"—in short, the world of *film noir,* a world similarly explored in postwar American film, a kind of post-traumatic stress disorder of the national spirit. *The Blue Dahlia* (1946) is the perfect marriage of *film noir* and PTSD. But self-knowledge leads to safety, at least in this film, and being home helps the recovering veteran who can experience the healing effects of love.

Perhaps it was precisely the message that only love could cure the wounded spirits of these soldiers that led to the now-notorious banning of the film from public viewing. On one level, the film's antiwar message might have been appropriate to a world trying to recover from the devastation the war had wrought. On the other hand, it is equally true that with the cold war already under way even before the hot war against the Nazis was won, the sight of psychologically damaged soldiers would work against recruitment for the very possible war in the very possibly near future. Soon thereafter, the imagery of the Korean War in popular discourse, and in certain later films, most brilliantly, *The Manchurian Candidate* (1962), would be that of deliberately psychological warfare: the so-called brainwashing of American POWs. Psychology points the way toward recognizing that underneath this significant prowar level, we might find yet another explanation for the film's banning. Here is Huston's own interpretation:

"What I think was really behind it [the banning of the film] was that the authorities considered it to be more shocking, embarrassing perhaps to them, for a man to suffer emotional distress than to lose a leg, or part of his body. Hardly masculine, I suppose they would say."[8] Thus, *Let There Be Light* inaugurates Huston's rethinking and revisioning of traditional American modes of masculinity and male behavior, which would reach fruition in such films as *The Red Badge of Courage, Moulin Rouge,* and *Fat City* (discussed in detail in later essays in this volume).

In 1948 Huston was already reconceptualizing notions of masculinity and the heroic in his two remarkable films of that year: *The Treasure of the Sierra Madre* and *Key Largo. Key Largo*'s Maj. Frank McCloud, a returning veteran in need of recovery, like the psychologically war-wounded vets of *Let There Be Light,* may have his masculinity called into question because of his reluctance to fight. He is at loose ends on the home front following war's end, taking a trip to Key Largo to bring some comfort to a comrade's father and widow. We learn a few pertinent facts about Frank— he has not returned to his prewar job (a journalist); he is unmarried; he is, in some sense, drifting, since he has held odd jobs since returning home; and he would like to own a boat. McCloud's attitude thus mirrors that of the patients in *Let There Be Light.* As Scott Hammen has it, "Bogart [i.e., Frank McCloud] . . . suffers from a kind of malaise . . . a kind of general despair about the soul of postwar America."[9] And to what does the film credit this malaise? Well, we learn that McCloud and his friend, George Temple, fought at the battle of San Pietro, where George acted the hero. Later, we learn that the story Frank told of George's heroism was a reversal of the facts—that Frank was the real hero. But he is disillusioned now. For Hammen this disillusionment may stem from survivor guilt: "The survivor [of the battle of San Pietro] shares the plight of the subjects of *Let There Be Light,* asking himself why he lived while all around him died and how he can go on to reintegrate himself into a peacetime society."[10] But this analysis seems wrong. The peacetime society is completely unimplicated in *Let There Be Light.* There is no notion in that film that the world outside the hospital is somehow not worth returning to. In the documentary, returning home (we might better say "coming home" to anticipate the disillusionment in a later film by that name about war, though not one of Huston's), is unambiguously a positive goal. But that is not the case in *Key Largo.* Huston is dramatizing PTSD as a function of the world of *film noir.* Huston himself provides a better clue to Frank's disillusionment, his dark vision: "The high hopes and idealism of the Roosevelt years were slipping away, and the underworld . . . was once again on the move, taking advantage of social apathy. We made this the theme of the film."[11] As Frank, in that inimitable Bogart style, says about midway through the film, "I had hopes once, but I gave them up." This is to say that while the war experiences are implicated in a darkened vision, it is the postwar world that is to blame for the alienation of men like Frank, who (like Huston himself, perhaps, also a major at war's end) "returned from the war and found the unpleasantness unchanged in spite of the men he had seen die."[12]

But Frank does experience healing, is reintegrated into the postwar world. To be cured, he must act, he must oppose the villainous Johnny Rocco. Initially cynical in the face of Rocco's tyranny, he is drawn into the fray again. Not only is Rocco a symbol of the revitalized underworld, an index for the resurgence of crime and corruption (Kaminsky notes that Rocco resembles the then recently deported gangster Lucky Luciano), but also a stand-in for fascist dictators: "Allusions to home-grown Hitlers are evident, and the film includes frequent references to Rocco as a would-be Fascist dictator."[13] Yet it is possible, despite all these implications of crime and the public's apathy to it, to see crime as only an index of Frank's alienation, symbolic of the general malaise into which he has fallen. Or crime, perhaps more strongly, is only the *dramatic* sign of postwar disillusionment. As Huston himself said elsewhere about Frank, "This man had returned and already disenchantment had set in."[14] After all, Frank *begins* the film alienated, out of step, drifting. His confrontation with the gangsters is not responsible for his crisis of faith and his loss of values. Yet, it is only by resisting the gangsters and the inner angst and disillusionment they represent that Frank can be reintegrated into society.

Frank is led to action by a series of circumstances. He is accused of cowardice by Nora Temple, his buddy's widow, when he seemingly refuses the chance to shoot Rocco. (The gun Rocco gave Frank to do it was not loaded, but even Frank admits not knowing that when he seemingly chickened out. The deputy sheriff was not so cowardly, or was more foolhardy. He tries to shoot Rocco with the empty gun and is shot dead by Rocco.) Rocco's girlfriend, Gaye Dawn, remarks, "It's better to be a live coward than a dead hero." Frank says, "I fight nobody's battle but my own." Yet he fights Rocco, first when he defies him and gives Gaye a drink after Rocco refuses her one. Rocco slaps McCloud, but McCloud takes the punishment silently. It is at this point that Nora reveals she knows that Frank was the real hero at San Pietro, not her late husband. McCloud seems most determined to kill Rocco when the sheriff kills the Indian Osceola brothers, after Rocco falsely implicates them for killing the deputy. Rocco's attitude toward the taking of Indian lives recalls Hitler's virulent racism, and McCloud's revulsion for Rocco reaches a breaking point. Also, Frank has been developing an attraction for Nora, although one that is remarkably restrained in the film; in fact it is almost nonexistent. (Audience knowledge of the Bogie-Bacall reteaming following *To Have and Have Not,* which *Key Largo* in many ways recalls; *The Big Sleep;* and *Dark Passage,* and their offscreen marriage in 1945 substitutes for any onscreen sparks.) Thus we might say that love heals the trauma of the spirit.

But before love can conquer all, violence must conquer the gangsters. It is a violence for which the film has been preparing us by the claustrophobic setting and theatrical staging. Frank's sublimation of his violent impulses is mirrored in Huston's repression of cinematic space. Oddly, however, while Frank is allowed to give free rein to this violence, Huston does not simultaneously open up the space. The theatrical staging and setting are in themselves rather odd, since the film was shot on location. The predominant nighttime and interior setting work well in establishing and maintaining the claustrophobic intensity of the drama (despite the location shooting). So that in the penultimate, climactic scene, Frank's violent actions on board the get-away boat might be accompanied by an equally violent opening up of the cinematic space, both for dramatic purpose and to take advantage of the location shooting. Yet no such opening up occurs. The scene is shot much like the shipboard sequences in *Across the Pacific,* where it was precisely the limitations of the soundstage and Warner's budgetary penuriousness that led to the suggestive, *noir*-like atmosphere. In fact, Frank's confrontation with Rocco and his henchmen on the speeding boat even more clearly recalls Howard Hawks's staging of Harry Morgan's climactic violence in *To Have and Have Not.* This, too, is partly attributable to house style and lack of location shooting. But Huston's almost exact reproduction of Hawks's staging is not. Rather, by invoking those two earlier *noir*-war films, he relates his postwar film to them. It is not until the final scene, in fact the final image of this claustrophobic film shot mostly at night, that natural sunshine bursts through the hotel room. And the sun shines literally and symbolically when Nora learns that Frank is all right, a moment that could have been scripted by the direction: Let there be light.

31

## NOTES

1. Stuart Kaminsky, *John Huston: Maker of Magic* (Boston: Houghton Mifflin, 1978), 25.

2. Ibid., 20.

3. Ibid., 33.

4. Gerald Pratley, *The Cinema of John Huston* (South Brunswick, N.J.: A. A. Barnes, 1977), 46.

5. John McCarty, *The Films of John Huston* (Secaucus, N.J.: Citadel, 1978).

6. Gary Edgerton, "Revisiting the Recording of Wars Past: Remembering the Documentary Trilogy of John Huston," *Journal of Popular Film and Television* 15, no. 1 (Spring 1987): 32. Reprinted in this volume.

7. John Huston, *An Open Book* (New York: Alfred A. Knopf, 1980), 125.

8. Pratley, *Cinema of John Huston,* 56.

9. Scott Hammen, *John Huston* (Boston: Twayne, 1985), 40.

10. Ibid.

11. Huston, *Open Book,* 151.

12. Kaminsky, *John Huston,* 62.

13. Ibid.

14. Pratley, *Cinema of John Huston,* 64.

# Revisiting the Recordings of Wars Past: Remembering the Documentary Trilogy of John Huston

## GARY EDGERTON

> I went through the war more as an observer than a partici-
> pant. But I saw enough of it that it shaped something in me.
> —Bill Mauldin, in *The Good War: An Oral History of World War II*

Through the exploits of his characters Willie and Joe, Bill Mauldin spoke for and mirrored the sentiments of many of America's GIs in his enormously popular and Pulitzer Prize-winning syndicated cartoon, "Up Front." His understated and sardonic attitude appealed to and reflected a generation of enlisted men and women who would be profoundly shaped and changed by the grit and trauma of their war experience. John Huston was one of the individuals; and it was not by coincidence that he cast Bill Mauldin and Audie Murphy, two famous ex-GIs and virtual nonactors at the time, as his leads in *The Red Badge of Courage* (1951), a motion picture that Huston had passionately wanted to make ever since the end of World War II.

Similar to Mauldin, Huston's role in the Second World War was essentially that of an observer, although he directed film crews under fire in both the North Pacific and Italian theaters. He likewise used his observation to record resonant and meaningful documents in response to what he was seeing and experiencing. John Huston's three wartime documentaries—*Report from the Aleutians* (1943), *The Battle of San Pietro* (1945), and *Let There Be Light* (1946)—are pivotal works in the evolution of Huston as a moviemaker as well as seminal in the history and development of the nonfiction film form. The intended and subtextual messages within these motion pictures, along with the stories behind their subsequent distribution and reception, certainly afford a privileged view of a wider spectrum of feelings, insights, and attitudes about living through and fighting the "good war" than those provided by any other American documentaries produced in this period.

## DOING HIS DUTY

> Several of the best people in Hollywood grew, noticeably,
> during their years away at war; the man who grew most
> impressively, I thought, as an artist, as a man, in intelli-
> gence, in intransigence, and in an ability to put through fine
> work against difficult odds, was John Huston, whose
> "San Pietro" and "Let There Be Light" were full of evidence
> of this many-sided growth.
> —James Agee, *The Nation*, January 31, 1948

As is well known, several of Hollywood's most talented and successful filmmakers—Frank Capra, John Ford, Anatole Litvak, William Wyler, and others—entered war service in late 1941 and early 1942 to make documentaries for various sections of the U.S. Armed Forces. John Huston soon followed suit by reporting for duty to the U.S. Army Signal Corps in April 1942. His first assignment was to proceed to the Aleutian Islands for the purpose of documenting the conflict there for both civilian and enlisted audiences. The working title of this film was *Alaska—1942*, and it was part of the "War Department Historical Series" and was essentially designed as a public relations and informational piece about the major theaters of combat attended to by Allied forces.[1] What resulted was a conventional military documentary that can be characterized as effective advocacy, conservative in ideology, and traditional in film form and style.

The intentions of *Report from the Aleutians* unmistakably echo the clichés of the customary World War II documentary, while also showcasing a number of conventions that we have come to expect from the Hollywood war film, such as the proverbial melting pot; the bugler blowing Taps; busy, smiling soldiers, singing and playing harmonicas; scores of American flags waving; and heroic background music. The primary impressions that the movie imparts are "morale is first-rate . . . and getting stronger," and the Japanese are being kept at bay in the North Pacific while the Americans rapidly rebuild their sea power after the tragedy of Pearl Harbor. As Huston himself explained in a 1981 PBS interview, "It was a simpler period."[2]

The film itself outlines the day-to-day experience and routine of manning a remote outpost while occasionally flying bombing missions. The usual and commonplace events of the motion picture eventually culminate in a stirring and successful attack on the Japanese where "our bombers found the target. Nine bombers went out and nine are coming home." In point of fact, this final ending and declaration were a result of poetic license. Huston and his production crew went on several bombing raids, and as is typical of the authoritarian style, the filmmakers recreated this final sequence during the editing process from footage taken over a number of missions into one action-packed climax, providing the audience with a rousing, obligatory happy ending. Huston later confessed, "This was not a routine flight [the episode depicted in the film's denouement]. Planes were lost on this mission, but the War Department wanted it to be a completely successful mission . . . it was a propaganda film—definitely."[3]

This admission by Huston is, of course, no surprise; like the aforementioned Hollywood filmmakers, he was "very anxious to enlist . . . and honored with the invitation to get a commission."[4] Authoritarian documentaries had moreover been the standard approach to nonfiction filmmaking throughout the 1930s and into the war years, and Huston was understandably in tune with the spirit of the country at the time by following orders and doing his job and duty. John Huston's attitude about the nature of war and how to film and understand its complexities only began to take shape during the production of *Report from the Aleutians*. Spending six months in the rain and almost constant fog of Adak, Huston did in fact pepper the overall structure of his documentary with numerous scenes of enlisted men doing mundane tasks and ultimately fighting the routine and boredom of army life. In an otherwise ideal propaganda film, these shots of idleness and digging latrines are the only parts of this movie that may be construed as portraying the underside of being at war; in other words, "war isn't hell" in *Report from the Aleutians,* "it's just a drag."[5]

Since there were genuine censorship problems with both *The Battle of San Pietro* and *Let There Be Light,* much has been made in retrospect of the delayed distribution of *Report from the Aleutians.*[6] The public exhibition of the film was indeed postponed two to three months because of a bureaucratic disagreement between Army Public Relations and the domestic motion picture division of the Office of War Information. The minor controversy surrounded the OWI's support of the preference by U.S. movie theater owners of only booking shorts of two reels or less. The full-length forty-seven-minute version of *Report from the Aleutians* would have therefore needed to be cut anywhere from fifteen to twenty-five minutes. Army Public Relations balked at this proposal, and thus backed the wishes of the Signal Corps and John Huston.[7]

The assertions that the film was held back because it either contained military secrets or too graphically documented the boredom of manning a remote outpost in the North Pacific, "as if Huston knew that the banalities of Army life in his first war film would gain poignancy and meaning when paired with its successor, *The Battle of San Pietro,*"[8] is simply a matter of making this documentary out to being more subversive and controversial than it really is. *Report from the Aleutians* is in most ways a traditional and undistinguished effort. What it does show us in hindsight, however, is how dramatically Huston matured in vision, attitude, and style as a nonfiction filmmaker by the time he made *The Battle of San Pietro* and *Let There Be Light.* In comparison to *Report from the Aleutians,* it is clear in his later documentaries that he soberly learned through the experience of making these films that war can be more than dull; instead, Huston exactingly communicates in these ensuing efforts that it can undeniably be hell.

## HUSTON'S UNSPARING GAZE

I realized it *[The Battle of San Pietro]* wasn't any picture
about combat or any military film that they had ever seen. I
knew they were in for something of a surprise, but I wasn't
prepared for the shock with which they received it.
—John Huston, "John Huston: A War Remembered"

*The Battle of San Pietro* needs little introduction; the public has always embraced it as one of the very best war documentaries ever made. The

*The Battle of San Pietro:* Huston was a pioneer in the art of combat photography.

power and poignancy of its imagery still speak eloquently about the horror and futility of war and the resiliency of the human spirit, despite the film's melodramatic and propagandistic storyline. Indeed, this latent tension in *The Battle of San Pietro* between intentions that are doctrinaire and reactions that are personal, sensitive, and spontaneous is also implied in Huston's later explanation that "we knew what we wanted to say, but the story told itself."[9] *The Battle of San Pietro* is unique in that the winning is constantly underplayed while the suffering and sacrifice is accorded tantamount attention.

This result was clearly not what the high command had in mind when it originally ordered Huston in the fall of 1943 to produce a film that would document the successful liberation of Rome by the Allies. When in fact the Italian campaign didn't proceed as smoothly as anticipated, Huston's mandate was adjusted to his making a film specifically for American audiences on why the advance of the U.S. Army in Italy had been slowed to a virtual halt. Proceeding to the front and learning firsthand how to tell his story was an experience that had a profound effect on Huston, the man and film artist. The tragedy of the Italian campaign was a ripe stimulus for such soul searching and rethinking of priorities; this phase of World War II was marked by useless battles, herculean body counts, and seemingly endless sieges with a retreating German army that stubbornly entrenched itself in the rugged and mountainous Italian terrain.

*The Battle of San Pietro* is actually a mixture of two documentary film styles. Like *Report from the Aleutians,* the movie has many authoritarian aspects; on the other hand, *The Battle of San Pietro* also exhibits formal elements that are closely associated with the cinema vérité movement of the 1950s and 1960s, such as longer takes, hand-held- and mobile-camera work, and on-the-spot interviewing. Huston's approach to filmmaking benefited greatly from his temporary, war-imposed sojourn from Hollywood; he had come to rely too heavily on working in a studio and doing adaptations from literary sources. In this way, his war experiences provided him with opportunity to broaden his filmmaking repertoire by essentially forcing him to create original motion pictures on location. The liberating effect of these changes in setting and context cannot be underestimated when explaining the reasons behind Huston's attitudinal and stylistic development in the nonfiction mode which begins to noticeably take hold in *The Battle of San Pietro* and later continues to have an even greater impact on the results of *Let There Be Light.*

The battle for San Pietro took place between December 8 and December 15, 1943. The bloodletting and body counts were relentless as Allied forces slowly battled both the geography and the German resistance. Huston's documentary has its share of diagrams, maps, and a narration that is intended to describe the strategy behind the conflict and explain how this struggle developed. The American army eventually triumphs over the terrain and the retreating Nazis while John Huston's voice-over announces the victory; still, the overall tone of the film is inconclusive. The audience is never told why San Pietro is so important or what justifies the death and sacrifice of more than one thousand GIs in the combat surrounding this tiny village.

Several Vietnam-era critics have from their mindset interpreted this disquietude on Huston's part as being full-fledged "pacifism" and "antiwar" in sentiment.[10] Huston himself has said, however, that "it was anything but done out of hatred of war on my part. It was done out of a profound admiration for the courage of the men who were involved in the ghastly thing."[11] In other words, Huston's direct familiarity with a battleground as brutal as San Pietro further demystified the war experience for him beyond just the boredom that is communicated in *Report from the Aleutians;* combat makes most soldiers suspicious of warrior legends. Instead of presenting his comrades within the romance and artificiality that frames most World War II documentaries, John Huston accorded his fellow GIs the compliment of recording their actions as honestly and as unencumbered by hyperbole and official doctrine as he could.

Huston first unveiled *The Battle of San Pietro* to a screening room filled with his superiors and other army officers during October 1944. The reaction was nearly unanimous: Members of the audience began to walk out about three-quarters of the way through the documentary.[12] Despite the fact that *The Battle of San Pietro* is still a propaganda film that portrays the conflict exclusively from the American point of view, the pain inherent in many of the images is both poignant and unmistakable. As the sometimes sardonic narration provides a step-by-step accounting of the Allied victory, graphic pictures in this first cut of the documentary included handheld shots capturing falling and wounded GIs in battle; a close-up of a single boot attached only to the fragment of a leg and foot; an occasional world-weary or even shell-shocked stare from a U.S. enlisted man or Italian civilian; and finally an ending composed most powerfully of several easily recognizable American soldiers now being placed by fellow comrades into body bags as their previously recorded words are heard in voice-over speaking about what they thought the world would be like after the war. In Huston's mind he had constructed, in the most personal and expressive terms he could, a tribute to these soldiers that revealed the enormity of the horror that they were forced to face and endure, and in turn the resulting sacrifice that they all had made in the war effort. His initial audience of Pentagon officers interpreted the motion picture differently, and a move was quickly expedited to either censor or shelve this documentary.

The controversy surrounding *The Battle of San Pietro* actually heated to a level that the army's chief of staff and newly appointed five-star general, George C. Marshall, asked to see the film. His reaction to the subsequent viewing was generally positive, much to the relief of Huston. General Marshall did, however, suggest a number of cuts, including the shot of the bloodied boot and more significantly the entire final sequence highlighting the dead faces of the GIs and their voice-overs. In the film's final edit, in fact, the only dying stares that remain are those that are frozen on Nazi soldiers; in contrast, the fallen Americans are typically shot from the back as they are hoisted into their body bags. All of these shots are still

Too many American soldiers filling body bags caused the censorship of portions of *The Battle of San Pietro.*

disclosive and moving; the illustrative and vivid impact of these pictures is not easily censored. Nevertheless, the released version of *The Battle of San Pietro* is somewhat watered down from the original, although this film still remains the most graphic and honest account of combat during World War II ever documented on celluloid.

John Huston "more or less agreed" with General Marshall's deletions, including the ending sequence, which Huston found in hindsight to be "rather too emotional I think."[13] What remains is a camera-eye that begins to step back at times from the usual authoritarian posture of most World War II documentaries in order to record in fascinating detail men under the pressure of live fire; this time, though, the violence and danger saps the spirit and wreaks devastation. The test of combat in *The Battle of San Pietro,* therefore, is one of survival, not some rite of passage. In his own way, Huston successfully exposes a good deal of the reality that underlies this traditional adolescent fantasy of proving one's worth and toughness in battle. In so doing, he offers a more understated and compassionate memorial to the men who fought and died at San Pietro; and in the process, he violates and demystifies what the Pentagon had wanted to believe about the heroism and glamour of GI Joe and the grand significance enveloping each American victory in the Italian campaign.

Huston also adopted more "objective" strategies, such as mobile, probing camera work, and the filmed interview. In the former instance, World War II precipitated the more rapid refinement of 16mm film equipment; this gauge became more common and widespread throughout the duration of the global conflict. Developments in technology, therefore, made it possible for Huston's troops to gather a majority of the combat footage in *The Battle of San Pietro* at close range and under fire. Some question has been raised recently about whether most of the sequences in this documentary are in fact reenactments.[14] Reviews of the film's outtakes at the National Archives in Washington, D.C., do demonstrate that some of the battle scenes as well as the final sequence involving the Italian civilians coming out of hiding and returning to San Pietro after the Germans had been driven from their town were actually shot as late as January 22, 1944, or five full weeks after the battle ended.[15] Still this stock footage has a more artificial and unhurried look than what is evident in most of the explosive, vérité-like fighting sequences. It is reasonable to literally accept the final title in *The Battle of San Pietro,* which states, "All scenes in this picture were photographed within range of enemy small arms or artillery fire. For purposes of continuity a few of these scenes were shot before and after the actual battle of San Pietro." Whether or not more footage was indeed staged than is readily apparent through a review of the surviving outtakes remains to be seen. This possibility, however, still doesn't detract from the overall "poetic truth" of *The Battle of San Pietro;* this film clearly is more honest, insightful, and complex than any other combat documentary of its era.

*The Battle of San Pietro* was not the only World War II nonfiction film to employ hand-held combat footage taken at close range. What is significant, though, is that John Huston at times strikes the pose of an observer rather than a propagandist, and lets these pictures stand on their own without interpretation. He was also wise enough to give voice to the American foot soldiers through the aforementioned interviews. As cited before, these recordings, used as voice-overs in the first edit, were eliminated in the final cut. In this way, the technique itself provided a final sequence that made the thrill of victory unconvincing, if not the purpose of the battle questionable; the vérité aspects of these interviews were frankly ahead of their time and downright taboo in 1944.

On balance, John Huston willingly "agreed with the cuts," and stated in 1981 that "the body of the picture was left intact."[16] Huston's growing awareness about the essential nature and impact of warfare on the humans involved enabled him to reach beyond his contemporaries in the Armed Forces Pictorial Service to produce a lasting document of inspiration and subtlety in *The Battle of San Pietro* that audiences today respond to with more than feelings of mere nostalgia or a passing historical curiosity. Overall this film was highly progressive in breaking beyond the bonds of what was acceptable to think and speak about in a public forum during 1943–1944, and in the process this motion picture provides future generations with the most honest appraisal available that fighting the "good war" could indeed be as overtaxing and heart-wrenching as fighting a "bad war" like Vietnam.

*The Battle of San Pietro* was finally released to the general public across the United States between May 21 and July 1945, or seven months after the final version was completed; this delay also followed on the heels of V-E Day, which occurred on May 7.[17] As a small consolation and vindication, however, Huston did receive a promotion from captain to major for his efforts. His troubles with army censorship were far from over though; he would venture even further into the realm of challenging official and acceptable attitudes about the American GI in the shaping and design of his next project, *Let There Be Light*.

## SEARCHING FOR THOSE MOMENTS OF REVELATION AND DISCOVERY

In the thick of the Sicily campaign and not far from the front,
Patton was touring hospital tents near San Stefano.
He went the rounds commending wounded soldiers.
Then he came upon one who sat on the edge of his cot.
"Where are you wounded?" asked Patton.
The soldier, a "shell-shock" case, mumbled something
about hearing shells that never landed and
guessed it was his nerves. Well known for his disbelief

in the reality of "shell-shock," Patton flew into a rage,
called the soldier "yellow-bellied," and gave him a back-handed
cuff that knocked off the man's helmet lining.
A nurse lunged at the general but was restrained and led away
weeping. As he was leaving, Patton heard the soldier
sobbing. He strolled back and slapped the private again.
At about the same time, Patton similarly upbraided
another "shell-shocked" victim.
—"Patton's Slap," *Newsweek*, December 6, 1943

The American war most associated with the "shell-shocked," or the mentally fatigued, disabled, or even disturbed soldier is Vietnam; this linkage has as much to do with unknowingness and the suppression of information surrounding these kinds of disabilities in respect to World War II as it has to do with the character of the war itself in Southeast Asia. The raw and gritty nature of *The Battle of San Pietro* offers some explanation to the contemporay viewer on why "20% of all battle casualties in the American Army during World War II were of neuro-psychiatric nature."[18] Huston's charge to produce a documentary about the "Returning Soldier—Nervously Wounded (or Psychoneurotic)" offered him a project that continued logically from the lessons that he had learned and the darkness that he had encountered in his battle experience in the Liri Valley; now he was ordered to investigate and record the rehabilitation process of those war-wearied GIs who had themselves become casualties of the mind in the face of their own personal "San Pietros" in theaters throughout Europe and the Pacific.

The above incident involving General Patton also is meant to give some indication into the general ignorance and naiveté of most Americans about mental illness in 1945–1946. Granted, the general population was typically not as savage in its nescience and inexperience with neuropsychiatric disorders as George Patton. Still, there was evident backlash that manifested itself in the American mass media in the form of hysterical newspaper and magazine articles designed to address the worst fears of people at the home front about the returning state of GI Joe's mind: "Any former serviceman who got into trouble was seized upon as empirical support of the War-Crazed Veteran theory. Daily newspaper headlines exploited the fears, and the following were not atypical: 'Veteran Beheads Wife with Jungle Machete'—'Ex-Marine Held In Rape Murder'—'Sailor Son Shoots Father'—'Crazed Vet Goes Berserk.' "[19]

The ultimate irony about this feverish outpouring of distrust is that "the veteran problem turned out to be no problem at all. Except for a troubled handful, most veterans wanted nothing more than to pick up where they had left off before induction, or to make up for civilian joys lost while in uniform."[20] William L. O'Neill performed this diagnosis decades after the fact in the introduction to his book, *American Society since 1945;* the War Department's orders of May 7, 1945, engaged a problem that appeared to be all too real at the time:

> The film on the "Nervously Wounded (or Psychoneurotic)" should
> (1) point out what a small proportion fall into this category; (2) eliminate the stigma now attached to the psychoneurotic through explanation of the conditions of what it really is—thus to offset the exaggerated picture that has already been given to the public through the press, magazine and radio stories; and (3) explain that in many cases the reason that makes a psychoneurotic unsatisfactory for the Army is the very reason for which this same person could be a real success in civilian life. (It has been stated by separatees that those qualities which made them a success as a civilian were the very things that made them *crack up* [my emphasis] as a soldier.)[21]

By June 25, 1945, Major John Huston was assigned to produce *The Returning Psychoneurotics* with the specific command that, above all else, the documentary should convince prospective employers that they have nothing at all to fear in hiring one of these ex-GIs. Like most everyone else in American society at the time, Huston admits that "beyond a superficial acquaintance with the ideas of Freud, Jung and Adler, I was completely uninformed regarding the new science of psychiatry."[22] Indeed, the level of the army's unsophistication and naiveté concerning the area of psychoneurosis is clearly evident in its May 14, 1945, directive to obtain a print of RKO's *The Enchanted Cottage* (1945) as a means of doing background research on the topic of mental disturbances and their relationship to the soon-to-be-discharged World War II veterans.[23]

To put this order into perspective, *The Enchanted Cottage* is a well-meaning but contrived melodrama about an injured army flier who is struggling to cope with civilian life. The role of the discharged veteran is played by Robert Young, whose injury is a nasty scar on the left side of his face; his trial in life, therefore, is "to face life as ugly." The heroine is Dorothy McGuire, who proves that love transforms personal hardship by eventually bringing the hero out of his shell. *The Enchanted Cottage* was one of four similar morality tales about disabled or disturbed veterans that were produced by Dore Shary for RKO and United Artists between March 1945 and July 1946.[24]

The reassimilation of shell-shocked or injured GIs was obviously a popular issue to many Americans during the months that served as the production period for Huston's developing documentary on neuropsychiatry; still, it is a telling index to the attitudes about mental illness at the time that one of John Huston's commanding officers in the Signal Corps would actually direct him to a Hollywood potboiler as being good source material for further understanding of the subject matter at hand.

As much as *The Battle of San Pietro* was an education for Huston into the ravishes of war and suffering, the evolution of *Let There Be Light* out of the initial order to produce a film about the "Returning Soldier—Nervously Wounded" was even more of a growing and learning experience for him. Psychoanalysis had been somewhat of a fad in the Hollywood community just before World War II; therefore, Huston's knowledge of psychiatry up to this point was a result of what he had been able to pick up informally through his conversations with his friends in the movie colony.

He began the research phase of *Let There Be Light* by visiting a number of military hospitals on both the east and west coasts. He quickly decided to use Mason General Hospital on Brentwood, Long Island, for a number of reasons: First of all, Huston was impressed by the openness and receptivity of the doctors and staff that he met there; Mason General was also the biggest and most modern facility of its kind on the East Coast; and finally, the hospital itself was conveniently located near the army motion picture production center at Astoria Studio in Queens, New York. Huston next spent ten weeks on location executing a strategy that was designed to follow one group of soldiers suffering from war-induced neurosis from their entry into this particular military clinic until the time they would have completed the necessary therapy, and were thus ready to be discharged back into civilian life.

As with his previous documentaries, the structure of *Let There Be Light* is typical of the conventions of its era, such as a predictable storyline and an obligatory happy ending. Even more so than with *The Battle of San Pietro* before it, however, there are sequences in *Let There Be Light* that transcend the characteristic melodramatics with a hard-edged and emotionally authentic camera-eye. The integrity and compassion of Huston's

45

point of view is well honed at this point after his experiences in the Liri Valley as he now communicates an intimate understanding and sympathy for the predicament in which these GIs find themselves.

Huston incontestably had orders to follow, and *Let There Be Light* is still a propaganda film with a cumulative design that is meant to quell the fears of prospective employers. Huston nevertheless went much further in experimenting with both the form and content of his final wartime documentary than he had with his previous efforts. Despite the finely judged irony in the narration and the clarity of perception within certain scenes of *The Battle of San Pietro, Let There Be Light* is uncompromising in letting people and events be seen for what they are in the film's vérité segments; this time, no scenes are staged.

Like *The Battle of San Pietro* before it, *Let There Be Light* is a hybrid of both the authoritarian and cinema vérité styles; still, there is more of the "objective," probing camera in the latter motion picture as Huston had become more accustomed to this approach of photographing nonfiction footage. The director and his crew exposed approximately 375,000 feet of celluloid for *Let There Be Light,* which computes into an astronomical shooting ratio of 72 to 1 for this fifty-eight-minute documentary. By this time, Huston was obviously more taken with the joys of discovery through his use of the motion picture medium than with his lone charge to dictate a specific message and thus produce a film of influence and propaganda; in the final analysis, *Let There Be Light* is much more than a work of public relations.

The plot structure of this documentary is meant to put the "nervously wounded" veteran in the best possible light. The motion picture begins with the usual voice-over interpreting a montage of mentally injured and combat-exhausted soldiers being admitted for rest and rehabilitation to Mason General Hospital. Each group is typically composed of seventy-five patients who the film presents as "casualties of the spirit" that "in the fulfillment of their duties as soldiers, were forced beyond the limit of human endurance." Huston evidently confronted some of his own limitations and recognized those of his comrades at San Pietro; he was therefore perceptive enough, sensitive of what was to come, and consequently inclined to stand back and improvise with his film technique to allow the impact of the next important sequence to unfold on its own.

Huston thereupon sets up one camera on a doctor and another on a series of incoming GIs and then lets the technology record the subsequent proceedings as each patient responds to questions about the whys and wherefores of his present disability. The resulting twelve minutes is arguably the best footage in *Let There Be Light* and reason enough to earmark this film as an exceptional human and social document.

The style of this segment predates the British free-cinema and American vérité movements by more than a decade, as Huston relies solely on "talking heads" and the inherent drama in each of these disabled soldier's individual stories to hold interest in the sequence. He is successful as twelve different GIs recount their various fears, as well as the horror of seeing friends and acquaintances killed before their eyes; in the process, these men exhibit a number of psychoneurotic symptoms, such as whispering, mumbling, crying, stuttering, shaking, wandering concentration, and a tendency to avoid their doctor's gaze. It is a genuinely sad and poignant sequence filled with rambling conversations, faraway looks, and startling self-appraisals like "I guess I just got tired of living" and "I used to always have fun. I used to be going places . . . I don't go no more."

The rest of the documentary evidences a pattern of checkerboarding where a conventional montage sequence, which describes the action in a voice-over, is interspersed with a more neutral and observational vérité segment of much longer takes and ambient sound. This strategy ultimately makes certain parts of *Let There Be Light* far more satisfying than the whole since the artificiality of the authoritarian style clashes with the inherent spontaneity of those sequences that speak for themselves.

Besides the aforementioned sequence of interviews, there are five scenes in *Let There Be Light* that are predominantly vérité in style. These five sections constitute forty-three of the film's fifty-eight minutes, or nearly three-quarters of the screen time, This percentage is a substantial stylistic change from *The Battle of San Pietro,* which is composed of a running voice-over that accompanies most of the text, interpreting the action and images.

The five scenes in *Let There Be Light* that contain elements of vérité filmmaking are: a young soldier unable to walk is administered an injection of sodium amytol as "a short cut to the unconscious mind," which successfully begins his therapy by dramatically allowing him to walk again; a room full of men undergo group psychotherapy and talk about their "inner conflicts"; a GI who lost his memory during a shellburst at Okinawa is hypnotized and begins to recall his fear and terror of battle; another soldier who stutters is also given sodium amytol to induce a state

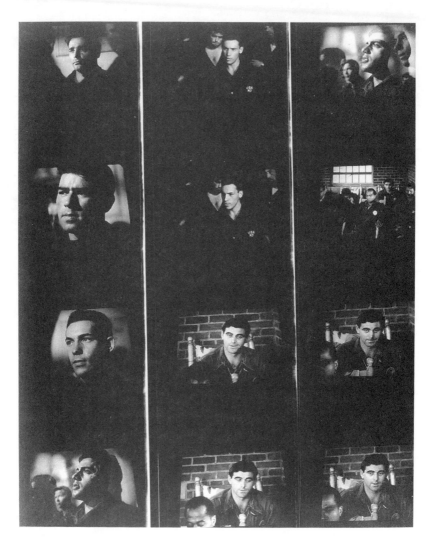

*Let There Be Light:* the agonized faces of the psychoneurotic soldiers.

similar to hypnosis that emphatically brings him to tears as he clearly states, "I can talk! Oh, God, listen! God, I can talk!"; and a final group meeting that is actually less an exercise in therapy than it is an opportunity for the men to speak directly to the camera about how they want to be treated, how they think the world will react to them after they are discharged, and what they believe they have to offer to future employers.

Several critics have rightly pointed out that the above scenes in *Let There Be Light* create a strong impression that many of these patients are quickly and miraculously cured despite several sections in the narration that qualify the dramatic turnabouts on the screen as merely first steps toward total rehabilitation.[25] The major flaw in the film certainly is this strong disposition to believe in the unfailing powers of the various military psychiatrists at Mason General. This sense of blind faith about the wonders of psychiatry is indeed reinforced by the very title of the film, *Let There Be Light,* which at times deflects the film's focus from its premiere strength: Huston's undaunted and unadorned gaze at the struggle of each of these GIs with his own personal neurosis.

The highlight of the final sequence, for example, is a baseball game where painful and telling segments from the opening interviews are cross-cut with the vigorous displays of energy and enthusiasm that are presently being brandished on the ballfield, most particularly, the stutterer is now portrayed as an assertive umpire, while the young man who couldn't walk speeds around the bases for a home run. The implicit conclusion in this documentary's final, upbeat sequence is clear: These shell-shocked soldiers have been taken care of and transformed by a caring and understanding army that won't abandon its men.

Unfortunately, this specific use of parallel editing diverts attention away from the men's pain and the potential to further explore in depth the process of their recoveries. No doubt, the propaganda imperative of *Let There Be Light* will always give contemporary audiences pause, as viewers today are much less inclined to accept without question that these men have recovered so thoroughly and completely in just ten short weeks.

To put the film into perspective, *Let There Be Light* is simply not as pure an exercise in cinema vérité as audiences are now accustomed to after more than three decades of development and maturation of this form; the film is, however, a hybrid example and precursor to the eventual emergence of this style in the late 1950s. Moreover, *Let There Be Light* offers much more than the predictability of the official military position. Huston's honesty, intelligence, and sensitivity also allowed him to select and focus on those telling moments that those in the army typically ignored, didn't notice, or frankly wouldn't admit. The sight of sincere though tormented GIs left crying, stuttering, or shaking in the wake of their combat experiences flies in the face of the " 'warrior' myth, which said that our American soldiers went to war and came back all the stronger for the experience, standing tall and proud for having served their country well."[26] Huston's message was, in its own way, patriotic but with a different twist: He exposes us to the unabashed pain and anguish of World War II's forgotten GIs and implies in the process that they too "served their country well."

Huston went further to assert that a psychoneurotic impairment is no more disgraceful than a physical injury. This point of view is all the more remarkable when it is remembered that most people in the America of 1945–1946 were traditionally indifferent or even antagonistic toward the "the returning soldier—nervously wounded." Mental illness was still a taboo subject in American society, and the shell-shocked soldier was considered by many in the armed services to be a malingerer, a quitter, or a coward. Dr. William C. Menninger's pioneering study about the extent and reality of the army's psychiatric casualties during World War II, *Psychiatry in a Troubled World,* was still nearly two years away from publication.[27]

Huston, therefore, was well ahead of his time in taking pains in *Let There Be Light* to reveal the truth, as he knew it, about the prevalence and ordinariness of being a psychoneurotic casualty of World War II; in so doing, he was also wise enough to gravitate slowly to a newer, more probing, and observational film style that was necessary to let these veterans, in a sense, speak for themselves. The reaction of the Department of the Army to such an unfettered picture of veteran GIs in psychological distress far surpassed the alarm and outrage elicited by *The Battle of San Pietro.* What resulted was a long-term ban of the film that in effect successfully inhibited and suppressed the future influence of *Let There Be Light* on the subsequent evolution of both the style and content of nonfiction filmmaking in America during the 1950s and 1960s; it would be nearly a decade after the completion of this documentary before similar vérité experiments began to appear in either England or the United States.

## THE AUTHORITY OF THE MILITARY IS PARAMOUNT

To this day I don't know who the opponents of this picture
were, or are, but they have certainly been unflinching in their
determination that it shall not be seen.
—John Huston, *An Open Book*

In the second and final group therapy scene in *Let There Be Light,* one of
the GI patients sums up his feelings and hopes about the prospective employers he believes he will likely encounter after his discharge: "Well, if
he's an intelligent man . . . why he's going react the same way as any other
normal human being would. He's going to say . . . I'll try him out." The
irony of this statement, in hindsight, is that the army, his then present support group and association, would itself come up short in having the necessary faith and intelligence to accept these recovering psychoneurotic
veterans for who they were, as well as trust that the civilian population
across the United States would be able to understand and respond appro-
priately to the intended message of this documentary.

No one, of course, got the chance to prove that Army Public Relations was wrong in suppressing this motion picture. On February 14, 1946,
Maj. John Huston was ordered to hand carry a release print of *Let There
Be Light* on a trip from New York to Washington for the usual approval
showing the next day.[28] Huston obeyed this directive, and the film was approved verbally for public release by the Army Pictorial Service the following week.[29] Sometime between the end of February and the beginning
of March, however, the policy group of Army Public Relations convinced
the United States War Department to restrict he distribution of *Let There
Be Light* from each and every public and military concern except seven
military hospitals in America, the Veterans Administration, the U.S. Department of the Navy, any service command Signal Corps libraries, and all
overseas theaters of battle for viewing by relevant military personnel.[30]

The official order limiting the release of *Let There Be Light* was issued on March 11, 1946; this dictate contained no reasons whatsoever for
the ban. In a letter sent the same day by Lt. Harry P. Warner, post legal
officer of the Army Signal Corps, mention is made of a telephone call to
the Pentagon in reference to the existence of "clearances on [the] subject."
Lieutenant Warner moreover states that "all personnel who appear in the

film have authorized showing of the film on a world-wide basis."[31] On April 2, 1946, Capt. David Burman of the Signal Corps mailed two photostatic copies of each of the military personnel releases for *Let There Be Light* to the Pentagon; by this time, though, he also makes mention of the fact that four of the enlisted men who appeared in the film had not "executed releases."[32] In addition, these veterans had already been discharged from the army and no effort was made henceforth to secure clearances from them. It appears that Army Public Relations now had found its first official rationale for restricting the subsequent distribution and exhibition of *Let There Be Light;* the Pentagon began to use this question of the film's waivers as a means of arguing for its prohibition.

John Huston and the Army Pictorial Service were next informed by Army Public Relations that their documentary was deemed an invasion of privacy for the shell-shocked patients depicted in the picture; consequently, *Let There Be Light* was subject to policy censorship. Huston's reaction was adamant: "It was decided by the policy department. The film was 'unsuitable.' They said they felt it was unfair to the patients, to the men. In that case, I could see no justification for the film ever having been made at all. The original purpose, you know, was stated by the same people. Their argument is rather a paradox."[33] What makes this claim even more paradoxical in retrospect is the fact that the Pentagon had approved the publication of photographs made from certain frames of *Let There Be Light* as pictorial accompaniments for articles related to the topic of psychoneurotic veterans in two major, mass-circulated, American magazines. The first of these instances, it should be noted, occurred before the entire controversy seemed probable, or even possible. In early October 1945, Helen Robinson, an editorial staff member of *Life,* contacted the army to secure clearance for 241 frames of the film that Huston and Gene Fowler were then editing.[34] *Life* needed the photographs to support a short story written by John Hersey about the dramatic treatments that were being experimented with and developed by the army at the time to treat psychiatric casualties. Since Hersey's article was a work of fiction, no actual soldiers were identified by name; nevertheless, eleven stills appeared with the text: nine pictures of the young soldier who could not walk, and two shots of the chronic stutterer.[35] Both men had been located at their homes after being discharged by officials of the U.S. Signal Corps, and each cabled a release to *Life* by Western Union.[36] On October 29, 1945, this issue of *Life* reached the newsstands, and photographs in close-up and medium shot of the two relevant parties were then available for millions of readers to see.

More surprisingly, the same scenario replayed itself during the six weeks that approval for the standard, domestic distribution of *Let There Be Light* was being debated and reviewed. On January 27 and again on February 1, 1946, Dorothy Wheelock, associate editor of *Harper's Bazaar*, wrote the chief of Army Public Relations at the Pentagon to acquire frames from *Let There Be Light* in order to make photographs that would be used to reinforce a favorable commentary of the documentary that had been written by Frances McFadden.[37] In deference to the army and in good faith, Wheelock enclosed a copy of McFadden's review so Pentagon officials could inform the magazine of "any deletions which [they] wished made."[38] Wheelock, McFadden, and *Harper's Bazaar* art director, Alexey Brodovitch, had seen a rough-cut of the film at Astoria Studio in early January at the personal invitation of John Huston. Maj. Dallas Halverstadt, chief of Army Public Relations, next informed Wheelock by phone that permission would only be granted when he received the appropriate releases from the men appearing in the motion picture.[39] As mentioned earlier, photostatic copies of these clearances did not reach his office until April 12, 1946, or nearly three weeks after the official ban was imposed.[40] Quite clearly, the argument about holding back the film because of the four missing releases had not been formulated yet because, preposterously, approval was relayed to Dorothy Wheelock at *Harper's Bazaar,* and three close-ups of the young veteran who couldn't walk accompanied publication of McFadden's commentary in the May 1946 issue of the magazine; again, the soldier was not identified by name, but his face was ever present for millions to witness.[41]

Why would Army Public Relations ban the distribution of *Let There Be Light* to the general public on March 11 and then release frames of the film in early April for the purpose of eventual publication in *Harper's Bazaar*? The reason for this seeming contradiction appears to be twofold: First, the Pentagon's argument that *Let There Be Light* was an invasion of privacy had indeed not been formulated yet. Consequently, Army Public Relations was not thinking in terms of the fact that they too would be "invading a patient's privacy" by releasing pictures of him to a magazine that had national exposure. Second, there had to be a misstep or oversight in the decision-making process by what Huston calls "that bureaucratic morass [at] the War Department."[42] Why else would Army Public Relations agree to release pictures to accompany a review of a film that they had no intention of releasing domestically?

On orders in April 1946, the Signal Corps sent the original releases from *Let There Be Light* to the Pentagon. Huston later reported that "the War Department decided that they would pay no attention to any releases. And then the releases themselves became 'mislaid' there, or lost in the shuffle at the Pentagon."[43] Obviously, there was no fighting the jurisdiction of the Pentagon; the authority of the military is always paramount in matters that fall within its own purview. Huston himself had been shocked by the entire controversy; he had from the start believed that *Let There Be Light* was a hopeful and inspiring film. He instead found some solace in the fact that he had taken one of the first two release prints back with him to California, much to the chagrin of the War Department; at least he would now have a copy of his own motion picture for safe keeping.[44] Huston was also left with a modicum of consolation in the belief that someday the ban on *Let There Be Light* would be lifted; unfortunately, this reprieve took thirty-five years.

*Let There Be Light* became a cause célèbre with several New York film critics, especially James Agee of *The Nation* and Archer Winston of the *New York Post,* when the motion picture curators at the Museum of Modern Art tried to have a special screening of this documentary during the early summer of 1946. Huston requested and received permission from Army Public Relations to schedule and screen his picture. On the afternoon of the showing, however, just minutes before the appointed starting time of the viewing with an audience assembled, two military policeman arrived and confiscated the print; the Pentagon had changed its mind at the very last minute, and much of the New York film community was outraged by the action.

What resulted was a vigorous effort by Arthur Mayer, a prominent New York exhibitor and importer-distributor of both notable international and controversial domestic motion pictures, to rescue and release *Let There Be Light* for public consumption in 1947. The time was not propitious for such a coup, though, as the War Department only allowed the documentary to be seen during 1947 and 1948 by three groups or individuals other than those who were originally authorized in the aforementioned March 11, 1946, directive that had limited the scope of the picture's distribution and exhibition: Not surprisingly, two of these parties were respected members of the American psychological establishment, while the third was a Hollywood producer who was researching a film on psychoneurotic behavior.[45]

The U.S. Army Pictorial Service actually produced a docudrama in the summer and fall of 1947 that was based on *Let There Be Light. Shades of Gray* (1948) was released in January and was entered by the U.S. Signal Corps in that year's best documentary category for the Academy Award; the film was not selected, nor was it nonfiction. The army wanted to recreate the impact and immediacy of *Let There Be Light,* but this time they decided to use actors in a drama employing documentary stylistics that would be based on actual case histories of psychoneurotic patients. The result is tepid, overly sentimental, and superficial when compared to the original. This time the "powers that be" controlled the characterizations of the shell-shocked GIs, and the result was a picture of fictionalized courage and valor, rather than the reality of disabled and distressed veterans who were overwhelmed and sometimes out of control. John Huston thought little of the film when he saw it.

The concern about the suppression of *Let There Be Light* subsided considerably after 1948. The issue of psychoneurotic GIs was obviously no longer current or pressing; the attention of most Americans went elsewhere. John Huston himself enjoyed one of the greatest successes of his career in 1948 with the production and release of *The Treasure of the Sierra Madre;* with this film, he returned to making adaptations, although his war experience would in the future incline him toward shooting most of his subsequent motion pictures on location.

Some twenty-five years after the initial ban of *Let There Be Light,* James B. Rhoads, head archivist at the National Archives and Records Service, conceived of a program that would be a "Salute to John Huston" during the first week of October 1971. He intended to promote and screen for the public each of Huston's wartime documentaries, including *Let There Be Light.* On September 9, 1971, nevertheless, Mr. Rhoads was notified by the Pentagon that the ban on this documentary was still in effect because "it is believed that a public release now would constitute an unwarranted invasion of privacy."[46] Not enough of the right people had applied the necessary pressure to free the film this time; the process to recover and extricate *Let There Be Light* would actually begin in earnest nine years later during the final year of the Carter administration.

The course of events that ultimately led to the documentary's release really began at the instigation of Ray Stark, who at the time was developing the motion picture adaptation of *Annie* with Huston, and who had produced three of the director's previous films: *The Night of the Iguana* (1964), *Reflections in a Golden Eye* (1967), and *Fat City* (1972). Stark, then head of Raystar Productions, spent months carrying his personal crusade to both industry and government officials. On Stark's suggestion, Jack Valenti, president of the Motion Picture Association of America, requested a print of the film from the Pentagon and screened it at his Washington office on November 7, 1980. Valenti's reaction was, "I was so moved by the film. I think it's a really seminal documentary"; and in turn, he began to use his considerable influence in the nation's capital to lobby for the release of *Let There Be Light* once and for all.[47] On November 8, the Los Angeles County Museum of Art held the first-ever public exhibition of the picture in an unauthorized screening during a Huston retrospective that the institution sponsored.[48] Joseph McBride contributed to the renewed interest in this documentary by writing a series of articles for *Variety* that championed the merits of the film and functioned to keep the issue of the ban in the public eye. *Let There Be Light* was a cause célèbre again after more than three decades.

During the second half of November 1980, Valenti convinced Army Secretary Clifford L. Alexander, Jr., to preview the motion picture in the context of reconsidering its prohibition; Valenti even obtained Vice President Mondale's assistance in his lobbying effort. Alexander, who was an old friend and associate of Valenti's from their days together in the Johnson administration, "lifted the ban after viewing the once controversial film and conferring with other Pentagon officials and legal counsel."[49] The order for the release of *Let There Be Light* was executed on December 16, 1980, by Brig. Gen. Lyle Barker, deputy chief of public affairs for the army. The film then had its first commercial, public opening at the Thalia in New York on January 16, 1981. Response by the New York film critics was generally mixed with a few even wondering "what the fuss is about."[50]

*Let There Be Light* had a very successful run in revival theaters across the country that year; and afterwards, the motion picture was shown with Huston's other wartime documentaries, along with an interview with the director on the topic of these productions, in a PBS broadcast that was syndicated to stations nationwide in late 1981 and 1982.[51]

In the succeeding years, *Let There Be Light* has been paired with *Report from the Aleutians* and *The Battle of San Pietro* to form one of the most popular distribution packages in the history of the National Audio

Visual Center. This agency, which functions under the aegis of the National Archives and Records Service, serves as a central clearinghouse for all federal motion pictures, audio recordings, and videotapes. In the words of William J. Blakefield, a research administrator at the center, the Huston "trilogy has met with overwhelming critical and popular response when shown before standing-room-only audiences at international film festivals, universities, and film societies . . . seen together they reflect an evolving awareness of the true nature of war."[52]

Beginning with the patriotic conviction and unselfconscious optimism of *Report from the Aleutians,* a straight-thinking and bitter sense of irony springs forth with *The Battle of San Pietro.* This second documentary is more questioning, exploratory, and upsetting than the first work. It is therefore little wonder that this film was cut down from five reels to three, and the controversial footage destroyed; *The Battle of San Pietro* had edged into those equivocations and subtleties that are always off limits for the official army version, and contrary to the myth of the invincible warrior. Lastly, *Let There Be Light* picked up where *The Battle of San Pietro* left off: Huston clearly understood from his own combat experience why the greatest number of psychoneurotic war casualties are always among the first troops going into fire; moreover, he now understood first-hand that the shell-shocked soldier was not a second-class citizen. With *Let There Be Light,* then, the clarity and compassion in John Huston's gaze became even sharper and more riveting than it had been in his previous documentaries.

Taken together, these three motion pictures are both a story and record of personal growth as well as a lucid index of their era and culture.[53] Huston's penchant toward a direct, unsentimental, and hard-boiled view of people and the world was well served through his trilogy; in hindsight, Huston's production of these war documentaries was a simple and elegant example of the right artist tackling the appropriate subject.

## NOTES

1. Col. K. B. Lawton, "Memorandum to Officer in Charge, Signal Corps Photographic Center, Western Branch," Dec. 19, 1942, in production case file for *Report from the Aleutians,* Film AF-114, National Archives and Records Service, Washington, D.C.

2. "John Huston: A War Remembered," KCET-TV (Los Angeles: Raystar Television, 1981). During this program, which was syndicated on PBS, John Huston was interviewed by Clete Roberts about his documentary trilogy. These films were then shown in their entirety.

3. Ibid.

4. Ibid.

5. Richard Corliss, "The Disasters of Modern War," *Time,* Jan. 19, 1981, 80.

6. Ibid; Scott Hammen, "At War with the Army," *Film Comment,* Mar. 1980.

7. Theodore Strauss, "The Signal Corps' Fine Film on Aleutians Was Held Up by Lamentable Argument," *New York Times,* Aug. 8, 1943.

8. Hammen, "At War with the Army," 20.

9. "John Huston: A War Remembered."

10. Hammen, "At War with the Army"; Lawrence H. Suid, *Guts and Glory: Great American War Movies* (Reading, Mass.: Addison-Wesley, 1978), 181–83.

11. Richard Griffith, "The Courage of the Men: An Interview with John Huston," in *Film Book 2: Films of Peace and War,* ed. Robert Hughes (New York: Grove Press, 1962), 29.

12. John Huston, *An Open Book* (New York: Alfred A. Knopf, 1980), 119.

13. "John Huston: A War Remembered."

14. David Culbert, "The Making of John Huston's *The Battle of San Pietro,*" a presentation of the University Seminar on Cinema and Interdisciplinary Interpretation, Museum of Modern Art, New York, Feb. 23, 1984.

15. "Source Film: Captain Huston's Team Coverage—San Pietro, Italy," 111, ADC, 636, Signal Corps MP, silent, 980 feet, National Archives and Records Service, Washington, D.C.

16. "John Huston: A War Remembered."

17. James Agee, "Films," *The Nation,* May 26, 1945, 608; Bosley Crowther, " 'San Pietro' Is Given A 'Bell,' " *New York Times,* July 15, 1945; Manny Farber, "War without Glamour," *New Republic,* July 30, 1945, 133; Philip T. Hartung, "The Stuff of Heroes," *Commonweal,* May 25, 1945, 141–42; and "San Pietro," *Time,* May 21, 1945, 94, 96.

18. Opening graphic in *Let There Be Light,* 91946, Army Pictorial Service, Signal Corps, U.S. War Department.

19. Joseph C. Goulden, *The Best Years: 1945–1950* (New York: Atheneum, 1976), 38.

20. William L. O'Neill, ed., *American Society since 1945* (Chicago: Quadrangle Books, 1969), 5.

21. Maj. A. M. Whitlock, "Memorandum to the Chief, Army Pictorial Service, the Pentagon," May 7, 1945, in the production case file for *Let There Be Light,* PMF-5019, 111, M, 1241, National Archives and Records Service, Washington, D.C. (This production case file will hereafter be referred to as PCF-Light.)

22. Huston, *An Open Book*, 122.

23. Maj. J. C. Blaustein, "Memorandum to the Director of the Training Films Division—What Is a Psychoneurotic?" May 14, 1945, in PCF-Light.

24. Besides *The Enchanted Cottage* (1945), Dore Shary produced the following three films involving the theme of shell-shocked or mentally disturbed GIs between 1945 and 1946: *I'll Be Seeing You* (1945), *They Dream of Home* (1945), and *Till the End of Time* (1946).

25. Corliss, "Disasters of Modern War"; Hammen, "At War with the Army"; Stanley Kauffmann, "Old but New, New but Old," *New Republic,* Jan. 31, 1981, 20; and Andrew Sarris, "Hobgoblins of Reality," *Village Voice,* Jan. 21–27, 1981, 45.

26. Huston, *An Open Book*, 125.

27. "Minds and War," *Newsweek,* May 24, 1948; and William C. Menninger, *Psychiatry in a Troubled World* (New York: Macmillan, 1948).

28. Capt. John G. T. Gilmour, "Memorandum to Mr. Harburger, Editorial Branch," Feb. 14, 1946, in PCF-Light.

29. Capt. John G. T. Gilmour, "Memorandum to Director, Control Division," Feb. 21, 1946, in PCF-Light.

30. Lt. and Col. K. McClure, "Memorandum to Chief Signal Officer, Army Pictorial Service," March 11, 1946, in PCF-Light.

31. 1st Lt. Harry P. Warner, "Memorandum to the Chief, Army Pictorial Service, the Pentagon," Mar. 11, 1946, PCF-Light.

32. Capt. David Burman, "Memorandum to the Chief, Army Pictorial Service, the Pentagon," Apr. 2, 1946, in PCF-Light.

33. Griffith, "Courage of the Men," 32.

34. Helen Robinson, letter to Maj. Warren Wade, Oct. 13, 1945; and Maj. Warren Wade, "Memorandum to Chief, Film Library Branch," Oct. 18, 1945, in PCF-Light.

35. John Hersey, "A Short Talk with Erlanger: The Army Is Using a Dramatic Treatment Called Narco-Synthesis to Help Psychiatric Casualties," *Life,* Oct. 29, 1945, 108–22.

36. Robert A Gerardi, telegram to Hildegard Maynard, "A Release to Publish Photographs of Gerardi," Oct. 12, 1945, in PCF-Light; and Eric M. Hofmeister, Jr., telegram to Hildegard Maynard, "A Release to Publish Photographs of Hofmeister," Oct. 12, 1945, in PCF-Light.

37. Dorothy Wheelock, letter to the chief, Army Public Relations, the War Department, Jan. 27, 1946, in PCF-Light.

38. Dorothy Wheelock, letter to Maj. Dallas Halverstadt, chief, Army Public Relations, the War Department, Feb. 1, 1946, in PCF-Light.

39. Dorothy Wheelock, letter to Colonel Barrett, commanding officer, Signal Corps, Photographic Center, Long Island City, N.Y., Feb. 1, 1946, in PCF-Light.

40. Capt. David Burman.

41. Frances McFadden, "Let There Be Light," *Harper's Bazaar,* May 1946, 116–17, 177.

42. Huston, *An Open Book,* 126.

43. Griffith, "Courage of the Men," 33.

44. Capt. John G. T. Gilmour, "Memorandum to Mr. Harburger, Editorial Branch," Feb. 27, 1946, in PCF-Light.

45. Col. R. E. Burns, "Memorandum to Chief, Motion Picture Branch—Authorization for Dr. Benjamin Simon, Clinical Director of the Connecticut State Hospital and Member of the Committee on Occupational Therapy of the American Psychiatric Association," Aug. 29, 1947, in PCF-Light; Emil A. Gutheil, M.D., letter to Lt. Col. James B. Buchanan, Signal Corps Photographic Center, a thank-you note for authorization accorded to the Association for the Advancement of Psychotherapy, Feb. 28, 1948, in PCF-Light; and Col. R. E. Burns, "Memorandum to Chief, Motion Picture Branch—Authorization for Mr. Joseph Seidelman of Universal International," May 8, 1947, in PCF-Light.

46. Jerry W. Friedheim, letter to Mr. James B. Rhoads, archivist of the United States, Sept. 9, 1971, in PCF-Light.

47. "Huston's Suppressed Army Film Prompts Valenti Plea to Pentagon," *Variety,* Nov. 19, 1980, 5.

48. "Suppressed 35 years. [sic], Huston's 'Let There Be Light' Is Great," *Variety,* Nov. 12, 1980, 26, 44. Bootleg prints of *Let There Be Light* had been circulating among private collectors ever since the mid-1970s. One of these unauthorized copies was shown at the Los Angeles County Museum of Art.

49. "Huston's 'Let There Be Light' Gets Green Light from Army," *Variety,* Dec. 17, 1980, 7, 28.

50. Vincent Canby, "Film: 'Let There Be Light,' John Huston vs. the Army," *New York Times,* Jan. 16, 1981; Corliss, "Disasters of Modern War"; Kauffmann, "Old but New"; Sarris, "Hobgoblins."

51. "John Huston: A War Remembered."

52. William J. Blakefield, *Documentary Film Classics* (Washington, D.C.: U.S. Government, 1984), 35.

53. The following are credits for Huston's documentary trilogy: *Report from the Aleutians* (1943), forty-seven minutes, color; producer: Army Pictorial Service, Signal Corps, U.S. War Department; director and writer: John Huston; camera: Jules Buck, Freeman Collins, Herman Crabtree, Buzz Ellsworth, and Rey Scott; and narrators: Walter and John Huston. *The Battle of San Pietro* (1945), thirty-three minutes, black and white; producer: Army Pictorial Service, Signal Corps, U.S. War Department; director, writer, and narrator: John Huston; camera: Jules Buck, John Huston, and many other Signal Corps cameramen; musical performances: Army Air Force Orchestra, Mormon Tabernacle Choir, and St. Brendan's

Boy's Choir. *Let There Be Light* (1946), fifty-eight minutes, black and white; producer: Army Pictorial Service, Signal Corps, U.S. War Department; director: John Huston; writers: Charles Kaufman and John Huston; camera: Stanley Cortez, John Doran, Lloyd Fromm, Joseph Jackman, and George Smith; editor: Gene Fowler, Jr.; music: Dimitri Tiomkin; narrator: Walter Huston (released to the general public on Dec. 16, 1980).

# Havana Episode: The Revolutionary Situation of *We Were Strangers*

ROBERT SKLAR

**B**etween *Key Largo* of 1948 and *The Asphalt Jungle* of 1950, two of his most famous post–World War II pictures, John Huston directed a film that has disappeared almost completely from history or memory. Resurrecting *We Were Strangers* (1949), however, is only of passing interest as a simple act of authorial revisionism. What marks *We Were Strangers* as a film worth recovering is its place within broader narratives of United States film history—the surprisingly ample subgenre of Hollywood films about Third World revolutionary situations, to which it belongs; and the specific conjuncture of its production and reception, a period of escalating anti-Communist repression following the imposition of the Hollywood Blacklist. Huston's role as author is inseparable from these industrial and ideological contexts.

The historical setting for the narrative of *We Were Strangers* was the overthrow of Cuban dictator Gerardo Machado y Morales in 1933. By

*We Were Strangers:* Third World revolutionary situations as imagined by Hollywood.

itself this subject matter might not have been so surprising. Latin American political rebellions had been occasional subjects of Hollywood filmmaking, often in the framework of adventure stories about American military or newspaper men. Frank Capra's *Flight* (1929), set in Nicaragua at the time of Augusto César Sandino's guerrilla war against U.S. marines, and the Howard Hawks/Jack Conway film, *Viva Villa!* (1934), on the Mexican revolution, are two earlier examples. By the late 1940s, however, in the midst of rising cold war hysteria, at a time when even intellectual discourse on the subject of revolutionary overthrow of governments was regarded by some as treasonable, a film on the subject was likely to be inflammatory in the extreme—particularly when, as with *We Were Strangers,* its principal focus was an act of terrorism.

Predictably, some critical responses did regard the film as virtually an act of treason. The influential trade paper *Hollywood Reporter* was shrillest in its denunciation, calling the film, memorably, "the heaviest dish of Red theory ever served to an audience outside the Soviet" and "a shameful handbook of Marxian dialectics."[1] A writer in a periodical called *The Tidings* gave the opinion that "the objectives of the independent company responsible for this production . . . invite public disapproval and official investigation. It is a shocking, depressing, and evil film."[2] The Los

Angeles chapter of the California Federation of Women's Clubs protested to the film's distribution company, Columbia Pictures, that it was "cleverly disguised propaganda to advance the Communist party line" and added this authorial note: "Mr. Huston's consistent support of Pro-Communist causes and programs has received much publicity."[3]

Indeed, it is likely that all of these comments were addressed not only to the film's contents and modes of representation but also to its director/coscreenwriter's recent political activities. In fall 1947, in response to the scheduled House Committee on Un-American Activities (HUAC) hearings into alleged Communist infiltration of the motion picture industry, Huston had been one of the founders (along with writer Philip Dunne and director William Wyler) of the Committee for the First Amendment, a liberal group opposed to the investigation on civil liberties grounds. The Committee for the First Amendment sponsored nationwide radio broadcasts defending free speech for the motion picture industry and sent a delegation of prominent Hollywood figures to Washington to attend the HUAC hearings. Their visit turned into something of a debacle, however, when HUAC rescheduled its witnesses so that the First Amendment notables arrived just in time for the tumultuous testimony of the first "unfriendly" witness to be called, writer John Howard Lawson, and the liberals became tainted by association with those defiant witnesses who were to become the Hollywood Ten.[4]

As the clubwomen's letter attests, Huston's political views had become subject to distortion and vilification. This does not seem to have fazed him, however, nor caused him difficulties within the motion picture industry. In the aftermath of the HUAC hearings and the beginning of the blacklist in December 1947, he seems to have made no public gestures of expiation to assure that he could continue his career (in contrast, say, to Humphrey Bogart, perhaps the biggest star name among the First Amendment travelers to Washington, who wrote a mea culpa of sorts in *Photoplay* under the title, "I'm No Communist.")[5] Huston was able to inaugurate without apparent hindrance an independent production company with producer Sam Spiegel, attract the interest of the well-known conservatives at Metro-Goldwyn-Mayer, finally take a better deal at Columbia for *We Were Strangers,* and then sign a lucrative MGM contract for other projects.[6] His *Treasure of the Sierra Madre* (1948), a strong political film beneath its adventure-genre exterior, was nominated for best picture, and Huston won Oscar awards for directing and screenwriting.

So presumably Huston could do no wrong in the eyes of the Hollywood establishment. Still, one might have thought someone would warn him about the potential for political trouble in making a film about revolution. However, it was not to be the film industry's watchdog and censor, Joseph I. Breen of the Production Code Administration, who in other circumstances had no difficulty harassing would-be makers of political films. The PCA's attitude toward the project was remarkably forthcoming. Though it requested script revisions before giving approval to the production, its tone was unfailingly supportive. "The purpose of this re-writing," as the board explained its specific suggestions, "is to establish in the minds of the audience that this revolutionary body is a legitimate enterprise, and to get away from any flavor that what they are engaging in is murder. More particularly, it seems to us important to establish clearly that the regime in office is a tyrannical one, in power by usurpation, and infringing upon the rights of its citizens."[7] In closing, the letter cautioned, "You will readily understand that a picture which sympathetically presents revolution by force may well meet with difficulty as regards its release in a number of countries."[8] No difficulty in the United States was suggested, however, none at all.

A paranoid film historian, if such a person exists, might wonder at this point if Huston was putting his head in the noose of some elaborate trap to ruin him through a political misstep. Rest easy, this was not at all the case. Indeed, such strong supporters of reactionary politics as the New York *Mirror* and Hearst columnist Louella O. Parsons gave positive reviews to the film. In response to the clubwomen's protest, it was a simple matter for Columbia Pictures to cite these impeccable sources of praise.[9]

Not all of this support, however, was necessarily for Huston. Though the director's brief remarks about the origins of the film in his autobiography suggest that the choice of a source was casual and inadvertent, from a political perspective it was also shrewd. The text was a section from a novel, *Rough Sketch,* by Robert Sylvester, a newspaper columnist then working as drama editor of the New York *Mirror.*[10] Sylvester's involvement seems likely to have assured that his own newspaper and perhaps others of similar right-wing ilk might resist the knee-jerk anticommunism that animated the *Hollywood Reporter.* (It also, however, might give us pause to consider whether the perspective on revolutionary action in the film might also stem from a right-wing source.)

Another buttress of the film's establishment respectability was the behind-the-scenes participation of producer David O. Selznick, after his pro-tégée and companion, Jennifer Jones, was cast in the film's leading female role. In the post-production phase Selznick sent the filmmakers one of his legendary memos, eleven single-spaced pages largely concerned with de-tails of cutting continuity and sound matching. He complained several times about the title, suggesting as alternatives *Havana '33, Havana, Cuba, Memory of Havana, Memory of Cuba, Incident in Havana, Havana Incident, Cuban Incident,* and *Havana Episode.*[11]

If the sort of praise *We Were Strangers* received from the contempo-rary discourse has proven insufficient to keep the film alive in Huston's canon, one might think the sort of condemnation it garnered would have activated more interest in the film during the politically revisionary 1970s and 1980s. Perhaps all points on the ideological spectrum have taken their cue from Huston's dismissal: "It wasn't a very good choice," he wrote in his autobiography, "and it wasn't a very good picture."[12] Whether it was a good picture is one matter, what kind of choice it was, quite another. That a producer as canny as Spiegel and a director as accomplished as Huston, to launch their independent production company, should have selected, in haste and without much thought, in a political climate so inhospitable, a subject so controversial and potentially dangerous, seems inherently im-probable. We need to give attention to what conscious purpose this film might have served. Certainly it is possible that Huston, with his strong record of support for free expression, was allegorically addressing the po-litical repression in the United States. Even more probable is the notion that the director, by his choice of subject for his first independent film, was declaring his fearlessness in the face of those who had accused him, at the least, of naiveté about communism.

The critic Vernon Young may have possessed some insight into Hus-ton's attitude when, in a letter to the director, he called *We Were Strangers* "certainly the definitive 'revolution' movie I've seen, probably the best of its kind Hollywood has done—yet not Hollywood—John Huston versus Hollywood and versus everyone else."[13] Huston's defiant mood perhaps found expression in a note he wrote to the *Hollywood Reporter*'s editor af-ter the trade paper's scathing attack on the film. "It may amuse you to hear," Huston told the editor, "that the only other paper that was unsympa-thetic to *We Were Strangers* was New York's *Daily Worker.*"[14]

What? The Communist daily newspaper also panned the film? From a tactical perspective, this was, so to speak, a godsend. The combination of praise from the right and condemnation from the left could, and did, render harmless the *Hollywood Reporter*'s reckless rhetoric. (Columbia Pictures' official, Lester Roth, also cited the *Daily Worker* criticism in his response to the Los Angeles clubwomen.) But what does it say about a film's ideological perspective—its representation of a Third World revolutionary situation—if the work wins friends on the right and critics on the left? The *Daily Worker*'s critique of *We Were Strangers* deserves closer attention, but before that we need to consider in more detail the film itself.

*We Were Strangers* opens with a lengthy scrolling text establishing the historical setting as Machado's Cuba in 1933:

> Something began to go wrong with the stars of nations in 1925. Tyranny
> and brutality were making their debut in the world—again. Among the first
> casualties was the lovely island of Cuba. A clique of corrupt politicos led by
> President Machado drove all liberty from the tropic shores. They throttled
> its press, gagged its voice, hanged its soul, paralyzed its honor and reduced
> its people to beggary and despair. With gibbet and gun they made a mockery
> of human rights and looted its industries and plantations. This is the story of
> the White Terror under which the island of Cuba cowered for seven long
> years until its freedom-loving heart found its heroes in 1933.

After this prologue concludes with a quotation from Thomas Jefferson—"Resistance to tyrants is obedience to God"—the first scenes present evidence both of tyranny and of resistance. A supine legislature votes to make the assembling of more than four people an act of treason. Police confiscate leaflets headlined "Viva Cuba Libre!" and beat bystanders with clubs. They shoot at a car distributing leaflets and wound the driver. A secret agent assassinates a student on the steps of a university building.

Jennifer Jones's character, China (pronounced "Cheena") Valdes, is a sister of the murdered student. Vowing vengeance, she joins an underground movement committed to revolutionary action. The leader of their secret cell is an American, Tony Fenner (played by John Garfield), whose presence in Cuba is ostensibly explained by his work as a theatrical agent (it later turns out that he was born in Cuba and that his efforts are supported financially by Cuban exiles in the United States). The other members are a dock worker, a bicycle mechanic, and an intellectual.

The group develops an ambitious scheme to assassinate the president and his entire ruling junta. The Valdes home is located near a cemetery.

The underground cell, led by the American (John Garfield), fomenting revolution.

They scout the graves until they find the family plot of a leading political figure. From the Valdes basement they will dig an underground tunnel to the grave site, pack it with explosives, and then murder the politician they have selected. When the president and his entourage gather by the grave for the burial, they will light the fuse and . . . blam!

Much of *We Were Strangers* focuses on the tense, painful, often gruesome struggle to dig the tunnel. They work in near darkness, covered with dirt and grime, amid the stench of the corpses they unearth from other graves. Though a major subplot involves a growing love interest between China and Fenner, these are hardly glamour roles for either of the star performers. When they are not digging, they agonize over the certainty that innocent people will be killed in order to eliminate the regime's leaders. The cruel agent who shot China's brother torments their above-ground hours—a tour-de-force performance of sadistic villainy by the Mexican actor Pedro Armendariz. The intellectual can't stand the pressure and runs off to confess, but he is heedless in his panic and is (conveniently) run over by a truck.

Jennifer Jones and John Garfield eschewing glamor for revolution.

"Sure the people may rise up and do the job themselves, tomorrow, or in a year," Fenner says. "We can't depend on that. We can't pull out now." At last the tunnel is ready, and the time for the assassination is at hand. Carried out by allies in the underground, the politician's murder takes place almost in a separate visual world. In contrast to the shadowy, tightly constricted interiors of the tunnel diggers, the assassination occurs outdoors on a highway, in long shot, with stunning sunlit clarity.

But irony intervenes. Despite the brutal success of the murder and the cruel labor of the tunnel, the dead man's relatives inadvertently foil the plan when they decide to bury him in a country graveyard. By that point the secret of the Valdes house has been uncovered. Police close in on the plotters. China and Fenner grimly fight back with machine guns and dynamite; she continues to fire even as he is mortally wounded. Suddenly, bells ring out, and a quick sequence shows "the people" overrunning the presidential palace and police headquarters, taking guns, and seizing power. The president's statue topples, the secret agent hangs upside down. Fenner died five minutes too soon, someone laments, and *We Were Strangers* ends.

One way to gain perspective on *We Were Strangers* is by comparing it to a film regarded as a preeminent cinematic representation of a Third World revolutionary situation, Gillo Pontecorvo's *La Battaglia di Algeria (The Battle of Algiers,* 1966). Clearly Huston's film does not share the didactic ideological purpose of Pontecorvo's. Yet there are a number of important similarities between the two works. In *The Battle of Algiers,* terrorism against innocents is also presented as an inevitable, if tragic, revolutionary strategy; the principal revolutionary figures are hunted down and killed; and the film ends with a spontaneous popular demonstration, undirected by the revolutionary leadership (although a closing voice-over makes clear that it is not the moment of national liberation, which, the voice says, came two years later).[15]

The major difference between *The Battle of Algiers* and *We Were Strangers* lies in the former film's effort to construct what the director called a "collective protagonist"—a spectator identification with the movement of an entire people rather than with individual protagonists.[16] The spectator of Pontecorvo's film is not left to puzzle out the crucial political questions that remain unanswered in the swift conclusion of Huston's: Where did "the people" come from, and how does their uprising relate to the underground cell's assassination plot? Were the defeated tunnel-diggers the heroes whom, according to the prologue, freedom-loving Cubans found? Or are we to understand their failure as a condemnation of their form of terror and its sacrifice of innocents?

One might argue that it is unrealistic to pose a comparison between a work made with the codes of Hollywood narrative in a reactionary political moment and a work that deliberately broke with such codes in an era far more hospitable to radical ideas.[17] But even a positive review of *We Were Strangers* in *Variety* (contrasting with its trade paper counterpart, the *Hollywood Reporter*) made note of a lack of connection between the film's individual protagonists and its collective action. "Machado overthrow," the *Variety* reviewer wrote, "occurring without relationship to the film's plot development (and without explanation), is anti-climactic and too pat.

Film could have packed considerable more documentary wallop if the revolt *which did in fact occur* [emphasis added] had been woven into the main story."[18]

The *Daily Worker*'s reviewer, José Yglesias, made a similar critique from ideological rather than aesthetic grounds. "We feel constrained," he wrote, "to object here to using a putschist bombing as characteristic of the fight for national independence."[19] Yglesias did not elaborate on this point, or the failure to link the revolutionary plot to the popular uprising, because he had an even stronger objection to the historical implications of the film's conclusion. Unlike the *Variety* reviewer, who (as emphasized above) accepted the outcome as historically factual, Yglesias argued with its basic historical premise:

> For its happy ending *We Were Strangers* contends that freedom returned to Cuba with Machado's ouster. That was not the case; Wall Street simply commanded with another figurehead. It was years before any political democracy was gained. This misrepresentation is typical of the movie. Its lack of intellectual backbone is responsible for its failure. Huston appears to think that he can film a revolution without feeling any responsibility for historical facts.[20]

Recent theories concerning historical discourse, as well as the representation of history in fiction films, make considerably more complex the standard of "historical facts" that Yglesias applies to the film.[21] The past is a field of discursive contestation in the present, conducted upon a body of documentation (which is also frequently in dispute). Historical films cannot be assessed by their adherence to an accepted, fixed, past "actuality," but are interpretations no different from other treatments of the past, to be read for their formal and ideological tropes. Within this framework, a first step in analyzing *We Were Strangers*'s perspective on Cuban history is to see how historical scholarship constructs the events of 1933.

It turns out, recent historians, if not quite echoing the *Daily Worker*'s rhetoric, generally support its view of the determining factors in Machado's ouster. A revolutionary situation did exist in Cuba in 1933. There were demonstrations and a crippling general strike. Acts of revolutionary terrorism and state terrorism frequently occurred. "Bombs exploded in central places of Havana," writes Luis E. Aguilar in *Cuba 1933: Prologue to Revolution,* "killing and injuring many persons; bursts of machine gun fire spread terror in the streets; in many ingenious and terrible ways soldiers, officers, and functionaries received the deadly message of the opposition."[22] In July 1932 a government official had been assassinated by automobile, much as depicted in *We Were Strangers*.

But if historical accounts emphasize the gravity of the revolutionary situation, they also stress that a revolution did not occur. The determining factor lay in diplomatic activities carried out by the United States. The new Franklin D. Roosevelt administration, coming to office in March 1933, faced in Cuba, writes historian Louis A. Perez, Jr., "nothing less than a crisis of hegemony."[23] The United States had been losing economic power over Cuba through the impact of the Great Depression and increasing foreign competition in the Cuban market. "It was clear," Roosevelt's ambassador to Havana, Sumner Welles, later wrote of his mission, "that the immense market for American agriculture and industrial exports should be restored to us."[24] Welles's specific instructions were to prevent the revolutionary situation from erupting into revolution.

Machado himself had pursued economic policies inhospitable to United States interests. Getting rid of him was central to United States aims. But among his opponents were many even more hostile to the United States than the dictator. With the threat of United States military intervention in the foreground, Welles pursued the goal of engineering Machado's removal with a minimum of turmoil and without threatening the power of those segments of the ruling classes friendly to the United States. "The real threat in August 1933," writes Perez, "as Welles readily understood, was contained in the deepening social struggle on the island and expressed most dramatically in the August general strike. Once again the United States rescued the social system threatened with revolution and prevented the displacement of its local political allies, thereby preserving intact the classes and structures essential for continued U.S. hegemony."[25]

Machado was removed, not by popular upheaval, but by behind-the-scenes United States political maneuvering. The popular uprising, the looting of government offices, the violent reprisals against Machado's secret agents, depicted as revolutionary rebellion in *We Were Strangers*, all occurred in the days *after* Machado's departure from office, rather than as part of the action that led to his overthrow.[26] The turmoil did help to bring down the figurehead who was Welles's choice as Machado's successor and put in place a government with more revolutionary aims. But the United States refused to recognize this radical government, a tactic that brought about its replacement in early 1934 by leadership more amenable to

United States interests. Ambassador Welles found congenial to his purposes in this period an emerging military figure, army sergeant Fulgencio Batista, whom United States sponsorship launched toward his future career as the dictator who brought "White Terror" back to Cuba.[27]

The most extensive contemporary discussion of *We Were Strangers,* by Gavin Lambert in the British film journal *Sequence,* takes up these issues not from the viewpoint of history but of film history and the historical film. "An American critic has remarked that historical films can be divided into two opposite categories," Lambert's review begins, "those like *Potemkin* which interpret political events as the outcome of a popular movement, and those like *Napoleon* which show history as the instrument of a great national hero. Films about groups of people actively involved in significant events are uncommon in the American cinema, which prefers to address audiences through a particularised figure, hero or villain." *We Were Strangers,* in Lambert's view, *is* one of those uncommon American films that makes a "collective study of men in crisis."[28]

From this general perspective, however, Lambert's review quickly shifts focus to issues of authorship. His interest in what the film reveals about the director's personality is as elaborated as the approach we identify with the 1950 French *politique des auteurs.* "Structurally it is a taut, exact, almost flawless piece of work," he writes. "It lacks depth at times because of Huston's attitude to people; he concentrates his passion on physical attention and detail, on exterior climaxes, and the rest he observes and records, excitingly but imperviously." The problems of *We Were Strangers* were not of history or ideology, Lambert asserts, nor of stylistics or performance, but of the director's "limitations of feeling." Huston does not identify with his protagonist, according to the critic, he reserves his sympathy, he holds back. Lambert's review concludes that "the personality behind the film remains at last elusive."[29]

If *We Were Strangers* remains a perplexing film, however, it is not necessary to attribute its problems to the director's psychological propensities. Nor are they solely a result of the complexities of its torturous times. Among the film's multiple determinations, perhaps the strongest is its conception of Third World revolutionary situations, and this is attributable less to an individual director or a specific conjuncture than to a broad ideological consensus that has found expression over decades in the subgenre to which it belongs.

The elements of this consensus include an abhorrence of tyrants but a decided ambivalence toward movements that oppose them; an incapacity to represent the decisive role of the United States government; and an obsession, ultimately obfuscating, with the tragic fate of individual Americans who get in the way. In recent years, such films as *Under Fire* (Roger Spottiswoode, 1983), *The Year of Living Dangerously* (Peter Weir, 1983) and *Salvador* (Oliver Stone, 1986) have extended the subgenre of Third World revolutionary situation films to settings in Nicaragua, Indonesia, and El Salvador, respectively, while exhibiting contradictions similar to those of *We Were Strangers*. Cuba was again the scene for *Havana* (Sydney Pollack, 1990), although that film's treatment of the events of December 1958, when dictator Batista fled the country and rebels led by Fidel Castro took power, owes more to the cinematic intertexts of *Casablanca* and *The Godfather, Part II* than to any concern for representing history.

Most of the heroes of recent Third World revolution films have been newspapermen, rather than active participants in revolutionary struggles, such as Tony Fenner. A 1990 addition to the subgenre, *A Show of Force* (directed by Bruno Barreto), marked several new tangents—a woman as the American journalist, and a public struggle over issues of representation during production. The film's subject is the murders by police of two young supporters of Puerto Rican independence at Cerro Maravilla in 1978. Although the murders were revealed by Puerto Rican journalists, the film gives credit to a North American woman television reporter portrayed by Amy Irving. Protests by Puerto Ricans may have led to changes during production.[30] In the film, the reporter is the widow of a Puerto Rican political activist, thus giving her a Hispanic surname.

The film also breaks with the *We Were Strangers* model of ignoring United States involvement in Third World revolutionary situations. It suggests that an FBI agent was at the scene of the murders and possibly directed the police. Though an end title carefully notes that the FBI agent character was "wholly fictional," his appearance may have made the film considerably more controversial than earlier works in the subgenre. A report in the *Village Voice* accused the distributor, Paramount, of killing the film by giving it a limited release without press screenings or advertising.[31] The struggles over *A Show of Force* indicate that the 1990s may be no less torturous a time for films treating Third World revolution than the repressive post–World War II era was for *We Were Strangers*.

## NOTES

1. *Hollywood Reporter,* Apr. 22, 1949.

2. W. H. M., *The Tidings,* May 6, 1949, clipping in *We Were Strangers* file, Production Code Administration papers (hereafter PCA), Margaret Herrick Library, Academy of Motion Picture Arts and Sciences (hereafter AMPAS).

3. Virginia E. Williams, California Federation of Women's Clubs, Los Angeles District, to Harry Cohn, May 9, 1949, *We Were Strangers* file, PCA, AMPAS; see also "Clubwomen Assail Film," Los Angeles *Examiner,* May 12, 1949, clipping in *We Were Strangers* production file, AMPAS.

4. See John Huston, *An Open Book* (New York: Alfred A. Knopf, 1980), 131ff.; Philip Dunne, *Take Two: A Life in Movies and Politics* (New York: McGraw-Hill, 1980), 193ff.; and Larry Ceplair and Steven Englund, *The Inquisition in Hollywood: Politics in the Film Community, 1930–1960* (Garden City, N.Y.: Anchor Press/Doubleday, 1980), 275–90.

5. Humphrey Bogart, "I'm No Communist," *Photoplay,* Mar. 1948, 52–53, 86–87.

6. Huston, *An Open Book,* 163–65, 174.

7. Joseph I. Breen to Harry Cohn, Sept. 3, 1948, *We Were Strangers* file, PCA, AMPAS.

8. Ibid. PCA records indicate the film was banned in Portugal and Egypt.

9. Lester Wm. Roth, Columbia vice-president, to Virginia E. Williams, May 16, 1949, *We Were Strangers* file, PCA, AMPAS.

10. Robert Sylvester, *Rough Sketch* (New York: Dial Press, 1948); Huston, *An Open Book,* 163.

11. David O. Selznick to Harry Cohn, John Huston, Sam Spiegel, and Lester Roth, Feb. 1, 1949, *We Were Strangers* file, Folder 1, John Huston Papers, AMPAS. On the title see also Selznick to Roth, Jan. 28, 1949, and Selznick to Huston and Spiegel, Jan. 29, 1949. The Spanish language title became *Rompiendo las cadenas (Breaking the Chains);* E. P. Smith (Cuba office, Columbia Pictures) to Huston, Sept. 20, 1949. Selznick and Jones were married July 13, 1949. See Jeffrey L. Carrier, *Jennifer Jones: A Bio-Bibliography* (New York: Greenwood Press, 1990), 20.

12. Huston, *An Open Book,* 163.

13. Vernon Young to Huston, Sept. 8, 1949, *We Were Strangers* file, Folder 1, Huston Papers.

14. Huston to Billy Wilkerson, May 10, 1949, Huston Papers, Folder 1.

15. For an English translation of the screenplay see *Gillo Pontecorvo's "The Battle of Algiers": A Film Written by Franco Solinas,* ed. PierNico Solinas (New York: Scribner's, 1973). Text of the voice-over is at 158.

16. Interview with Pontecorvo in Solinas, *Gillo Pontecorvo's "The Battle of Algiers,"* 166–67.

17. Pontecorvo relates how he and scriptwriter Franco Solinas began with a conventional concept of the "Third World revolutionary situation" subgenre, telling the story through the ideas of a European journalist visiting colonial countries. Ibid., 163–64.

18. *Variety* weekly, Apr. 27, 1949.

19. José Yglesias, "Huston Fails with Movie of 1933 Cuban Uprising," *Daily Worker* (Apr. 28, 1949), 13. Born in 1919 in Tampa, Florida, of Cuban background, Yglesias became a novelist and memoirist. He wrote a book about Cuba after the 1959 revolution, *In the Fist of the Revolution: Life in a Cuban Country Town* (New York: Pantheon, 1968).

20. Yglesias, "Huston Fails."

21. For theoretical perspectives on historiography and historical discourse, see, among many recent works, Dominick LaCapra, *History and Criticism* (Ithaca, N.Y.: Cornell University Press, 1985) and Michel de Certeau, "History: Science and Fiction," in *Heterologies: Discourse on the Other,* trans. Brian Massumi (Minneapolis: University of Minnesota Press, 1986), 199–221. Leger Grindon, "The Representation of History in the Fiction Film," Ph.D. diss., Department of Cinema Studies, New York University, 1986, discusses theoretical perspectives on the historical film.

22. Luis E. Aguilar, *Cuba 1933: Prologue to Revolution* (Ithaca, N.Y.: Cornell University Press, 1972), 125–26. A day-to-day account of this period by a *New York Times* correspondent appears in R. Hart Phillips, *Cuba: Island of Paradox* (New York: McDowell, Oblensky, 1959). See also Justo Carrillo, *Cuba 1933: Estudiantes, yánquis y soldatos* (Miami: Instituto de Estudios Interamericanos, University of Miami, 1985).

23. Louis A. Perez, Jr., *Cuba under the Platt Amendment, 1902–1934* (Pittsburgh: University of Pittsburgh Press, 1986), 301.

24. Sumner Welles, *Two Years of the "Good Neighbor" Policy* (Washington, D.C.: GPO, 1935), 5–6, as quoted in Perez, *Cuba under the Platt Amendment,* 302.

25. Perez, *Cuba under the Platt Amendment,* 317.

26. These events are vividly described in Phillips, *Cuba,* 38ff.

27. These events are summarized in Perez, *Cuba under the Platt Amendment,* 301–32, and treated in greater detail in Aguilar, *Cuba 1933.*

28. Gavin Lambert, *"We Were Strangers," Sequence* 9 (Autumn 1949): 127.

29. Ibid., 128–29.

30. See Ron Howell, "Where Credit Is Due," *Newsday,* July 2, 1989, pt. 2, 3.

31. James Ledbetter, "Media Blitz," *Village Voice,* June 12, 1990, 9. *A Show of Force* has appeared on cable television and is available on video cassette.

# Traven, Huston, and the Textual Treasures of the Sierra Madre

## JOHN ENGELL

With every ounce of gold possessed by [Dobbs, Curtin,
and Howard] they left the proletarian class and neared
that of the property-holders, the well-to-do middle class. . . .
They had reached the first step by which man becomes
the slave of his property.
—B. Traven, *The Treasure of the Sierra Madre*

Ever since, I've had a hankering to be a fruit grower.
Must be grand watching your own trees put on leaves,
come into blossom, and bear . . . watching the fruit get
big and ripe on the bough, ready for picking.
—Curtin in John Huston's shooting script for
*The Treasure of the Sierra Madre*

I n 1948 John Huston adapted B. Traven's *The Treasure of the Sierra Madre* for the screen. Though Huston's screenplay and film are faithful to the book in most particulars, the transition from verbal to visual narrative shifts the ideological center of the text. Traven's tale of Germanic "individualistic anarchism" and primitive agrarian communalism becomes, in Huston's hands, a sentimental representation of American Jeffersonian individualism. In this article, I wish to examine how this ideological shift occurs and why.

79

The trail left by the life of Traven is as difficult to track as an Indian in the rocky Mexican mountains where Huston shot his film. Various detectives of literature and history have claimed that Traven was a German, Czech, Scandinavian, or American. Recent textual and biographical evidence suggests that he was Ret Marut, an actor, essayist, editor, and short-story writer living in Germany between 1907 and 1923. Marut—like Traven years later—claimed to be an American citizen. But his name, like Traven's, was pseudonymous. In the late 1970s British television journalist Will Wyatt traced Marut back to Schwiebus, Poland, a small town where Marut/Traven was born in 1882 as Otto Wienecke.[1] From about 1924 until his death in 1969 Traven lived in Mexico, there assuming several other names, among them Hal Croves, though he wrote as B. Traven. His works appeared first in German; he himself translated most of them into English, though they needed extensive stylistic revisions. *The Treasure of the Sierra Madre,* for example, was published in Germany as *Der Schatz der Sierra Madre* in 1927, eight years before the first American edition.

The ideological implications of the fictions written by Wienecke/Marut/Traven/Croves are easier to track than his life. Recent scholarly studies of both Marut and Traven suggest that this man—whatever his name or names at various times—was influenced by the radical intellectual anarchist tradition of nineteenth- and early twentieth-century Germany. Michael Baumann, perhaps the finest Traven scholar, proves that Marut was a follower of Max Stirner, a contemporary of Marx and Engels who espoused a brand of anarchism dubbed "individualistic anarchism." In *The Ego and His Own,* Stirner attacks all institutions and ideas that lie outside the ego. Baumann summarizes the work in this way:

> Stirner condemns all ideas *as* ideas, maintaining that they chain us; he shows that adherence to them makes hypocrites of us because we deny ourselves, our *genuine* selves, in the *name* of these ideas. Stirner's is a fight against the tyranny of absolutes and universals. He pleads for each individual human being; he will have nothing to do with the concept of Man, or with any doctrine, religious, political, social, or humane, that either hypothesizes on, believes in, or acts for the sake of the abstraction "Man." Stirner undermines and critically destroys every piety by which men live in bourgeois society; he proposes that they live honestly, in accordance with what they, as individual men, as "egoists," need and desire; he urges individuals to take what they need, to "own" it.[2]

Stirner's radical views are a curious and arguably decadent fruit of German romanticism. *The Ego and His Own* won Stirner few disciples in his day; Marx felt he was both naive and bourgeois. But the rise of German militarism and the debacle of the First World War revived intellectual interest in Stirner. The writings of Marut between 1907 and 1923 affirm the "individualistic anarchism" and egoism preached by Stirner.

Under the name B. Traven, Rex Marut wrote novels and stories promulgating, in part, individualistic anarchism. *The Treasure of the Sierra Madre, The Death Ship, The Bridge in the Jungle, The White Rose,* and the later "Jungle" novels are anticapitalist and anti-institutional. Traven reserves his greatest disdain for governments, religious institutions, oil companies, and other corporations. He believes social structures and ideologies destroy the individual by perverting and eventually negating ego. But Traven's fictions are also communalistic in a primitive, agrarian way. Traven respects most the tribal, communal life of Indians in isolated Mexican villages, which he had experienced during some of his early years in Mexico. His later works especially emphasize the moral and social superiority of this way of life.

How can Traven's respect for Indian communalism be reconciled with the individualistic anarchism of Stirner and his disciple Marut? Stirner's ideology is grounded on the pervasive romantic myth of the individual as a free agent whose ego can transcend social and historical imperatives. In the bourgeois, capitalistic, militaristic world of Germany in which Ret Marut lived, such a myth could be sustained and illustrated only through the egoist's retreat from social values or the anarchist's destruction of social institutions. But in the Mexico where B. Traven lived, the bourgeois, capitalistic, and militaristic model of the state was juxtaposed with an Indian world antedating and in most ways antithetical to the former. Traven clearly believed that the tribal life of Mexican Indians was superior, both socially and morally, to the hegemony of European social and political institutions. He may have felt that the precapitalist commune liberated the ego and the individual by subsuming them. But such liberation is philosophically and historically problematic since the agrarian commune cannot accommodate the romantic notion of the ego. No Mexican Indian in the context of historical reality or Traven's work could be called an individual anarchist or egoist. None could be called an "individual" in the Romantic sense of the word. Communal agrarianism (as Nathaniel Hawthorne discovered at Brook Farm) affords no space for the transcendent self and therefore must clash with the notion of the "transcendental" Western self that seeks to create or penetrate communal life. Traven's *Treasure of the Sierra Madre* thus contains the seeds of ideological confusion.

In *The Treasure of the Sierra Madre,* as in a number of his other novels and stories, Traven chooses down-and-outers for his central characters. These are men on the fringes of modern capitalist society who are radically alone: friendless, penniless, without family, virtually without identity. Dobbs, Curtin, and Howard—the three American gold miners who strike it rich in Mexico, then lose their fortune—illustrate through their aloneness the inexorable dehumanization of the individual by institutions. Their lives dramatize the way in which political, social, and moral bonds among men have been severed in the modern world. Their lives show that the individual cannot combat either institutionalized power or the personal greed and corruption encouraged by that power. If these men followed the dictates of individualistic anarchism, they might retreat from their world through intellectualizing it, or they might attempt to overthrow it. Neither of these options seems remotely possible in Traven's fiction. Rather, after Dobbs has been destroyed by his greed, Howard and Curtin go to live with a tribe of Indians. They thereby escape the familiar power of Western-style institutions and the social forces enslaving their egos, their individuality. Yet the communal agrarian community they enter appears to absorb their individuality.

Huston began his Hollywood career as a screenwriter and subsequently wrote or cowrote the screenplays for all feature-length films he directed between *The Maltese Falcon* (1941) and *Heaven Knows, Mr. Allison* in 1957. A close inspection of his many screenplay adaptations of novels, including *The Maltese Falcon, The Treasure of the Sierra Madre, The Asphalt Jungle, The Red Badge of Courage, The African Queen, Moby Dick,* and several later works, especially *The Man Who Would Be King* (based on a Kipling short story), proves that he habitually lifted much of his dialogue from the fiction being adapted. Even when Huston did not write the screenplay for a film he directed—as with *The Dead,* written by his son Tony—he inevitably worked with adaptations verbally similar to the original literary texts. More importantly, an inspection of Huston's screenplays and films suggests that he always strove to "capture the spirit" as well as the letter of his literary source.[3] Thus, in *The Treasure of the Sierra Madre,* the narrative line remains close to Traven's; a majority of

Tim Holt, Walter Huston, and Humphrey Bogart bring B. Traven's symbolic characters to life.

speeches in the film are taken verbatim or nearly verbatim from dialogue in the novel. Huston's screenplay descriptions and visual renderings of locations often recreate descriptive passages in the novel detail by detail, and the actions and motives of the central characters are in most particulars unchanged.

As both screenplay and film, Huston's *Treasure of the Sierra Madre* does on occasion diverge from the text of Traven's novel, but a majority of these divergences are deletions.[4] Huston deletes entire scenes and chapters of the novel to attain narrative economy and rhythm. Two stories told by Howard, chapters 3 and 16 of the novel, concerning the history of gold mining in Mexico, do not appear in either the screenplay or film. Huston also deletes several minor characters, numerous brief incidents, and many nonnarrative, authorial passages. Though the cumulative effect of these deletions is to move the focus of Traven's novel away from society as a whole and to rivet it on the three central characters, most individual deletions in the script and film seem motivated by the transition from 300-page novel to 126-minute film; from expansive verbal tract to more economical visual narrative. Yet, interestingly, few of these deletions are related to or transform Traven's ideological conflation of individualistic anarchism and tribal communalism.

In shaping the final film Huston also makes a number of changes, as distinct from deletions. Again, a majority of these changes seem motivated by a wish to achieve narrative economy and rhythm. The most important such change concerns the role of Mexican bandits. In Traven's novel, Howard especially, but the other characters as well, fear bandits and tell stories about them. Bandits lurk around the edges of the novel's narrative, always about to threaten Dobbs, Curtin, Howard, and their gold mine. But Traven's bandits actually appear only once, when they attack miners and are finally driven away by government troops. In his screenplay and film, Huston introduces the bandits before Dobbs (Humphrey Bogart), Curtin (Tim Holt), and Howard (Walter Huston) discover gold. Huston's bandits attack the train to Durango (scenes 20 and 21 of the shooting script). Their leader, Gold Hat (Alfonso Bedoya), rides beside the train. Dobbs tries to shoot him but tells Curtin and Howard, "The train gave a jolt and I missed, dammit. Sure wish I'd got him." Later, this same Gold Hat and his band appear at the mine (scenes 80-98 of the shooting script). Here the action is similar to that described in Traven's novel, though not identical; in both novel and film the miners are saved by "Federales." Finally, after Dobbs has tried to kill Curtin and is fleeing alone with the sacks of gold, three of these bandits, Gold Hat and two confederates, taunt, then kill him (scene 125 of the shooting script). Here, Huston lifts most of the dialogue and action from the novel, but in Traven's text the three men are not the bandits; they are local bums. Though this change from novel to film somewhat obscures the sense of random social violence emphasized by Traven, Huston presents Gold Hat and his band three times and consequently achieves a heightening of the economy and rhythm of the narrative. Not only can the audience identify a single antagonist who need not be introduced with each appearance, but the three incidents involving Gold Hat are spaced to create maximum tension and contain an ironic twist: Dobbs has two chances to kill Gold Hat before the bandit kills him. However, in both film and novel, the bandits serve a similar ideological function. They are indigenous people ("Indians") tainted by the colonialist society's greed and institutionalized corruption. As a result, they serve as foils for the primitively communalistic, unselfish Indians with whom Howard and (in the novel but not the film) Curtin go to live.

Though most of Huston's deletions and changes may appear to emphasize narrative, rather than thematic concerns, several deletions and several additions profoundly alter the ideology of the novel. The most significant deletions of this kind occur in the early chapters. With significant detail, Traven pictures the oil fields of Mexico as an exploitative venture of Yankee entrepreneurs. These fields are built and manned by Americans like Dobbs and Curtin, the rabble of industrialized society, and by demoralized, displaced Indians. With another American named Moulton (who is deleted from the film), Dobbs goes looking for work in the fields, accompanied by a nameless Indian. During the wanderings of these three men, the reader learns that the oil fields are about to go bust. The huge underclass of workers are now without work, food, or hope. The Indians who have left villages to toil in the oil fields have been severed from both their heritage and the land. The nameless Indian with Dobbs and Curtin is so out of touch with the world of his ancestors that he can no longer distinguish the difference between the night sounds of a grazing burro and a stalking tiger. Moreover, Traven uses this search for work, together with several other incidents early in the novel, as opportunities to have his characters discuss politics. Dobbs, Moulton, and Curtin verbally flirt with what they call bolshevism. They attack capitalists. They revile "the system." In this talk Traven intends the reader to recognize the fundamental social naiveté and political ignorance of the capitalist underclass. These men are trapped in institutional systems they do not understand. They spout vague condemnations and still vaguer slogans—slogans cribbed from bankrupt ideologies that destroy individuality. Theirs is a hopeless political, and therefore personal situation.

Though the substantial cuts Huston makes in these early sections of the novel may be motivated primarily by what he believed were narrative considerations, the *effect* of these deletions is decidedly ideological. The viewer of his film is never asked to scrutinize, even to recognize the larger social and political context that, according to Traven, creates men like Dobbs and Curtin. In the novel we see these oil-hands-turned-gold-seekers in a specifically political and surprisingly naturalistic context. The individual cannot combat hegemonic capitalism. Thus the individual "escapes" by becoming an extension of such hegemony: He seeks gold. For Traven the departure of Dobbs, Curtin, and Howard in search of gold represents not a triumph of the individual, but the triumph of a capitalist system inimical to individual ego. Dobbs, Curtin, and Howard are tools—the picks, shovels, and strong backs of the society from which they seek to flee.

There is no shred of this bleak political vision in Huston's film. Rather, the viewer assumes—quite rightly, given the world Huston depicts—that Dobbs and Curtin are lured into mining by the stories of Howard; that they make a choice to go; that they change their lives by making such a choice. Therefore, when Huston deletes social and political material from the novel's early chapters, he begins the transformation of Traven's radical ideological fable into a traditionally bourgeois moral fable. Traven's fable hinges on a choice. Dobbs and Curtin go to live with Indians. By so doing, Traven suggests that they escape the corruption of a capitalist system and free their individual egos. Huston's fable also hinges on a choice, but this choice begins when the three Americans decide to hunt for gold and culminates when Curtin returns to Texas to become a peach farmer. Through this transformation Huston suggests that Curtin escapes the lure of gold and becomes a good man. Consequently, Huston's moral fable emerges as comfortably bourgeois, not radically anticapitalist.

The moral fable Huston wrests from Traven's text hinges on three additions Huston makes later in the film.[5] In the first (scene 47 of the shooting script), Curtin tells Howard what he wants to do after they finish digging for gold and go home.

> One summer when I was a kid I worked as a picker in a peach harvest in the San Joaquin Valley. It sure was something. Hundreds of people—old and young—whole families working together. After the day's work we used to build big bonfires and sit around 'em and sing to guitar music, till morning sometimes. You'd go to sleep, wake up and sing, and go to sleep again. Everybody had a wonderful time. . . . Ever since, I've had a hankering to be a fruit grower. Must be grand watching your own trees put on leaves, come into blossom, and bear . . . watching the fruit get big and ripe on the bough, ready for picking.[6]

In Traven's text Curtin never speaks of peaches, of fruit harvesting, or of owning a farm.

Immediately after the bandits attack the mining camp, Huston makes a second, larger addition. In Traven's novel a man named Lecaud follows Curtin, who is returning to the mine from buying supplies. Lecaud, a shadowy figure in the novel, a scientific miner who conceals his past, becomes Cody (Bruce Bennett) in Huston's film. Whereas Lecaud stays behind when Dobbs, Curtin, and Howard finally leave the mine in Traven's novel, in Huston's film Cody is killed during the attack of the bandits. Dobbs discovers his body, and the three men search him for personal effects. They find, among other things, a letter from Cody's wife. Howard begins to read the letter. He falters, and Curtin takes over.

> Dear Jim: Your letter just arrived. It was such a relief to get word after so many months of silence. I realize, of course, that there aren't any mail boxes that you can drop a letter in out there in the wilds, but that doesn't keep me from worrying about you. Little Jimmy is fine, but he misses his daddy almost as much as I do. He keeps asking "When's Daddy coming home?" You say if you do not make a real find this time you'll never go again. I cannot begin to tell you how my heart rejoices at those words if you really mean them. Now I feel free to tell you. I've never thought any material treasure, no matter how great, is worth the pain of these long separations.
>
> The country is especially lovely this year. It's been a perfect spring—warm rains, hardly any frost. The fruit trees are all in bloom. The upper orchard looks aflame and the lower like after a snow storm. Everybody looks forward to big crops. I do hope you are back for the harvest. Of course, I'm hoping that you will at last strike it rich. It is high time for luck to start smiling upon you, but just in case she doesn't remember we've already found life's treasure. Forever yours, Helen.[7]

Once again, there is no such letter in Traven's novel.

Finally, at the very end of the film, after Dobbs has been killed by the bandits and they have scattered the sacks of gold, thinking it is dust, Curtin and Howard sit and decide what they will do. As in the novel, Howard decides he will live with the Indians as a kind of medicine man. But Curtin, who doesn't decide anything in Traven's novel, hears this advice from Howard in the film: "Tell you what. You can keep my share of what the burros and hides'll bring if you use the money to buy a ticket to Dallas. Seeing her in person and telling her what happened would be a lot better than writing a letter . . . Besides, it's July and there might be a job for you in the fruit harvest . . . Well, what do you say?" In response, Curtin says, "I'll do it."

In his speech about harvesting peaches in the San Joaquin Valley, Curtin describes hundreds of families working, singing, and sleeping together in a kind of primitive communal bliss.[8] This mythic sense of community, of equals doing a task and enjoying it, is at first glance similar to the conclusion of Traven's myth, to his depiction of the Indian village Howard visits and returns to. But before the speech is over Curtin says he would like to become a "fruit grower . . . watching [his] own trees . . . watching the fruit get big and ripe on the bough, ready for picking."

What Huston describes is not the primitive communalism of Traven, but a vision that might be called Jeffersonian: the vision of the small farmer. The letter from Cody's wife increases this disparity of ideological vision. Helen moralizes to her husband. Dear, she says, all this searching for treasure (significantly, she uses that word twice) is beside the point. We know what real treasure is: It's loving one another, being close, watching the orchard come into blossom on our own little farm. The bliss of love, of family, and of ownership. This is Jeffersonian bliss, as American as peach pie; bourgeois bliss of an ennobling kind. Gold, money, and power are vices. Land, family, and self-fulfillment are virtues.

It could be argued that passages in Traven's novel suggested to Huston both the letter found on Cody's body and the peach orchard motif. Early in the novel, Traven describes the office of a flophouse where Dobbs is living. Here,

> [a] shelf with little compartments was filled with letters for patrons. Bundles of letters, many of them from a mother, a wife, or sweetheart, were piled up, covered with thick dust. The men to whom they were addressed might be dead, or working deep in the jungles clearing new oil-fields, or on a tramp in the China sea, or helping the Bolsheviks build up a workers' empire, with no time to think that the letter writers back home might be crying their eyes out over a lost sheep.[9]

But in Traven's text, the letters never reach their destinations. The men intended to receive them have been swept away by capitalist conditions or Bolshevik ideology. Unlike Cody in Huston's film, they do not carry these letters pressed to their hearts; after all, they cannot go home. Most important, in the novel Curtin neither reads one of the letters nor decides to act on it. No man will ever read the letters described by Traven.

Another passage in the novel specifically suggests Huston's peach orchard motif. In chapter 16, the second long story Howard tells about the history of gold mining, he introduces an Indian chief, Aguila Bravo, who disdains the wealth of a great gold mine. A Spaniard asks Aguila Bravo why he has not exploited the mine. The Indian replies:

> I do not need gold nor do I want silver. I have plenty to eat always. I have a young and beautiful wife, whom I love dearly and who loves and honors

me. I have also a strong and healthy boy, who now, thanks to your skill, can see and so is perfect in every way. I have my acres and fields, and I have my fine cattle. I am chief and judge, and I may say I am a true and honest friend of my tribe, which respects and obeys my orders, which they know are for their own good. The soil bears rich fruit every year. The cattle bring forth year in, year out. I have a golden sun above me, at night a silver moon, and there is peace in the land. So what could gold mean to me? Gold and silver do not carry any blessing. Does it bring you any blessing? You whites, you kill and rob and cheat and betray for gold. You hate each other for gold, while you never can buy love with gold. Nothing but hatred and envy. You whites spoil the beauty of life for the possession of gold.[10]

Both the pastoral images and moralistic tone of this speech resemble the three peach orchard additions Huston makes to his text. In Traven's novel, however, the words are spoken by an Indian, a leader who wishes to preserve centuries of communalistic and, therefore for Traven, individualistic tradition. Curtin's visions of the migrant worker in California or of the small farmer in Texas may sound something like the words of Aguila Bravo, but the social and ideological contexts of these speeches are incompatible. For Traven, happiness is unattainable in a capitalist society, where the individual is trapped, helpless. For Traven, ownership and love are incompatible. The radical German political philosophy and mythic communalism of Traven's text are thus transformed by Huston into nostalgia for nineteenth-century individualism, into the American frontier vision of the citizen-owner.

This transformation is most evident in the character of Curtin. For Traven, Curtin and Dobbs are identical in every way but one: Curtin is not consumed by greed. Otherwise, both men live hopeless lives; they control nothing, not even themselves. For Huston, Curtin becomes a moral protagonist, an alternative to Dobbs and the amoral, arid world of the Sierra Madre. Both novel and film contain a scene in which Curtin pulls Dobbs out of a mine cave-in. Traven writes:

> He knew then instantly that Dobbs was buried. He did not even take time to notify Howard, as he thought it might be too late then to bring Dobbs out alive. He went in, although the ceiling was hanging so that it might come down any second and bury the rescuer as well. He got Dobbs out and then called for the old man.[11]

Huston's shooting script describes a similar scene:

Curtin moves on to the next tunnel. There has been a cave-in. The ceiling is hanging so low at the opening that there is not enough room for a body to pass through. Curtin doesn't take time to yell to Howard but starts clawing rubble aside. When he has made a big enough opening he wriggles into the tunnel. . . . Dobbs is lying unconscious, half covered with rock. Curtin works Dobb's body free, then starts pulling him out. It is an inch-by-inch proposition getting the unconscious man through the narrow opening, but at last he succeeds.[12]

Both Traven's novel and Huston's screenplay convey the sense that Curtin makes no decision; he simply rescues Dobbs, not because Curtin is courageous or noble, but because there is nothing else to do.

In the film's final version Huston adds a highly significant shot. Curtin hears the cave-in and runs to the mouth of the tunnel. The camera, aimed from inside the tunnel, holds him in its field of vision. He calls for Dobbs but gets no answer. His face becomes irresolute. Finally Curtin turns and begins to walk away from the tunnel (and camera). Max Steiner's music swells. And then, shot still held, Curtin turns and rushes to the opening of the tunnel. Later, when Dobbs thanks Curtin for rescuing him, the camera again fixes him in its gaze. His face suggests inner turmoil, as if to say, "I was going to let him die. All for that damn gold. What's happening to me?" What is happening to Curtin, in Huston's film, is that he is becoming a moral protagonist of a kind impossible in Traven's fiction.

In the novel, when Howard and Curtin stay on to live with the Indians, they turn their backs on gold and greed. According to Traven, they also place themselves outside Western social and moral categories, outside the ideological constructs of the modern world. They become "individuals" by being subsumed into a primitive community. Within such an ideological framework there is no place for a bourgeois moral protagonist. Huston, on the other hand, shows the viewer that Curtin is worthy of owning a peach orchard and heading a middle class family. In Huston's *Treasure of the Sierra Madre*, Curtin becomes a typical American protagonist. Not particularly intelligent, articulate, or wise—just good. Good and just.

John Huston was an American bourgeois. His father, Walter Huston, was a great stage and screen actor; his mother, Rita, divorced Walter Huston and later married a vice-president of the Northern Pacific Railroad. Unlike Traven/Marut, Huston grew up not in the chaotic and terrifying world of Germany before and after World War I, but in the boom period of the American 1920s. Moreover, America's ideological base has always

Mexico's dangers menace the heroes of Huston's adaptation, but Huston himself came to love the country.

been narrow; it leaves little room for radical anarchism, even "individualistic anarchism," or for primitive communalism. The self-proclaimed and somewhat ironic "Christian anarchism" of an American Brahmin such as Henry Adams is a far cry from the impassioned Germanic views of Stirner or Marut. The experiments in communal living fashionable in the United States in the mid-nineteenth and twentieth centuries are tame imitations of the communal tribal life described by Traven.

How, then, could John Huston feel any kinship for the writings and ideology of B. Traven? It might be observed that, like Traven, Huston had no permanent home. As a boy, he traveled from one part of the United States to another, never settling. As a man, Huston made films in several dozen countries and lived much of his later life in Mexico. In his autobiography Huston describes his isolated home in Las Caletas, near the Chacala Indian community.[13] Moreover, Huston liked to be known for "personal" projects that often put him at odds with the studio system, though at times, when he needed money, he quickly abandoned such projects and filmed inferior studio-sponsored scripts.

But such similarities between Huston and Traven are superficial and

incidental. What links these men and their two texts most firmly is a fascination with, even a love for, the loner and the underdog—the individual
(always male) who either attempts to sever himself from society or believes he has been abandoned by the social and moral structures of it. As
with all of Traven's major fictions, each of Huston's major films—from
*The Maltese Falcon* to *The Red Badge of Courage* to *Fat City* to *The Man
Who Would Be King* and *Wise Blood*—centers on such men. Perhaps, then,
the ultimate ideological difference between Traven and his novel, Huston
and his film, is this: Traven, the German radical, espouses a form of intellectual individualism; he believes that the individual must break with the
modern capitalistic world to achieve selfhood. In his narratives, Traven
employs the myth of primitive communalism to signify this break, this
radical sense of self. Huston, the American "liberal," espouses a kind of
sentimental individualism; he believes that the individual must struggle
with this place, this time, this world to achieve selfhood. In his narratives,
Huston uses the myth of "rugged male individualism" to signify this struggle, this sentimental sense of self.

Here it is worth remembering a curious anecdote about Traven, Huston, and the making of the film *Treasure of the Sierra Madre*. Huston
wished to involve Traven, and in an interview with Gerald Pratley, he described his attempts to meet the reclusive and elusive writer:

> [Traven] was supposed to meet me in Mexico City and I wanted him to
> work on the picture with me as I made the film. . . . I was in my hotel room
> in Mexico City and I awoke early in the morning. I'm one of those people
> who never locks his door wherever he is. Standing at the foot of my bed was
> the shadowy figure of a man. He took a card out and gave it to me. I put on
> the light, it was still dark, and it said, "Hal Croves, Interpreter, Acapulco
> and San Antonio." I said "How do you do, Mr. Croves." Then he said, "I
> have a letter from you from Mr. B. Traven," and he gave me the letter,
> which I read. It said that he himself was unable to appear but that this man
> knew as much about his work as he himself did and knew as much about the
> circumstances and the country and he would represent Traven in every way.
> We had conversations, Croves and I, for the few days I was in Mexico City.
> I gave him the script, he read it, liked what he read and said he was sure
> Traven would like it very much.[14]

Croves agreed to be a technical adviser and attended much of the shooting.
Huston was not alone in suspecting that Croves might be Traven; Croves
became so disturbed by numerous conjectures linking him with Traven,

especially by articles in *Life* and *Time* magazines, that he eventually left the set. We now know that Croves and Traven (like Wienecke and Marut) were the same man, a man who approved the script for Huston's film and watched the shooting.

How can this story be reconciled with Huston's ideological transformation of Traven's text? There are several possible explanations. First, Traven may have failed to recognize Huston's transformation because his own novel chaotically combines the conflicts of German romantic "individualistic anarchism" and primitive agrarian communalism. Second, Traven may have been so eager to maintain his personal anonymity that he never noted the kind of individualism implicit in Huston's script. Third, both Traven and Huston may have been more concerned with the challenges, pleasures, and stimulation of the filmmaking process than with rigorous ideological analysis. Fourth, the various ideologies of "individualism" inherent in or growing out of the lives of Traven and Huston may, finally, have resolved into a disgust with capitalistic institutions and vulgar materialism. Both men, regardless of their different intellectual and social backgrounds, came to despise any person who was "the slave of . . . property" and to sympathize with any person who fought against the tyranny of money. As I have said, both men liked economic underdogs.

Such "individualism" does not constitute a cogent, consistent, or usable ideology, but it seems to have been sufficient to garner Traven's approbation of Huston's film adaptation. Perhaps we can learn from the "ideological reorientation" of the former Soviet Empire, or from the dramatic and quixotic ideological inconsistencies of so-called Marxist and capitalist nations in the past three-quarters of a century. The Marxist ideological model that has underscored much film (and literary) criticism in recent decades is precisely that—a model. Traven, though a German ideologue of sorts, and Huston, though an American liberal of sorts, were artists; they could not, in the creation of their art, precisely follow ideological models. Their texts, like all narratives, are ideological. But like all narrative art, these texts are fluid in form to a degree that cannot be accommodated or explained by any static model. The art of adaptation from one medium to another is a formalistic, aesthetic exercise of significant complexity and difficulty. Adaptation inevitably transforms the ideology of a text, though this transformation may be different in degree as well as in kind, depending on the nature of the original text, historical circumstance, and the intentions (or lack of intentions) brought to that text by the adaptor. Ideological critics might not be pleased with the fluidity of textual ideology, but B. Traven and John Huston apparently believed the textual treasures of their Sierra Madre could accommodate everything from pre-Renaissance communalism to post-Enlightenment peach orchards.

## NOTES

1. Will Wyatt, *The Secret of the Sierra Madre: The Man Who Was B. Traven* (Garden City, N.Y.: Doubleday, 1980), 299–336. Numerous works have been published on the identity of B. Traven. Wyatt's discoveries and general conclusions are now accepted by Traven scholars.

2. Michael Baumann, *B. Traven: An Introduction* (Albuquerque: University of New Mexico Press, 1976), 64. For further discussion of the influence of Stirner on Marut/Traven see Robert T. Goss, "From Ret Marut to B. Traven: More Than a Change in Disguise," in *B. Traven, Life and Works,* ed. Ernst Schurer and Philip Jenkins (University Park: Pennsylvania State University Press, 1986), 44–55.

3. Stanley Kubrick exemplifies a director who adapts specific fictional texts for his own ends, consciously and meticulously transforming the ideology of each text he adapts. See for example his transformation of William Thackeray's *Barry Lyndon* and Stephen King's *The Shining.*

4. "Screenplay" refers to John Huston, *The Treasure of the Sierra Madre,* ed. James Naremore (Madison: University of Wisconsin Press, 1979). All quotations of or references to Huston's screenplay are from this volume. In some instances the published script diverges from the final film version.

5. In his excellent introduction to the published shooting script of *The Treasure of the Sierra Madre,* James Naremore singles out these three additions for discussion, suggesting that they are part of the "Hollywood" elements of the film. He notes that the wife's letter found on a dead man is standard fare in World War II movies. But Naremore neither explains Huston's reasons for including what could be called the peach orchard motif nor shows how these additions to Traven's novel, taken with deletions, transform the ideological center of the text.

6. Curtin's and Huston's blissful agrarian vision is curiously at odds with, say, *The Grapes of Wrath,* written by John Steinbeck and directed by John Ford, and with the realities of western farm life during the depression, distanced by less than a decade from the making of *The Treasure of the Sierra Madre.* Clearly Huston, unlike Traven—or Steinbeck and Ford—had little interest in commenting on contemporary American economic realities.

7. Huston, *Treasure,* 145.

8. B. Traven, *The Treasure of the Sierra Madre* (New York: Hill and Wang, 1967), 11–12.

9. We "ideologically sophisticated" readers may believe that men like Curtin and Dobbs must carry their Western, bourgeois values into the communal culture in which they choose to live. But Traven clearly believes that men can change; that in extreme circumstances they can transform their selves, their egos.

10. Traven, *Treasure,* 194.

11. Ibid., 89.

12. Huston, *Treasure,* 94.

13. John Huston, *An Open Book* (New York: Alfred A. Knopf, 1980), 3.

14. Gerald Pratley, *The Cinema of John Huston* (New York: A. S. Barnes and Co., 1977), 59.

# The Undeclared War:
# Political *Reflections in a Golden Eye*

STEPHEN COOPER

B y the time John Huston came
to direct *Reflections in a
Golden Eye* (1967), he had
already distinguished himself with his treatment of American military
life and death. *Report from the Aleutians* (1943), *San Pietro* (1945), and
*Let There Be Light* (1946) comprise a triptych of World War II documentaries unsurpassed in their depiction—unflinching, engaged, and above all
compassionate—of men in battle and battle's uneasy aftermath. In *The
Red Badge of Courage* (1951), Huston had extended in fictional terms the
central preoccupations of his nonfiction films, using Stephen Crane's
classic novel as the basis for his further explorations into the horrors of
war and the redemptive potential of trial-by-fire.[1] In each of these works,
Huston demonstrated a thoroughgoing commitment not merely to some
abstract military code of honor but to the historicized portrayal of flesh-
and-blood soldiers caught up in the fury of war. The principled sympathy
for the American fighting man at the heart of these films had firmly

established what we might choose to think of as Huston's military-aesthetic credentials.

It is within this context that *Reflections in a Golden Eye* may well strike us as strange, even incongruous, for this is a film that employs American military setting and characters precisely to enact its grotesque drama of solipsistic perversions, sexual deceit, and murder. In the oppressively closed environment of this story, deviance is the norm: Masochism abounds, and both the cruel and the fetishistic are voyeurized to the point of obliterating all but the obsessive and the irrational. Gone is the declarative emphasis on the soldier's defining quality, his selflessness; gone too the profound show of respect for devotion to duty. These qualities, so characteristic of Huston's earlier military films, are replaced in *Reflections* by a ruthlessly ironic insistence on the army's atomizing effects on both its members and their dependents. It is as if, in returning to the military as primary diegetic world after pursuing other subjects for a decade and a half, Huston had radically changed his mind.

In this paper I shall be tracing out not the contours of John Huston's mind but the literary and cinematic aspects of *Reflections in a Golden Eye* against its context in time. I am aware of the admonitions of those critics who would discount as naive, if not improper, such forays beyond the secured boundaries of the theoretical. Nevertheless, I shall be following paths of connotation as various (but interconnected) as the narrative, the historical, and the technological—a traversive reading, if you will, in response to the film's transgressive tendencies. For certainly *Reflections in a Golden Eye* is about nothing if not the violation of boundaries imposed by the ruling ideology of convention. I will argue, in fact, that although it abstracts its concern with things military from the dominant context of its production and release—that is, the escalating American war in Vietnam—Huston's film can be taken as a strangely, even strongly political film. Through its insistence on the eye and the largely gender-related problems of looking, seeing, and (mis)understanding, the film implicates the viewer in its dreamlike interrogation of power, delusion and violence. The implications that emerge, however, do not exhaust themselves at the level of the merely personal. Rather, the theory of war that effectively envelopes the film's drama functions so as to raise those implications to the level of the social and the political, ultimately promoting a stance both critical and self-critical toward the intersections of history and art.

One such intersection, impossible to overlook in considering any act of adaptation, is that between Huston's film and the Carson McCullers novel upon which it is based. While others, including McCullers, have generally praised (or damned) the film for its so-called fidelity to the novel's provocative themes and gothic atmosphere, I choose instead to focus closely on the first paragraph of the novel, embedding it in my subsequent discussion of the film.

> An army post in peacetime is a dull place. Things happen, but then they happen over and over again. The general plan of a fort in itself adds to the monotony—the huge concrete barracks, the neat rows of officers' homes built one precisely like the other, the gym, the chapel, the golf course and the swimming pools—all is designed according to a certain rigid pattern. But perhaps the dullness of a post is caused most of all by insularity and by a surfeit of leisure and safety, for once a man enters the army he is expected only to follow the heels ahead of him. At the same time things do occasionally happen on an army post that are not likely to re-occur. There is a fort in the South where a few years ago a murder was committed. The participants of this tragedy were: two officers, a soldier, two women, a Filipino, and a horse.[2]

For a critical approach to Huston's film adaptation of the McCullers novel, we could hardly ask for a more suggestive set of guidelines than the one we have here laid before us. From the laconic rephrasing of the famous Santayana warning about the dangers of historical amnesia—"Things happen, but then they happen over and over again"—to the awareness of class, gender and race underlined in the categorical identification of central characters—"two officers, a soldier, two women, a Filipino"—the passage invites a political reading. No sooner do we note the suburbanized "peacetime" that seems to reign over this nameless military installation—a Pax Americana of tract housing arranged with ideological finesse about the principle loci of spiritual and physical worship[3]—than we must note as well the isolation and enforced repetitiveness from which the only escape is the murderous violation of order. That is as much to say that the "certain rigid pattern" that directs the eye in such regimented landscape belies the more deeply dreamlike pattern of narrative to come; for once the metaphorical boundaries have been dissolved between the fort's overdetermined schematics and the unchecked forces of the surrounding forest, a new view emerges perforce, and the "insularity" of the post is inundated with the terrors of the unbidden unrepressed. Before this dissolution can begin, to be sure, the setting must be established in all its dullness, the planned community, one might say, of some five-star super-ego. But within that very master plan of control lurks a dark inevitability, for this is a landscape that reeks of murder. As we are told at the outset, "There is a fort in the South where a few years ago a murder was committed." Literally transposed from the novel's first page to the beginning of the film (it closes the opening credits and returns at the end to open the film's close, suggesting the Santayanan "sentence" to which those who forget history are doomed), this piece of expository information privileges its readers with advance knowledge of the tragic potential contained in an army's peacetime "surfeit of leisure and safety." According to the logic of the narrative, the palpable absence of war and of war's mass production of human slaughter redounds to individualized murder most simple.

But what about that palpable absence? The date of the novel's original publication notwithstanding,[4] there can be no doubt that Carson McCullers resolutely avoids treating war. Instead, she focuses on a "peacetime" maelstrom of highly individual, even stylized psychologies.[5] Thus, Capt. Weldon Penderton, a professor of military science, has a personality that "differed in some respects from the ordinary. . . . In his balance between the two great instincts, toward life and toward death, the scale was heavily weighted to one side—to death." He collects facts and statistics with "scholarly exactitude," all of which add up not to a single idea but rather a hoarded trove of intellectual fetishes, not unlike his secret cache of stolen spoon and scavenged candy wrapper, phallic substitutes for his "basic lack" (8).[6] Against his impotent obsession for order at all costs, Penderton finds in his wife the sensual embodiment of everything that terrifies him. Leonora Penderton revels in the physical pleasures of eating, drinking, and sex; she rides a spirited stallion named Firebird, and she does not hesitate to laugh in the captain's face at the humiliating displays of his need for control. When he commands her to put on some shoes, for example, openly registering his disgust at what he considers her slatternliness, Leonora responds by performing a coldly sadistic striptease. "I will kill you!" Penderton gasps when the performance is complete; but the threat evaporates in Leonora's even icier response. "Son," she says from her superior position on the stairway, looking down on him as he trembles, "have you ever been collared and dragged out in the street and thrashed by a naked woman?" (10). Compressed as it is to hostile camps of one each, this might not be war in fact; but in war's absence it will certainly suffice.

This centripetal focus upon the personal in confrontation with the unresponsive, even defiant needs of others continues in the development of the novel's other central characters. Thus Maj. Morris Langdon and his wife, Alison, the equally mismatched couple who live across the street from the Pendertons in identical officers' quarters, mirror Weldon and Leonora in reverse. Langdon is the healthy animal with whom Leonora is openly carrying on an affair, while Alison is tormented with such self-loathing that she has recently mutilated herself, cutting off her nipples with a pair of garden shears. As dull to nuance as his wife is hypersensi-tive, Langdon encourages Penderton to join in the enthusiasms he enjoys adulterously with Leonora—riding horses, playing poker, going to the fights—blind to the irony of his thickheaded good intentions. To compen-sate for her husband's obtuseness, Alison turns to her devoted Filipino houseboy, the queenly Anacleto, who shares her passions for watercolors and classical music. In one especially rhapsodic moment, Anacleto deliv-ers himself of the novel's expressive counterpoint to the stolid pragmatism of the military mind, valorizing the artist's dissociation from all conven-tional ways of knowing.

> "Madame Alison," he said, "do you yourself really believe that Mr. Sergei Rachmaninoff knows that a chair is something to be sat on and that a clock shows one the time? And if I should take off my shoe and hold it up to his face and say, 'What is this, Mr. Sergei Rachmaninoff?' then he would an-swer, like anyone else, 'Why, Anacleto, that is a shoe.' I myself find it hard to realize." (42)

It is a telling mark of the story's distaste for the military stamp of confor-mity that its ration of sympathy is reserved for Alison and Anacleto, fe-male hysteric and open homosexual though they be. And when Langdon mulls aloud over getting Anacleto into his battalion to straighten him out, the ironic gulf between his received perception of the world and the reali-ties of its inhabitants is nothing short of abysmal. Anacleto's aliveness could never be deadened sufficiently to conform with the army's require-ments, nor does Langdon ever come to an understanding of that fact.

It is that aliveness that contrasts most directly with the states to which Pvt. L. G. Williams is prey, trancelike moments during which the young soldier stands still and does nothing but gaze "unblinking into space" (6). As far as Private Williams manages to adapt this blank stare to any kind of focused use is his ritualized vigil, first outside the Penderton house— where on the night of her cruel striptease he has glimpsed Leonora naked—and then inside Leonora's bedroom, which he enters with the aid of a switchblade. Once inside, however, he does little more than smell the perfumes and undergarments of the beautiful Leonora, who sleeps oblivious to his nightlong watches. Having been subjected to the paralyzing fire-and-brimstone of his father's wisdom about women—they all have some terrible disease—Williams can do no more than stare raptly at the beautiful otherness of Leonora, incapable of penetrating its mystery. Williams is a virgin, and in spite of his nightly opportunity to alter that fact, he remains a virgin until the end. Cut off from language to the point of virtual wordlessness, he carries within him "a deep reflection of the sight he had seen that night" (20)—a reflection Huston actualizes in the massive close-up of Williams's eye, at once the most striking and densely packed image of the film.

If I have dwelt at some length over the novel before looping back to the film, it is because I believe in regarding either side of any adaptation in the light of its formal other. More to the point, however, everything I have just said with respect to the novel can be applied with equal certainty to the film—everything, that is, except my earlier assertion about the novel's thoroughgoing avoidance of war. Strictly speaking, the same cannot be said of Huston's film. True, the historical date of the film's story is never really specified; various elements of its content work to situate it in an uncertain time after World War II. The automobiles, for example, are of early 1950s vintage, but civilian fashions, notably clothing and hairstyles both male and female, suggest, as they so often do in films, the time of the film's production—in this case, the mid to late 1960s. Nevertheless, we are never given to understand that there is any American war in progress, either in Korea or in Vietnam. On first glance, then, this abstraction from history would appear to be an integral part of the film's vaunted "fidelity" to its novelistic source, an element of its putatively timeless universality.[7] And yet that abstraction is incomplete. For even as we begin to surrender to Toshiro Mayuzumi's mesmerizing score and to the highly stylized performances of the principles—the rod of steel in Brando's back, Taylor's lip-smacking Southern accent, the "thousand-yard stare" forever clouding Forster's eyes[8]—the apparently closed aspect of the film's narrative arrangement gives way to wider perspectives. This shift occurs initially in a scene that is merely hinted at toward the end of McCullers's novel, but which in Huston's adaptation is given pride of place, near the beginning, and suggestive, even provocative development.

Corporal Williams' (Robert Forster) nocturnal vision—we watch the voyeur.

In the scene, Captain Penderton (Marlon Brando) is lecturing to a classroom full of attentive junior officers. His subject is the theory of warfare, which, in his faultlessly jargonized definition, "tries to discover how we may gain a preponderance of physical forces and material advantages at a decisive point." The scene has begun with what seems an innocent enough bit of business, as Penderton erases a diagram of an attack from a chalk-crazed blackboard. But the portion of the blackboard being erased is blocked to occupy the exact quadrant of the film screen where a moment before Leonora and Langdon have lain down to make love behind the convenient screen of a blackberry bush—the transitional link between the two scenes being a slow dissolve. Now while this piece of irony is available to neither Penderton nor his students in their functions as story exigents, it is one that cannot be lost upon the attentive viewer.[9] The simple point, of course, is that Captain Penderton is a cuckold—a cuckold, moreover, in the pitiless grip of denial. Another point, however, is also being made, one not confined to the narrative world of the story. This small moment in the film is an important element of its discourse, for it undermines by underlining—erases, but in erasing, calls our attention to—the conventionally unreflected distinction between the fictional events projected upon the screen and the material fact of that screen itself.

We are given this glimpse of the self-reflective commitments of *Reflections* when, turning from the blackboard and rapping the book in his hand pedantically, Penderton says, "Let's have a look at a few things that Clausewitz says." He is speaking of Carl von Clausewitz (1780–1831), the Prussian general and military strategist whose classic work *On War* (*Vom Kriege,* 1832) remains "a basic text" for serious students of the problems of war and peace.[10] In particular he is speaking of the tactical efficacy of the surprise attack, which, as he says, Clausewitz considers to be "one of the strongest weapons of defensive warfare." But Penderton is not content to submit to the authority he has invoked; he must add his own two-cents' worth. "Now I would not want to improve upon Clausewitz," he continues, with a professorial flourish of false modesty, "but I would say that the night attack is one of the strongest weapons of defensive warfare."

Now, this scene is not only an adaptational improvement upon McCullers, who never mentions Clausewitz, and who, moreover, never enters Penderton's classroom via scene, it is also a bridge between the excessive psychological interiority of the film and the contextual world of fact so seemingly absent therefrom. Cued as we are by the transitional dissolve between this scene and its predecessor (blackberry: blackboard: the act of erasing) to the simultaneity of film art and apparatus, we necessarily attend to the doubled valence—diegetic and beyond—of any such de facto historical reference.[11] On the one hand, Penderton's pompous improvement upon Clausewitz (wrongheaded, as we shall see) foreshadows Private Williams's nocturnal forays into Leonora's bedroom, the last of which will culminate in Williams's death: Penderton's murderous response to his own blindingly desperate vanity. On the other hand, it opens the film up to implications impinging upon not only the basic theories that buttress the nation-state practice of maintaining standing armies, but also the actual exercise of those armies in wartime and peace. As peripheral as these considerations may seem to the plot of onscreen story events, they are considerations that we fail to recognize only at the peril of our own understanding—our ability, that is, to see the film truly.[12] Clausewitz helps us to do just that.

Central to Clausewitz's theory of war, if not indeed paramount to it, is his concept of *Kritik*.[13] For Clausewitz, *Kritik* is the tool by which strategy is constructed, and strategy, no matter how Olympian it might strike the casual observer with its seeming detachment from the exigencies of the field, relates always to the concrete uses of tactics. Neither dogma nor theory, *Kritik* is bivalent in its simultaneous engrossment in the details of battle and its constant search for higher ground from which to view ever larger planes of the specific. It does not evanesce into theory because it never leaves the particular, comprehending more of the particular as it ascends. In order successfully to "judge conquest in terms of control"—for a tactical advantage inapplicable to larger purposes is in fact a strategic liability—the critic "rises above the particular battlefield to see the field in its theater, the theater in its campaign, the campaign in the war, and the war in the overall statecraft of the warring nation."[14]

What we have here, of course, is a blueprint for practical criticism, or what has been called the politics of interpretation, where "interpretation" is substituted for "war."[15] Taken that way, the emphasis in Clausewitz upon seeing and the controlling power of sight is not without relevance to *Reflections in a Golden Eye*. I have already mentioned the massive close-up of Private Williams's eye, with its titular reflection of the nude Leonora. Approached from the level of first-phase feminist criticism,[16] this shot is emblematic of the film's overall excess, a tendency that has earned for it the charge of "genuinely reactionary cinema."[17] At a somewhat higher level, the shot opens up the whole issue of the male gaze and its use in the narrative reification of its female objects.[18] While approaches as various as these are clearly welcome in the free exchange of critical ideas about the film, I prefer to concentrate on how the film's studied insistence on the eye in relation to power elevates *Reflections* above the plane of the merely "reactionary." Were it not for the unyielding quality of that study, and the consequent imbrication of the spectator's own eye, the "reactionary" charge might very well stick. But camera placement and editing collaborate to construct the spectator's point of view in such a way that we are finally not allowed mere passive identification with Private Williams in his voyeurism. Thus while Williams stands outside raptly gazing up toward Leonora's second-story bedroom window, it is not Williams but the spectator who is allowed to see what is going on inside, as, for example, when Penderton puts the drunken Leonora to bed, unzipping her dress and removing it.

The point here is that an inaugural gap is being constructed between the on-screen voyeur and the spectator in the theater, even as the spectator is being turned toward the voyeuristic. The spectator-voyeur must deal

105

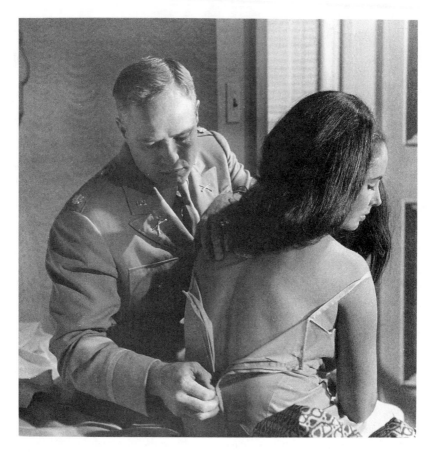

We watch what the voyeur cannot possibly be seeing.

with a voyeurism problematized precisely by the construction of that narrative gap in which Private Williams is seen seeing nothing more than an upstairs lighted window: This is no peep show, but a showing forth of the politics of cinematic looking, an implicit indictment of films that would suture their spectators into unquestioning passivity. True, we will soon gain entrance with Williams to that bedroom, and see the same sleeping Leonora that he watches, but the gigantic close-up of his gaze, which has earlier confronted our own eye, has alerted us to the self-consciousness built into the film and in turn imposed upon us. We are not looking, in other words, at the naked Elizabeth Taylor (or, more precisely, at Taylor's

Italian body double); we are looking at an enormous film image of an eye staring straight back into ours, so that our own eyes must be reflecting the nude reflection in its corner—and so on, ad infinitum.

Or so it would seem. But the metaphysical threat of infinity—an endless chain of reflections replicated forever—finally does not obtain. The reason for this is that the gargantuan eye there before us in all its unblinking excess, far from striking us as dumb as Private Williams, shatters the spell of disengagement that mere spectacle seeks to enjoin and returns us to the intersecting worlds of art, apparatus, and historical context.[19] Needless to say, paradox is never far from that particular intersection; nor does Clausewitz in his discussion of *Kritik* disregard that most compelling paradox at the heart of power and its exercise, namely, that in asserting one's power, one surrenders the freedom to disregard the next counter-assertion.

Here we are given to consider Penderton's absolute loss of control over Leonora's stallion, Firebird. The sequence of scenes culminating with Leonora's horsewhipping of Penderton commences with the scene in which he accompanies his wife and Langdon out riding in the forest, only to fall going over an easy jump. Woodenly regaining control of his horse, if not of his injured pride, Penderton sees the naked Williams cantering his own horse in graceful circles—"Bareback and bare-ass," is how the amused Leonora phrases it. But Penderton is not amused. His mouth pursed in anal outrage, he calls the sight "disgraceful," no doubt still smarting from his own equestrian disgrace. But his disgrace runs deeper than that, and we see it in his eyes. For while this is only the latest in a long line of affronts to his ability to exercise control, it is here, in mocking view of the naked Private Williams, that Penderton's freedom to disregard any such further challenges is effectively dissolved. It is here, too, that his hatred for the reversed image of himself suggested in everything about Private Williams—the rangy looseness of the enlisted man, his strong, capable hands—itself reaches the point of longed-for reversal, and hatred becomes desire.

The dissolution of Penderton's freedom is in fact so complete that he does not wait for the next challenge to his authority to come from without. Rather, ignoring what he knows about his own feeble horsemanship, he takes it upon himself to attempt the mastery of Leonora's beloved Firebird. The runaway ride that ensues charges the film with an exhilarating demonstration of the absolute loss of control, even as it terrifies Penderton. Having barely hung on until the end of the ride, Penderton beats the horse savagely, then breaks down and weeps, reduced to the fickle mercy of a control that is no longer his: The naked Private Williams appears and quietly walks the horse away, effectively taking charge from his commanding officer. The horsewhipping at the hands of the enraged Leonora—a surprise night attack undertaken in full view of Penderton's fellow officers and their wives—will follow in good enough time.

Now all of this relates less to Clausewitz's ideas on the night attack than to Penderton's muddled "improvement." Notwithstanding Leonora's sharp success with her riding crop, Clausewitz argues that the night attack must for the most part "be considered only as desperate means."[20] "Conditions rarely provide a night attack with much promise of success," for in a night operation "the attacker seldom if ever knows enough about the defense to make up for his lack of visual observation."[21] Of course, it is precisely the missing visual element that gives Penderton's would-be improvement the lie, adding an ironic footnote to his abbreviated lecture when he turns in his pacing at the head of the class to glance casually out the window. But the glance turns quickly into one of the film's signature actions—a fixed gaze through the blinds—as Penderton finds himself caught by the view of Leonora and Langdon riding happily across the post-coital drill field. The visual irony of this surprise daylight assault on Penderton's pride suffices to undermine his presumed authority, if not with his students, who are not privy to what he sees, then certainly with those of us in the audience, who are. As he does in the classroom, moreover, so Penderton does throughout the film, consistently misprisioning the world about him. From the theory of war to the practice of love, Captain Penderton bungles the officer's two most critical obligations, to judge correctly and to lead; so that by the time he delivers his lecture on leadership later in the film, revealing the depth of his undoing in the process, he has all but succumbed to the obsession of his secret desire for Private Williams, and in so succumbing abandoned both obligations.

In calling on Clausewitz my point has been to valorize neither war nor its masters, theoretical or otherwise, but to understand Penderton's emblematic crisis of leadership. That that crisis invests *Reflections in a Golden Eye* with extranarrative resonance is suggested in the emphasis on the visual, to which it repeatedly returns us. For as we have already seen, it is Clausewitz's central emphasis on visibility and seeing in their relation to power that permeates *Reflections,* from the voyeuristic eye of Private Williams to the eye of the peacock that Anacleto paints, with its ghastly green suggestion of the grotesque. Nor is that emphasis absent, though it is certainly reversed, in Penderton's self-blinding monomania to see what in reality is not there—the reflection, that is, of his desire—as he follows Williams through the rain-soaked streets of the post. By the time of that thunderstorm, the lockstep order of the novel's introductory paragraph ("once a man enters the army he is expected only to follow the heels ahead of him") has been turned in on itself, as the superior officer surrenders his leadership to the vagaries of obsession. Clausewitz talks of the irrationality of war, of how the need to control one's own troops can turn them into one's enemy; but exchange that control for the desire to become one's own inferior, as Penderton does in his wrenching speech about the "rough," "clean" "life of men among men" denied those of rank like himself, and the line between feared enemy and coveted object of desire becomes as blurred as a rain-streaked window pane, the same blinded window, say, from which the drugged Penderton peers through flashes of lightning, as Williams circles the house down below. In a gesture as simple as it is elegant, Penderton smooths his mussed hair and turns out the light, awaiting the lover he thinks has finally come for him. But Williams has come again for Leonora, to watch her in her sleep, and his virginal perversion amounts to betrayal in Penderton's eyes. Thus spurned in his own mind, Penderton empties his service revolver into the waiting body of the younger man, making him pay for all the bungled perceptions of deluded leadership— and leaving them to us with our *Kritik* to judge.

How such a film could be released in the fall of 1967 and garner not one mention of the Vietnam war in its major reviews is perhaps best seen as testimony to ideology's interpellative power to screen itself out of its subjects' consciousness. A mere glance, however, at the front-page headlines for October 11 of that year—the day on which *Reflections* premiered in New York—suffices to show how central to the American experience the war was in fact: "U.S. Drops First Bombs on Soviet Arms Depot in North"; "Cost of U.S. Raids on N. Vietnam 3-1 Over Hanoi Losses"; "Thieu Pledges Wider War If Search for Peace Fails."[22] And sharing the front page with Southeast Asia is this from South America: "U.S. Green Berets Remain in Bolivia to Train Regulars,"[23] and "Bolivia Confirms Guevara's Death; Body Displayed,"[24] accompanied by the famous photograph of Che in repose. An inside-page squib datelined Panama (AP) tells how an officer of the National Guard has prevented a dozen Panamanian

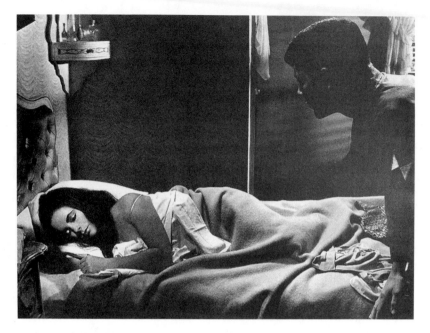

Sleeping Leonora (Elizabeth Taylor) is unaware of the intruding Williams (Robert Forster).

students from "setting the Flag [sic] afire," although it has been "ripped in the struggle."[25] Ten days later, in Washington, D.C., following a peaceful rally and march by more than 50,000 people protesting the presence of nearly 500,000 American troops in Vietnam, thousands of other Americans would storm the Pentagon; there would be tear gas, scores injured, and hundreds of arrests.[26] The war was no longer absent.

This then was the concrete moment in history into which John Huston introduced *Reflections in a Golden Eye,* one year before John Wayne introduced *The Green Berets.* Odious as it is, the comparison will stop there, before it is even begun; and yet I cannot help noting the emphasis upon color in either title, and the radical difference in the treatment of color within either film. Whereas Wayne served up his version of wartime heroism in conventional Technicolor, Huston went to great lengths to present his vision of peacetime antiheroism in a color scheme defying all traditional standards of Hollywood realism. His intention with *Reflections* was to "get into people's minds,"[27] and toward that end technicians at

Technicolor Italiana in Rome spent nearly six months experimenting, emerging finally with an effect called "desaturation."[28] In this process, all the colors of the film were rendered in an almost monochrome sepia, except for red hues, which were translated into varying tones of muted scarlet. No color other than red was interpreted realistically, so that only Leonora's dress in the prizefight scene, for example, or the lettering on the Baby Ruth candy wrapper, would register as anything other than a generalized amber.

The dreamlike effect of this color scheme defamiliarizes not only our received sense of film's palette but the experience itself of watching a film: again, self-conscious tactics serving the larger strategy of subversion at work in virtually every aspect of Huston's film. But the effect was too unconventional for the executives at Warner Brothers-Seven Arts, whose eyes were on the added profit to be made after general release from the television networks, which paid more for color films.[29] Within days of the film's premiere, the original desaturated prints were pulled from release and replaced by a conventional Technicolor version, to which Huston contemptuously referred as "standard, literal beer-ad color."[30] To this day the desaturated *Reflections in a Golden Eye* suffers the same effective fate imposed upon *Let There Be Light,* which was suppressed for nearly forty years.[31] Since Huston fought hard—and failed—to keep the desaturated version of his film available, it is only fair to quote from the long letter he wrote in its defense:

> Color in nature is very different from color on the screen. When you sit in
> a darkened theatre your attention is so concentrated on the screen that the
> images seem more fully saturated with color than they are in reality. Thus
> color effects are unnaturally heightened. This kind of color has been fine for
> extravaganzas and spectacular films. But when we are dealing with material
> of psychological content it becomes invariably distracting as it gets between
> the viewer and the mind he is trying to search into. Until now, the film-
> maker had a single choice, the use of black and white or of color. This is
> as though all painters were limited to either pure pigment or black india
> ink washes. This day and night difference is no longer the only choice as
> *Reflections in a Golden Eye* demonstrates.[32]

Huston did not shy from battle when the fight was a worthy one; but despite his workmanlike eloquence, *Reflections in a Golden Eye* stands in this regard as a casualty of censorship, all the more so for not being recognized as such for almost a quarter of a century.[33] If we are still prevented

The absence of blood on Private Williams' bullet-ridden body strikes us as strange.

from viewing the version intended by Huston, however, this aspect of the film's history allows us to see the telling red, which seeps through the limited black-and-white wash of its critical and popular reception thus far. For in that reception the excessive displacement into peacetime of perverse sexuality went unnoticed for what it also was: an effective cultural response, unconscious or otherwise, to the bloody perversions being wreaked on Vietnam.[34] In a film that highlights its reds, the absence of blood on Private Williams's bullet-riddled body strikes us as strange, and then makes us think: the real blood is being shed outside the theater, while inside we grapple with sight. With its compelling portrayal of military leadership gone murderously blind to the most basic principles of war—not to mention its suggestion, present in its absence, of a people's power to defeat those principles—*Reflections in a Golden Eye* deserves another look, and not only in retrospection.

## NOTES

1. Scott Hammen points out the many "uncanny" parallels between *The Red Badge of Courage* and the documentaries: "The uncertainty and impatience of untried soldiers in the first part of Crane's book correspond to that pictured in *Report from the Aleutians*. The horror of actual combat that Crane describes later is captured by Huston in *San Pietro,* and, finally, the inquiry into what happens to a man's spirit after exposure to such combat that is the novel's central subject is likewise that of *Let There Be Light*. It was as if Huston had already make a documentary version of *The Red Badge of Courage*." See Scott Hammen, *John Huston* (Boston: Twayne Publishers, 1985), 57.

2. Carson McCullers, *Reflections in a Golden Eye* (Boston: Houghton Mifflin Company, 1941), 3.

3. Chapel, gym, golf course and pools: "ideological state apparatuses" all. See Louis Althusser, "Ideology and Ideological State Apparatuses," in *Lenin and Philosophy,* trans. Ben Brewster (New York: Monthly Review Press, 1971), 127–86.

4. *Reflections in a Golden Eye* appeared originally in two installments, in the October and November 1940 issues of *Harper's Bazaar.* It was issued in book form the following year by Houghton Mifflin. All subsequent quotations from the novel will be taken from the Houghton Mifflin edition and identified in the text by page numbers within parentheses.

5. Virginia Spencer Carr tells us that *Reflections in a Golden Eye* owed its genesis in part both to D. H. Lawrence's story "The Prussian Officer" and to Freud, "in whose works [McCullers] also was steeped." See Carr, *The Lonely Hunter: A Biography of Carson McCullers* (Garden City, N.Y.: Doubleday and Company, 1975), 39.

6. I hope that the Lacanian psychoanalytic reading here clearly called for will be undertaken by someone else. Neglected as it has been, the novel-film axis presented to us by *Reflections in a Golden Eye* offers an embarrassment of critical riches.

7. Asked how the then-current escalation of the Vietnam war and the sharp division of public opinion on the matter affected the making of a movie about sexual deceit, impotence, and a murderous crime of passion on an army base during peacetime, the producer of the film replied, "Not at all. Our aim was to be faithful to the book." Author's interview with Ray Stark, Los Angeles, Oct. 26, 1989.

8. See Philip Caputo, *A Rumor of War* (New York: Ballantine Books, 1977), 93.

9. For his very helpful treatment of the elements of narrative, including story exigents, see Seymour Chatman, *Story and Discourse: Narrative Structure in Fiction and Film* (Ithaca: Cornell University Press, 1978).

10. See Michael Howard's preface to *A Short Guide to Clausewitz On War,* ed. Roger Ashley Leonard (New York: G. P. Putnam's Sons, 1967), ix.

11. Consider Terry Eagleton on the literary text: "Like private property, the literary text . . . appears as a 'natural' object, typically denying the determinants of its productive process. The function of criticism is to refuse the spontaneous presence of the work—to deny that 'naturalness' in order to make its real determinants appear." See Terry Eagleton, *Criticism and Ideology: A Study in Marxist Literary Theory* (London: Verso, 1978), 101. Notwithstanding my own critical efforts in this direction, I am suggesting that the text itself of *Reflections in a Golden Eye* actively collaborates in the unveiling of its own productive process and the underlying political influences.

12. Perhaps I should pause here to note that I hesitate to call these considerations "extra-cinematic" in any pejorative or even secondary sense, for even when the term of putative opposition, "cinematic," is made to refer "to all that goes on on the screen and to what happens between screen image and spectator," the distinction, less than sharp, between "all that goes on" and "what happens" fails to exclude the kind of intervention I am working to make. See E. Ann Kaplan, *Women and Film: Both Sides of the Camera* (New York: Methuen, 1983), 20.

13. This section of my analysis relies heavily on Gary Wills, "Critical Inquiry (*Kritik*) in Clausewitz," in *The Politics of Interpretation,* ed. W. J. T. Mitchell (Chicago: University of Chicago Press, 1983), 159–80.

14. Wills, "Critical Inquiry," 171, 170.

15. Mitchell, *Politics of Interpretation,* 1.

16. See Elaine Showalter, ed., *The New Feminist Criticism: Essays on Women, Literature and Theory* (New York: Pantheon Books, 1985), 5.

17. "Everything about this film, its characters, the acting, camera positions, subject matter, iconography, color, mise en scene, dialogue, use of the static close-ups [sic] as establishing shot, is *in extremis*. The relentless force of its audacity makes it genuinely reactionary cinema." Ann Laemmle, "Program Notes," *Cinema Texas* 21, no. 2 (Nov. 11, 1981: 36. In keeping with her analysis, Laemmle concludes with what might be taken as an equally reactionary recommendation: "To scream . . . seems a most appropriate reaction for anyone really paying the slightest attention to the film."

18. For the classic pronouncement on the male gaze, see Laura Mulvey, "Visual Pleasure and Narrative Cinema," *Screen* 16 (1975): 6–18.

19. "The will-to-spectacle is the assertion that a world of foreground is the only world that matters or is the only world that *is*. . . . Spectacle offers an imagistic surface of the world as a strategy of containment against any depth of involvement with that world." See Dana B. Polan, " 'Above All Else To Make You See': Cinema and the Ideology of Spectacle" in *Postmodernism and Politics,* ed. Jonathan Arac (Minneapolis: University of Minnesota Press, 1986), 61, 63.

20. Carl von Clausewitz, *Principles of War* (Harrisburg, Penn.: Stackpole Company, 1942), 27.

21. Wills, "Critical Inquiry," 168. Wills is quoting from Carl von Clausewitz, *On War,* ed. and trans. Michael Howard and Peter Paret (Princeton: Princeton University Press, 1976), bk. 4, ch. 7, p. 241, and bk. 4, ch. 14, p. 273. Needless to say, the theory and practice of the night attack since Clausewitz have been refined on fields of battle from Panama City to Baghdad.

22. The first two headlines are from the *Los Angeles Times,* the third from the *New York Times,* both Oct. 11, 1967.

23. *Los Angeles Times,* Oct. 11, 1967.

24. *New York Times,* Oct. 11, 1967.

25. *Los Angeles Times,* Oct. 11, 1967.

26. For a report on the Washington demonstration, see the *New York Times,* Oct. 21, 1967. The half-million troop figure is from Stanley Karnow, *Vietnam: A History* (New York: Viking Press, 1983), 681.

27. John Huston, quoted in Ernest Anderson, unpublished paper dated Apr. 15 (1967?), 3. John Huston Collection, Academy of Motion Picture Arts and Sciences, Beverly Hills.

28. This section of my paper takes its technical information and phrasing from Herb A. Lightman, *"Reflections in a Golden Eye* Viewed through a Glass Darkly," *American Cinematographer,* Dec. 1967.

29. Anderson, 3.

30. John Huston, unpublished letter to Eliot Hyman, an executive at Warner Brothers-Seven Arts, Sept. 25, 1967. John Huston Collection, Academy of Motion Picture Arts and Sciences, Beverly Hills.

31. My attempts to view the film in its original desaturated color process proved how effective this suppression continues to be. The Warner Brothers Archives themselves listed only Technicolor versions, and Ray Stark, who was very cooperative and helpful in answering questions about the film's production, did not know where a print could be found. Thanks to Steven Ricci of UCLA's Research and Study Center, I was finally able to view one ten-minute reel from the university's Film and Television Archives.

32. John Huston, letter to Eliot Hyman. This long passage is also quoted in Lightman, "*Reflections in a Golden Eye* Viewed through a Glass Darkly," 2.

33. And not only a casualty of censorship, but a curious precursor of the colorizing debate raging currently.

34. As Fredric Jameson tells us, the political unconscious never sleeps. See his *The Political Unconscious: Narrative as a Socially Symbolic Act* (Ithaca: Cornell University Press, 1981). For a Clausewitzian analysis of America's failure in Vietnam, see Col. Harry G. Summers, Jr., *On Strategy: A Critical Analysis of the Vietnam War* (Novato, Cal.: Presidio Press, 1982).

# Part Two

HUSTON AND THE PROBLEM OF MASCULINITY

# John Huston and
# *The Maltese Falcon*

## JAMES NAREMORE

J ohn Huston's reputation was in decline during the heyday of auteurism, chiefly because of *The List of Adrian Messenger, Casino Royale,* and *The Bible,* but also because of critics who attacked him in order to praise Vincente Minnelli or Howard Hawks. He was often described as an "adapter" rather than an auteur (his public statements about his craft tended to justify this description), and even his earliest success was subtly damned. Thus Andrew Sarris described *The Maltese Falcon* as an actor's picture, owing more to "casting coups than to directorial acumen." The film, he said, was an "uncanny matchup of Dashiell Hammett's literary characters with their visual doubles: Mary Astor, Humphrey Bogart, Sidney Greenstreet, Peter Lorre, and Elisha Cook, Jr. Only Stendhal's Julien Sorel in search of Gérard Philipe can match *Falcon's* Pirandellian equation."[1]

First let me say I have deep respect for Sarris. He is a remarkably fine critic, greatly responsible for our serious interest in American popular

119

*The Maltese Falcon:* an archetypal image.

cinema; but in this case he was in error. Even if his remarks were true, he should have given Huston more credit for assembling such presences. In fact, however, the actors can hardly be regarded as "visual doubles" for people in the novel. Consider Hammett's opening paragraph:

> Samuel Spade's jaw was long and bony, his chin a jutting v under the more flexible v of his mouth. His yellow-gray eyes were horizontal. The v motif was picked up again by thickish brows rising outward from twin creases above a hooked nose, and his pale brown hair grew down—from high flat temples—in a point on his forehead. He looked rather pleasantly like a blond satan.

Clearly Humphrey Bogart is the visual opposite of Hammett's Sam Spade. Spade, Hammett tells us, is a tall man with an "almost conical" body. When he takes off his shirt, "the sag of his big rounded shoulders" makes him resemble "a bear." Bogart's slight, swarthy appearance, his menacing smile, to say nothing of his famed low-life New York accent (he calls the falcon a "black boid") evoke an altogether different personality.

In a less absolute sense, the same point can be made about the casting of every actor in the film. Sidney Greenstreet, in a beautifully restrained performance, is not so flabby or bombastic as the Gutman of the novel, and he lacks "dark ringlets" of hair. Peter Lorre is properly Levantine, but less effeminate and less bejeweled than Hammett's Joel Cairo. Elisha Cook, Jr., has the right stature for the "boy" Wilmer, but he seems always to have had the pinched face of an old man. Most unusual of all is Huston's choice of Mary Astor, who, far from being a double, is actually cast against the grain of her character. Hammett's Brigid O'Shaughnessy is little more than a sexy dame; indeed, one problem with the book is that it gives us no good reason why Spade should be in love with Brigid. She is wonderful to sleep with, but she is obviously not to be trusted, her only quality besides good looks being her transparent deceitfulness. Mary Astor, on the other hand, has a lovely but almost matronly face and build, and she brings a sophistication to the role that is entirely lacking in the novel. She fits nicely Raymond Durgnat's description of Maggie Smith: a blend of "brimming feminine sensitivity, of superior intelligence, and of something mockingly autonomous."[2] Like the character in the novel she is a tease, but she is a tease of a distinctly upper-class sort. Perhaps that is why she never became a great star. In any case, the scenes between her and Bogart have a humor and intelligence that seem to run beneath the surface of the words, so that lines Hammett wrote flatly and seriously gain a new dimension. When Astor tosses her head back on a soft couch, gazes up at the ceiling, and gives a description of Floyd Thursby ("He never went to sleep without covering the floor around his bed with crumpled newspaper so nobody could come silently into his room"), her manner—and Huston's framing of her face—is so outrageous and chic that we smile with delight. As Spade would say, now she's *really* dangerous.

One could go on in this vein, celebrating the changes that the film makes in even the minor roles (Jerome Cowan is a different Miles Archer than the one described by Hammett—slicker, more ironically treated), but there is no need to mention all the ways that Huston's characters are different. If these discrepancies between text and film prove anything, it is that Huston has gained ascendancy over Hammett. It is easy to forget that Sam Spade was not actually the visual double for Bogart, because we feel he should have been.

Moreover, while many people deserve credit for the success of *The Maltese Falcon,* its special quality owes chiefly to John Huston's style, a style so recognizable and individual that it is anything but the sign of a "competent craftsman." This statement may seem paradoxical, since Huston is widely regarded as an oblique, nearly styleless director, and especially since the movie is a fairly literal rendition of the novel. Huston claimed that before beginning work on a screenplay he gave Hammett's book to a secretary, asking her to break it down into shots, scenes, and dialogue. A copy of the secretary's work was shown to Jack Warner, who, thinking he had a complete script, gave Huston his blessing for capturing the flavor of the original.[3] The finished screenplay is less an adaptation than a skillful editing of the novel, which is mostly dialogue anyway. Huston economizes beautifully, telescoping scenes, cutting away some of the minor characters (including Kasper Gutman's daughter), and making slight changes in a few places to get past the censors or heighten the irony. The picture is leaner, quicker than the novel, but with few exceptions the words are Hammett's own.

And yet the result is a phenomenon much like the one observed by Andre Bazin, speaking of Jean Renoir's *Madame Bovary* and *Une partie de campagne:* "What strikes us about the fidelity of Renoir is that paradoxically it is compatible with complete independence from the original. The justification for this is of course that the genius of Renoir is certainly as great as that of Flaubert or Maupassant. The phenomenon we face here is comparable then to the translation of Edgar Allan Poe by Baudelaire."[4] Huston was no Flaubert, but with the aid of cameraman Arthur Edeson, art director Robert Hass, and a brilliant group of players, he made from *Falcon* one of the classics of dark cinema, a film that is not only "faithful" but also constitutive of his own signature.

The very choice of *Falcon* was consistent with the personality Huston would convey in nearly all his subsequent work—perhaps *Falcon* even determined that personality to some degree. Notice how neatly it fits into the Huston oeuvre: Most of his good films—*The Treasure of the Sierra Madre, Key Largo, We Were Strangers, The Asphalt Jungle, The Roots of Heaven, Beat the Devil, The Misfits, Fat City*—depend on simple visual symbolism and sharp contrasts of character. They are all quasi-allegorical adventures about groups of exotic, eccentric people, and, as several commentators have observed, they usually end on a note of great, ironic failure. Even *The African Queen,* which isolates two completely different character types, is barely an exception to these rules; it merely has a smaller cast and a more optimistic comedy, an act of God intervening to save the protagonists. It would be a more typical film if it ended about fifteen minutes earlier, at the point where Bogart and Hepburn collapse with exhaustion as the camera rises above high grass to show the open sea only a few feet away. Ultimately, however, Huston was less interested in success or failure than in the moments of truth that an adventurous quest leads up to. As a result, the point in his version of *Falcon* is not the bird itself, nor the fact that it ends up being a phony. Huston wants to show the greed, the treachery, and sometimes the loyalty of his characters. The focus at the end of the picture is on Sam Spade's curious integrity, and on Sidney Greenstreet as he taps a bowler hat on his head and gaily wanders off in search of the real bird.

Huston's films also show his admiration for a male world, though he was sometimes more ambivalent toward that world than a director like Hawks. Raymond Durgnat has rightly pointed out that *"Treasure of Sierra Madre* and *The Misfits* are 'tragic critiques' of the Hawksian ideal, respecting it, fairly, but going beyond their tough conformism to a profounder humanism."[5] *Falcon* is hardly an example of profound humanism, but Huston does seem more conscious than Hammett of the male myth which underlies the novel. The film is more emphatic, more stylized than the book, and it shows us very clearly that the underworld characters are foils for Spade's masculinity. A single room tells us that Spade scorns luxury; he is not effeminate like Cairo, and he has no soft belly like Gutman. This contrast is elaborated by other details: Spade does not need to carry a gun, but the "boy" Wilmer—whose very name sounds prissy—ludicrously brandishes two big forty-fives in a desperate and unsuccessful attempt to assert manhood. More important, Spade's professional ethics, his willingness to turn in a woman he loves out of loyalty to a dead partner he never liked much anyway, is at bottom a victory for the "male" ethic. It is true that in the past he cuckolded Archer (mostly, we suspect, at the insistence of Archer's wife), but his behavior as we actually see it is fundamentally different from Brigid O'Shaughnessy's or Mrs. Archer's. As in most private-eye stories, the women in Huston's film are fickle and dangerous killers, and they have to be rejected or sent off to prison at the end if the hero wishes to survive. *The Maltese Falcon* is one of the purest examples of this classic form; significantly, the one trustworthy female in the movie is Effie Perine, whom Spade treats like a little sister. She sits on his desk and rolls his cigarettes, and at one point he calls her a "good man."

But if *Falcon* is typical of Huston's themes, it is also the finest achievement of his visual style. In this respect we can see most clearly the difference between his work and Hammett's. Hammett's art is minimalist and deadpan, but Huston, contrary to his reputation, is a highly energetic and expressive storyteller who likes to make comments through his images. In his treatment of settings, for example, he usually employs the same principle of vivid contrast that governs his approach to character. In *We Were Strangers* he takes us from the sunny, whitewashed streets of Havana to the inside of a house filled with revolutionaries, where the light has what James Agee called "the luminous pallor of marble." Beneath the house the conspirators are desperately burrowing a tunnel, and all we see in the darkness is an occasional sweaty face. In *Freud* we move from the dark, heavily draped and tapestried background of Freud's household to the sunny, spacious, flowered boudoir of a young blond patient. *Falcon* has a similar structure, though it is more subtly realized. Most of the action takes place inside four rooms—Spade's office, his apartment, and the hotel rooms of Brigid O'Shaughnessy and Kasper Gutman. These rooms are roughly the same size, and the last three contain ornate mantelpieces of the same proportions but with different designs, as if Huston and his decorator were stressing a parallel to establish a basic contrast. Spade's apartment embodies a tough, masculine ethos: it is predictably Spartan, except for a big chair upholstered in glittering leather and a series of horse-racing photographs in the far distance over his mantelpiece (a touch surely provided by Huston himself). There are a couple of lighted lamps and several unlit fixtures. Books and papers are scattered around, and to one side is a rumpled bed with a plain iron bedstead. A window is always open, though it is cold enough outside for everyone to wear overcoats. The rooms of Brigid and Gutman, on the other hand, are feminine and luxurious, the walls nearly as bare as Spade's, but the furniture all satiny and decorated with stripes. A fire burns in Brigid's hearth; the windows are closed, and flowers stand around in cut-glass vases. Gutman's room is similar but more expensive, with oriental lamps and a few French provincial furnishings. It is also the whitest room in the film, its lightness accentuating Greenstreet's bulky, black-clothed body.

These settings have been criticized as being less accurate than the ones in Roy Del Ruth's 1931 version of *Falcon*.[6] It is true that the sets in the Huston movie are extremely simple, and the exteriors in particular have a false, studioish aura that is typical of Warners in the early 1940s. Still, Huston uses the *mise en scène* with great intelligence, first to empha-

Huston contributes characters in their symbolic settings to Dashiell
Hammett's deadpan descriptions.

size the contrast between Spade's "maleness" and the "femininity" of the
other characters, and second to give the film much of its remarkable feeling of spatial unity. Ninety percent of the action is played out against the
same architecture, even though the decorative arrangement of each setting
is different, and we seldom see all of a room in a given shot. *Falcon* is not
so potentially claustrophobic a movie as *Twelve Angry Men* or *Lifeboat,*
but it does have the same circumscribed, nearly allegorical world and the
same technical problem of maintaining interest. Huston seems aware of
the problem—thus the pace of the acting, the speed of the editing, the variety of the camera setups—but he also knows that the *Black Mask* detective
genre is among the most fetishistic of fictions, and therefore close interiors
can be as important to it as open vistas are to the Western. The classic

private-eye story benefits from intimacy, and it fascinates us with all kinds of objects: In Huston's film, for example, we have the leather swivel chair in Bogart's office, his roll-your-own cigarettes, the gadget on his desk from which he can withdraw lighted matches, the little neon signs outside his window that glow KLVW or DRINK. We also have Brigid's fur wrap, Gutman's watch fob, Cairo's enameled cane, and of course Wilmer's pistols. The atmosphere is heightened, so that a splash of whiskey in a glass is more important than the sound of gunfire.

Even Dashiell Hammett, whose prose style is extremely bare, occasionally lends atmosphere to his tale by listing objects. For example, in the first awkward moment of Brigid O'Shaughnessy's interview with Spade, we find this description:

> On Spade's desk a limp cigarette smouldered in a brass tray. . . . Ragged
> grey flakes of cigarette-ash dotted the yellow top of the desk and the grey
> blotter and the papers that were there. A buff-curtained window, eight or ten
> inches open, let in from the court a current of air. . . . The ashes on the desk
> twitched and crawled.

A bit later in the novel, when Spade receives a phone call about the death of Archer, Hammett pays fond attention to the things in the room: "a packet of brown papers and a sack of Bull Durham tobacco," a "pigskin-and-nickel lighter," "a white bowl" suspended from the ceiling on "three gilded chains," a "tinny alarm clock insecurely mounted on a corner of Duke's *Celebrated Criminal Cases of America*," and "cold steamy air" blowing in from two open windows. The deep-focus lenses of the early 1940s were well suited for adapting this technique; they brought clarity and perspective into the movie image and allowed objects to take on the ambience of character. Thus, one of the most effective and memorable shots in Huston's film is our first view of Spade's room, a view which is suggested by the descriptions in the novel. We have just seen Archer's murder, and immediately we cut to an in-depth composition featuring a bedside table in the foreground, in the distance an open window, its transparent curtains waving slowly in the cold night breeze. At first we are in darkness, the objects on the table a shadowy pyramid sculpted by pale light from the window. We see an old-fashioned tall black telephone, Hammett's "tinny alarm clock," a legal book, a newspaper, a sack of Bull Durham, and the shade of an unlighted lamp. The telephone is ringing, and a hand comes into the picture to remove it. The camera keeps the table precisely framed while we hear Bogart's voice and watch the somewhat ghostly curtains waving in the background. At last Bogart sits up from his bed, the camera moving back slightly to get the edge of his face. He is learning about the murder. He puts down the base of the phone and switches on the lamp. Now the whole depth of the composition has been lighted; the clock face reads 2:05, as in the novel, and an old patterned drapery is visible in the distance behind Bogart's head. We see the shiny surfaces of the alarm and the telephone, Bogart's full profile up close, and swaying curtains in the background at the left of the frame. It is an extraordinary shot, one tiny section of the room evoking the entire hard-boiled style of life. Furthermore, as in Hammett's novel, none of the atmosphere is achieved at the expense of the story. The time of night is established, Spade's character is suggested, and the sinister consequences of Archer's death are conveyed immediately and powerfully.

Here, as nearly everywhere else, the film is even more economical than the novel, and the force of its imagery is simpler, more nearly symbolic. It is perhaps fitting that the black bird itself, fetishist object around which all the other objects are organized, should be presented to us at the very opening, beneath the credits, so that its dark exotic shape can preside over the later scenes like a symbol. Probably Huston is not responsible for the credits, but in some ways they are in keeping with the stylized quality of the rest of the film. Huston's approach in *Falcon* is neither utilitarian (as in Hawks's *The Big Sleep*) nor arty (as in Edward Dmytryk's *Murder, My Sweet*); and yet, for a director who was widely reputed to conceal his technique, he shows a decided flair for iconography. This was the only time in his career when he made preliminary sketches for the camera setups, and these resulted in a number of bold flourishes. Perhaps the most famous example of visual symbolism comes at the very end, where the iron bars of an elevator grille close across Mary Astor's beautiful tear-stained face, foreshadowing the years she is going to spend at Tehachapi. A long shot follows, and as the lighted elevator cage descends, Bogart, purely for the sake of the metaphor, walks slowly down a stairway at the left of the frame, descending to his own kind of sorrow.

There are several such moments, including the little tableau on the night table. Indeed, even the first sequence of the picture is stylishly rounded off by a pair of camera movements which underline the irony of Archer's subsequent death. It begins with a pan shot, moving downward from the reversed SPADE AND ARCHER sign of the window above Bogart's desk. At the end of the sequence, the camera is set very low, looking up at Archer as he stands examining the money left by Brigid O'Shaughnessy. His greed and lechery are stressed by the squint of his eye, his little smile, and the cigarette hanging from his mouth; above him, the odd line of a beam on the ceiling creates a disquieting note. As Bogart walks into the frame the camera pulls back and up to a more normal view; then, as the two men walk across the room we pull back even more, until they stop at their desks. Their figures are composed at either side of the screen, and Spade's cramped little office now looks as big as an empty ballroom. They sit down, the SPADE AND ARCHER sign between them and about three-quarters of the floor visible, with nothing between the camera and the far-off desks. It is an extremely unrealistic shot; the real space of the office has been violated, as if we were looking through a proscenium onto a stage. As Spade jokes with Archer ("You're got brains, yes you have.") the screen darkens a bit and the camera moves down again, panning to the floor, aimed at the lighted rectangle cast by a window, the SPADE AND ARCHER sign visible again in bold dark shadow, its letters returned by the light to their normal left-right order. In the next sequence, of course, we will see Archer's murder.

The close-ups, too, are deliberately stylized. In its own way, *Falcon* is nearly as preoccupied with the landscape of faces as Carl Theodor Dreyer's *Passion of Joan of Arc,* though Huston's images are sometimes more like good cartoons; they give the movie much of its grotesque comedy and its feeling of a moral tale. Nearly every close-up is designed to make a statement about character—Peter Lorre brushing the tip of his fancy walking stick across his lips; Elisha Cook's psychotic eyes brimming with tears; Greenstreet's countenance appearing just above his stomach. Our first view of Mary Astor's face is meant to contrast her with the drab walls of Spade's office: Daylight from a window at the upper right of the frame sets off the little black hat perched atop her head, her fur wrap, and the line of her shoulder. Most of the composition is in gray or black, except for Astor's white collar and her face, a soft triangle of flesh at the very center of the picture. At the end of the film, when Spade informs Brigid he is turning her over to the law, a harsh dawn light breaks through the windows of his room, the curtains waving still, but now seeming to underline the agitation of the characters. Bogart literally pushes Astor up against a white wall, flat light washing the shadows out of her face as, for the first time, she loses control.

Huston's expressive, almost comic-strip style can be seen best in a sequence that comes midway in the first reel, when Lieutenant Dundy and Detective Tom Polhaus (Barton MacLane and Ward Bond) pay a call at Spade's apartment to discuss the murders of Archer and Floyd Thursby. Dundy is a smart, rather mean cop who disliked Spade. Polhaus is relatively slower and very uncomfortable, caught between his superior officer and his old acquaintance. The interview begins on a fairly uneasy note and then leads to an aggressive exchange between Dundy and Spade. Ultimately, when Spade sees that the police are not sure he is the killer, he relaxes somewhat, and the scene ends with the three men having a drink together. It is not one of the more important sequences of the film, but it is relatively brief and extremely well realized, showing how a powerful narrative is generated from Edeson's photography and Huston's rather mannered placement of actors and camera. Those who are interested may compare the film treatment with the equivalent passage in Hammett's novel. Huston has cut some speeches, trimmed others to their essence, and added a new line at the end. Hammett writes very well (the monosyllabic talk and the tough accents of his characters are indispensable), but in comparison the book seems a bit pale, without the edge of visual wit and the almost electric tension of the film. The sequence begins with two leisurely panning movements, taken from different angles and accompanied by foreboding music, emphasizing the decor of Spade's room and the unfettered bodies of the actors. Thereafter we have a fairly rapid series of tight, three-figured compositions and occasional close-ups. The coats and hats of the policemen are made to contrast with Bogart's open white shirt and bare head, and the players are cunningly positioned within the frame. We see Bogart reclining on his bed in front of two seated figures or sitting up in the bed with a figure beyond each shoulder. We watch him rise and cross between his visitors, trying to escape their menace, or we look down on his hair as the hats of the two detectives gather around. The montage of relatively static images gives the scene a frustrated energy that is perfectly in keeping with the dramatic situation.

Throughout the sequence, Edeson's lighting effects are low-key and melodramatic, making full use of the lamps, overcoats, and pulled-down hats that are the stock-in-trade of detective films, but investing all this paraphernalia with an uncommon intensity. It is only through a willed alienation that we can be aware of his skill. He keeps the entire room illuminated, using an extremely short focal-length lens (21mm) to increase perspective, creating atmosphere with the *tone* of light and by ingeniously setting hats and coats off from their backgrounds. Except for occasional shots of night streets or completely darkened rooms, no shadows in *Falcon* are very deep—as they are, say, in Stanley Kubrick's heavy-handed, pseudo-Wellesian *The Killing,* where whole sections of a room will be blacked out while others are sharply lit, or where two characters will huddle ridiculously over the top of a lighted lamp in order to have a conversation. Throughout *Falcon,* the relatively cramped spaces of the interiors are completely visible; the strongest blacks and whites belong to the characters themselves, while the play of light and shadow on the walls makes subtler, grayer contrasts.

The film never sledgehammers us with effects, and yet Huston's camera is at once more energetic and more stylized than the lighting (which he left mainly to Edeson) or the acting. There is, for example, a relatively large amount of cutting in the sequence I have been describing—most of it toward the end, where the tempo of the editing matches the heat of the conversation—and also a marked propensity for shooting at the ceiling, for framing tight compositions, and for looking at faces from slightly odd angles. The camera jumps about the room, moving along with the characters and always making comments on the action by pointing up at a face or by peering through a doorway. It is this camera style, together with Huston's positioning of the actors, which creates overtly sinister effects and the feeling that we are viewing the scene through the eyes of some witty observer. Notice, for instance, how Huston makes the sequence a near comedy by exaggerating the contrasts between the characters. Bond and MacLane are set off from one another by their clothing, by the way they walk into the room, by the chairs they select, by their every move. As MacLane enters, he keeps his eyes trained hard on the back of Bogart's neck, his overcoat neatly belted and buttoned, his hands not too deeply in the coat pockets. Bond moves slowly, a few steps to the rear, coat spread open, hands in his pants pockets, his eyes sliding over and around the room. MacLane switches on a lamp and chooses Spade's comfortable leather chair, while Bond takes a hard seat off to the right. At first, the camera stands back and watches them, but then it begins to stress their respective traits by shooting up at one and down at the other. The close, three-figured compositions are just as expressive. The camera moves in to show the dark shapes of the police leaning inward toward Bogart's white shirt, or it sits back just far enough to show MacLane's hand resting idly on the leather chair while Bond nervously rubs his palms.

Some people, who strain to follow all the plot turns and the rapid flow of the dialogue in *Falcon,* regard the film as a bit talky; in fact, the important events are always clear, and the viewer does better to let many of the long speeches slide by while he reads Huston's sharp, simple images. Huston has been called a realist, but here and in much of the rest of the film his methods are closer to caricature. Though in casting the major roles he has been less flamboyant than Hammett, and though his camera is never radically expressive in the manner of an Orson Welles or a Max Ophuls, there is a streak of the showman in his character. He will not dolly a camera right past a wall, or photograph a character from behind a piece of furniture, as Kubrick does, but all the same his images tend to be rigidly stylized. Especially in his treatment of minor figures like Miles Archer and his wife, Huston likes to underline meaning: Jerome Cowan as Archer sits on the top of Bogart's desk, crosses his legs, and leers at Mary Astor. Later, Bogart walks into his office and meets the sudden embrace of Archer's widow, dressed all in black. Or compare the Barton MacLane role in the film with Hammett's version of the character. In the novel Lieutenant Dundy is a compact, round-headed fellow with a grizzled mustache, a five-dollar gold piece in his necktie, and a Masonic emblem pinned to his lapel. Huston, on the other hand, makes him a big, dark man with his hat brim jerked down—a wonderfully sinister image which is nevertheless dangerously near cliché.

The mannered style, which can be seen nearly everywhere in the film, is at odds with the common notion that Huston was an antirhetorical director. The late James Agee, one of Huston's best critics, was perhaps chiefly responsible for establishing such an idea. "He loathes camera rhetoric," Agee wrote. "In placing and moving his camera Huston is nearly always concerned above all else to be simple and spontaneous rather than merely 'dramatic' or visually effective." As an example of what Agee meant, here is his description of a moment he loved from *The Treasure of the Sierra Madre.* An intruder has been killed by bandits:

> The three prospectors come to identify the man. . . . Bogart, the would-be tough guy, cocks one foot up on a rock and tries to look at the corpse as casually as if it were fresh-killed game. Tim Holt, the essentially decent young man, comes past him and, innocent and unaware of it, clasps his hands and

looks down, in the respectful manner of a boy who used to go to church. Walter Huston, the experienced old man, steps quietly behind both, leans to the dead man . . . and gently rifles him for papers.[7]

It is a fine touch, true enough, and it may have been achieved by Huston's casual, nondirective approach to the actors, but even in Agee's description it sounds as calculated and symbolic as a ballet.

There are nearly equivalent moments in *Falcon*. For example, there is the scene where Elisha Cook, Jr., awakes from being knocked out by Bogart. As he looks around the room at the faces of the other characters (all shown in vivid close-ups), he realizes he has been made a scapegoat and will be delivered to the police. He buries his head in his hands, and subsequently in a medium shot Huston shows Greenstreet and Bogart discussing the price of the falcon while Mary Astor goes to the kitchen to make coffee. Only Peter Lorre, as the homosexual, pays attention to Cook's sorrow. The camera barely seems to notice Lorre as he stands withdrawing an unlit cigarette from his mouth, his great frog eyes staring with pity, a hand reaching down to pat Cook on the shoulder. Of such effects Agee remarks, "Huston can draw the eye so deep into the screen that time and again he can make important points in medium shots . . . for which most directors would require a close-up or even a line of dialogue."[8] The point is well taken. It is true that Huston's compositions are oblique compared to those of a director like Alfred Hitchcock, who focuses unremittingly on the center of visual interest. Huston will sometimes have an actor stand off to the side of the screen in a long shot and do an intimate bit of business. But this does not constitute the absence of rhetoric, and in any case the absence of rhetoric is not always a virtue (vide Hitchcock). Agee's emphasis on casualness and spontaneity creates a somewhat false impression; certainly next to a Hawks or a Roberto Rossellini, Huston seems an almost Mandarin stylist.

In the good Huston films, nearly everything—the actor's movements, the camera setups, the editing—works to create a somewhat emphatic quality. Huston's camera never retards or works against the power of a script by utterly meaningless bravura, and usually he generates such interest that we don't care to analyze his technique. But clearly he does not eschew rhetoric, and the effect he produces on the screen seldom looks truly spontaneous. Thus Manny Farber, the eulogist of tough guys and termite art, gives an account of Huston's style that is both radically different and in some ways superior to Agee's: Farber overdoes it when he calls Huston

A genius for casting star roles and supporting players marks *The Maltese Falcon:* Humphrey Bogart and Elisha Cook, Jr.

the "Eisenstein of the Bogart thriller" (though notice the montage of greedy faces and hands as the coveted falcon is being unwrapped by Greenstreet, Astor, and Lorre). Still, he is right in saying that Huston's work is characterized by a "statically designed image" and a "mobile handling of close three-figured shots." Farber does not much care for this style, but he is often good at describing it. He observes that Huston "rigidly delimits the subject matter that goes into a frame, by chiaroscuro or by grouping his figures within the square of the screen so that there is hardly room for an actor to move an arm."[9] Actually, Huston is somewhat less rigid in his late films, such as *Freud,* where he lets the camera slide a little here and there to catch an actor who has strayed out of the frame. In a movie like *Falcon,* however, the actors are used like models—an unusual attribute, coming as it does from a director who was always happy to let the characters find their own way.

I bring out these qualities of Huston's work not because they are defects but because they help define a temperament. L. B. Mayer believed that Huston was a realist because *The Asphalt Jungle* was filled with seamy detail and a morbid sense of humor. Actually, Huston's world was no more ultimately real than that of Hawks or Minnelli. His best films had tough, even grimy settings, and he always rigorously excluded Hollywood romance; but he could not avoid what Agee called a "romanticism about danger," and he loved to point a moral. Chiefly with his camera style, he loaded male adventure stories with allegorical significance, and many of his pictures, despite their superficial realism, are like existentialist morality plays. Even his filming of *Moby Dick* forsakes Melville's visionary manner and turns the novel into a typical Huston movie—a cautionary tale about a group of odd characters engaged in a quest. It is no surprise that the last line of *The Maltese Falcon,* Bogart's remark about the black bird ("the stuff that dreams are made of"), is Huston's invention. But the same quality of mind that put that sentimental comment in the film is responsible for much of what is good about it, namely the sheer liveliness of the images, the way they give Hammett's fairly straight crime novel the air of dark comedy. There is subtlety and understatement in some of Hammett's language, in the acting of players like Greenstreet and Bogart, and in Edeson's photography. Yet against all this, and somehow enhancing it, is the overt drama of Huston's camera. The film is just stylized enough to present the private-eye story as it has to be presented—as a male myth rather than as a slice of life; and Huston's wit is just sly enough to humanize the film without destroying the power of its melodrama.

## NOTES

This essay, which originally appeared in *Literature/Film Quarterly,* is nearly two decades old, and was my first attempt to write anything about the movies. I fear it has become something of an antique, even though it conveys the admiration I still feel for *The Maltese Falcon.* I have changed the tenses of a few sentences to indicate that Huston is no longer living, but otherwise I decided not to revise the text. Some of my later ideas about Hammett and Huston are contained in two other articles: "Dashiell Hammett and the Poetics of Hard-Boiled Fiction," in *Essays on Detective Fiction,* ed. Bernard Benstock (London: MacMillian, 1983); and "Return of the Living Dead," in the *James Joyce Literary Supplement,* May 1991.

1. Andrew Sarris, *The American Cinema: Directors and Directions, 1929–1968* (New York: E. P. Dutton, 1968), 156.
2. Raymond Durgnat, *Films and Feelings* (Cambridge: MIT Press, 1970), 149.

3. See William F. Nolan, *John Huston, King Rebel* (Los Angeles: Sherbourne Press, 1965), 40.

4. Andre Bazin, *What is Cinema?* vol. 1 (Berkeley: University of California Press, 1967).

5. Durgnat, *Films and Feelings,* 84.

6. John Baxter, *Hollywood in the Thirties* (New York: Paperback Library, 1970), 200–201.

7. James Agee, *Agee on Film,* vol. 1 (New York: Grosset & Dunlap, 1967), 327–29.

8. Ibid., 329.

9. Manny Farber, *Negative Space* (New York: Praeger, 1971), 33–34.

# Heroic, Antihero, Aheroic:
# John Huston and the
# Problematical Protagonist

## MARTIN RUBIN

He was, then, a hero. He suffered that disappointment
which we would all have if we discovered that we were
ourselves capable of those deeds which we most admire
in history and legend. This, then, was a hero. After all,
heroes were not much.
—Stephen Crane, "A Mystery of Heroism"

John Huston remains one of the most elusive artists in American film history. Outside of a few stock thematic "keys" ("the stuff that dreams are made of," stoic laughter), he is a difficult filmmaker to categorize. His filmography, unusually checkered even by the inevitably compromised standards of commercial cinema, indicates a restless and eclectic temperament that resisted general identification with any particular genre, such as that established between, for example, John Ford and the Western or Douglas Sirk and the melodrama. Nor is he associated with a particular formal device, as are Orson Welles (deep focus) and Max Ophuls (camera movement), or a commonly identified stylistic tendency (Nicholas Ray and kineticism, Otto Preminger and objectivity). The supreme litterateur of classical American cinema, Huston frequently based his films on strong literary sources, so that it is not easy to disentangle a "Huston point of view" from those of the authors he adapts, such as Dashiell Hammett, B. Traven, Stephen Crane, Herman

Melville, Arthur Miller, Carson McCullers, Malcolm Lowry, Flannery O'Connor, and James Joyce.

More crucially, Huston's credentials as a cinematic stylist are uncertain. His style tends to be rigid and redundant in his early period (1941–1951), rambling and erratic thereafter. His films lack the density and richness that characterize many directors' work in the style-conscious postwar period. His sporadic attempts at flamboyance often seem heavy-handed and schematic, yet he also falls short of the more fully articulated spareness and classical "purity" of a Howard Hawks or Budd Boetticher. Characterized by a certain flatness and monotony, Huston's style seems to aspire toward the litanic, antidecorative terseness of his literary homologue, Ernest Hemingway, but this dimension is at best fitfully realized, with the possible exceptions of *The Asphalt Jungle* and *Fat City,* his two most aesthetically satisfying films. For the most part, it remains open to question whether Huston's style can be described as "less is more" or simply "less is less."

There is one area, however, in which Huston's contribution to American cinema is more sustained and formidable than in any other. That area is his treatment of the heroic. Huston's use of problematical heroes constitutes a significant innovation in the Hollywood of his times. Huston was by no means an isolated innovator in this regard. Other directors and screenwriters were working along similar lines during the 1940s and early 1950s, such as A. I. Bezzerides, Ben Maddow, Joseph L. Mankiewicz, John Paxton, Otto Preminger, Charles Schnee, Preston Sturges, Orson Welles, Billy Wilder, and Charles Brackett. It could also be said that an entire generic movement of the era—*film noir*—foregrounded the problem of a questionable hero position.

These developments and others indicate the presence of a major interrogation of the traditional screen hero during this era, which, although it certainly did not displace the mainstream tradition, constituted an important counterpoint and contributed to its eventual redefinition.[1] In Huston's major films of the period *(The Maltese Falcon, The Battle of San Pietro, The Treasure of the Sierra Madre, The Asphalt Jungle, The Red Badge of Courage),* this tendency seems especially pronounced, in part because of the persistency with which he pursued it, in part because of the relative meagerness of other dimensions in his work.

This essay will pursue the assumption that John Huston's most distinctive characteristics as a filmmaker are his investigation of the traditional heroic model and his altering of several of its structures. It is in this area, rather than that of visual style, that Huston made an important contribution to the increased articulation of tension within the American classical system of cinema in the late 1940s and the 1950s. Huston's example also helped pave the way for the less heroic or more ambivalently heroic structures that flourished briefly during the "New Hollywood" interlude of the late 1960s and early 1970s.[2]

## CONCEPTS OF THE HEROIC

The dominant tradition of the heroic against which Huston and his fellow revisionists defined themselves is based on strategies largely inherited from nineteenth-century melodrama and popular fiction and adapted to cinematic forms in the formative periods of classical narrative filmmaking (ca. 1908–1940). This tradition is oriented toward strong and not excessively problematical identification with a central character (variant cases are described below). In the simplest cases, one will "lose oneself" in the character much as one loses oneself in the realistic world of the story.

Key developments in the adaptation of this tradition to classical cinema include the evolution of codes of cinematic point of view and psychological montage, commonly identified with D. W. Griffith; the accommodation of German Expressionist strategies to the conventions of Hollywood classicism, identified most closely with the émigré German director F. W. Murnau; and the enlistment of synchronous sound to solidify and "ground" the objective weight of the fictional world.

The development of a hero position within this system depends upon the construction of an accessible and stable platform for viewer identification. This is accomplished by linking the subjective and objective dimensions and negotiating coherently between them. Such an approach enables the film to give an impression of subjectivity that is stabilized within the framework of a consistently objective fictional universe. The exterior world can be enlisted to express character subjectivity without compromising that world's sense of independent solidity and reality. This maintains what Roland Barthes has termed the "limited plural" of the classic text, allowing for a circumscribed slide (or "glissando") between the symbolic and the "natural."[3] It enables the classical film to have it both ways—to utilize an environment molded by subjectivity and psychological significance while leaving an "out" for a predominantly realist/objective reading.

This system of what might be called "modified" or "Hollywood" Expressionism, based on a complex but ultimately contained tension between objective and subjective dimensions, was firmly established by 1940. Within this phase of the system, problems will be created for the establishment of a hero position if identification is blocked or weakened, creating an excessively objective reading (put simply, the viewer has difficulty identifying with a main character). On the other hand, problems will be also created if the film is tipped into an excessively subjective reading that undermines the stability and unity of the fictional world, as is often the case with full-fledged Expressionism and the European Art Cinema.

The type of revisionism to which Huston can be related is centered mainly on the first, excessively "objective" alternative. This involves the weakening or distancing of viewer identification with a main character in such a way as to problematize that identification without necessarily negating it or completely reconceiving it. The result is an increase of overt tension within this aspect of Hollywood classicism (what might be called a baroque inflection of the classical mode), but not a fundamental alternative to that mode.

The concept of the heroic upon which viewer identification is predicated, whether in a "high" classical mode or in a later revision of it, operates on two levels that are essentially quite distinct, although in practice they are often combined. The first concerns the functional sense of the heroic as it applies to the protagonist or central actant of narrative events. The second concerns the heroic in the qualitative sense, as it applies to a character who serves to represent qualities considered ideal, admirable, or remarkable according to the standards invoked or established by the text and its immediate historical context. These two levels of the heroic can be termed *presentation* and *traits,* respectively.

*Presentation* refers to questions of style and structure and generally concerns strategies of textual prominence. These strategies, derived from the cinematic extensions of nineteenth-century melodrama and popular fiction mentioned above, were still largely operative when they were challenged (but not displaced) by Huston and his fellow revisionists in the 1940s. In a zero-degree model of this phase of classical narrative cinema (upon which one would expect even the most conventional films to work some variations), the following stylistic or structural elements are among those commonly associated with the hero position: emphasis by certain visual codes (e.g., centering, foregrounding, keylighting), occupation of the lion's share of screen time, establishment in a position of prominence early in the proceedings (or, alternatively, anticipation preceding a moderately delayed entrance), central involvement in the major actions of the narrative, and consistent anchoring of the viewer's look through reaction shots and point-of-view configurations.

One would also normally expect a clear sense of hierarchy in the classic narrative, with the hero figure(s) clearly differentiated from the subsidiary characters. A variant case would be the use of multiple heroes, ranging from a central twosome (e.g., the romantic couple of *It Happened One Night*) or trio (e.g., the action-hero buddies of *Gunga Din*) to the more numerous protagonists of multicentered narratives (e.g., *Grand Hotel, A Letter to Three Wives*) and multigenerational sagas (e.g., *Cavalcade, How the West Was Won*). However, these are merely cases of the same heroic pie being cut into a greater number of slices. There are still standards, whether implied or overt, against which the heroic can be measured, with each co-protagonist serving as a focal point of her/his interlocking subdivision of the total narrative (for example, the dying man, Kringelein, is one of the heroes of *Grand Hotel;* the hotel porter, Senf, one of the supporting characters). More substantially anticonventional would be potentially aheroic narrative structures that create pronounced uncertainty over whether the concept of a protagonist-hero is applicable at all.

*Traits* refers to adjectival qualities (or, to use Roland Barthes's term, "semes") that cluster around the name (and, in cinema, the bodily presence) of a fictional character.[4] In terms of traits, it should be noted that the concept of the antihero, especially fashionable since the First World War, can be seen as a variant on the heroic norm rather than a true alternative to it. In many cases, the antihero is simply an anticonventional hero—heroic precisely for the way he transgresses reigning (and often declining) conventional notions of heroism. In the appropriate antiheroic context, such conventionally negative traits as cowardice *(Catch-22),* failure *(Death of a Salesman),* and self-serving violence *(An American Dream)* can become the very emblems of the heroic. Antiheroic traits, perhaps to an even greater degree than the more straightforwardly heroic ones, are highly dependent upon current conventions. Yesterday's villain can, through revisionism, become today's antihero and then, through familiarity, tomorrow's conventional hero.

The concept of the antiheroic can be taken further to imply not merely expanding the boundaries of current mainstream concepts of the heroic but, more fundamentally, problematizing and calling into question the very institution of heroism. Again, this operates on two distinct but often conjoined levels. First, the hero embodies traits that can be considered genuinely alienating for the reader/viewer, rather than just providing an alternate mode of identification. Second, because the boundaries of potentially antiheroic-cum-heroic traits seem capable of almost infinite expansion, the presentation of the characters can be more crucially reconceived to undercut the hero position or to dispense with it altogether. It is here that the antiheroic begins to shade into the realm of the aheroic.

Hollywood cinema is a fundamentally heroic cinema because of its allegiance to classical narrative forms and its economic dependence on the star system. The latter works hand-in-glove with the heroic mode because the value of the star as a commodity is reinforced by the attractiveness and prominence of the characters whom he or she plays. At the same time, input from extra-Hollywood sources (literature, foreign and alternative cinemas) and the commercial advantages of changing fashions will lead to periodic revisions of the heroic.

It is within the context of the heroic mode of classical Hollywood cinema and its revision in the 1940s that Huston's problematizing of the heroic can be located. In terms of traits, Huston's films generally operate in the more familiar antiheroic mode, in which anticonventional heroic traits provide an expanded basis for heroism, although at times these traits are pushed to the brink of the alienating and/or aheroic. Examples include Sam Spade's ruthlessness in *The Maltese Falcon,* Dix Handley's antisocial "hooliganism" in *The Asphalt Jungle,* Billy Dannreuther's extraneousness in *Beat the Devil.* In terms of presentation, Huston often revises conventional forms in such a way that a questioning of the heroic mode is inscribed more fundamentally in his films' structure and style.

Huston's films frequently involve a destabilization of the hero position. This can take two basic forms: to prevent, delay, or otherwise impede the establishment of a hero position; and to undercut or devalue a hero position that has apparently been established. These tactics create abnormal difficulties and strain in the maintenance of a hero position, although they do not necessarily negate it altogether.

For purposes of brevity and coherence, this essay will concentrate on two Huston films that represent relatively pure scenarios for each of the two options outlined above. *The Treasure of the Sierra Madre* (1948) creates considerable obstacles for the construction of a hero position. *The Red Badge of Courage* (1951) appears to signal clearly the establishment of a hero position but then proceeds to question it, to unsettle it, in a number of ways. Both films belong to what could be called Huston's postwar "classic period," when his reputation as an iconoclast was at its height and his anticonventional tendencies were most consistently and explicitly pursued. After 1951, his work becomes less sustained in this respect, although not necessarily of lesser artistic quality.

## THE TREASURE OF THE SIERRA MADRE

*The Treasure of the Sierra Madre* is probably Huston's most overtly unconventional film, the one that did the most to enhance his reputation as a Hollywood "rebel" and "maverick." Besides resisting identification with any familiar genre and eliminating any visible love-interest, the film steadfastly withholds the creation of a stable or clearly defined hero position. Instead, it keeps the issue of the heroic in constant question, presenting numerous false leads, unresolved feints, and teasing delays, and indicating a possible solution of the hero question only at the very end, after the main action of the narrative has been essentially resolved.

The main characters of the film are three Americans down and out in Mexico: Dobbs (Humphrey Bogart), a derelict reduced to bumming dimes in the streets of Tampico; Curtin (Tim Holt), a young drifter of indeterminate background; and Howard (Walter Huston), a loquacious old prospector forever in search of paydirt. After striking it rich, the trio fend off Mexican bandits and an inquisitive American prospector named Cody (Bruce Bennett). Dobbs tries to murder Curtin and keep all the gold. The bandits kill Dobbs, and the gold dust blows away in the wind.

Translated into traditional Hollywood terms, Curtin would be the hero, Dobbs the villain, and Howard the character actor. A possible variation would have Dobbs as the antihero and Curtin as the paler, more straightforward alternative against whom Dobbs is measured.[5]

The early portions of *The Treasure of the Sierra Madre* are clearly dominated by Dobbs. The film begins with Dobbs staring sullenly at a lottery poster. Then it follows him closely as he cadges money from an American tourist, wins a lottery prize, and serves as the catalyst that brings the three men together in the quest for gold.

However, Dobbs's greed and paranoia become increasingly alienating to the audience, and his prominence in the narrative is challenged by his two companions, especially Howard. In the initial stages of the gold-hunting expedition, Howard serves as the leader of the otherwise inexperienced trio and the key internal spectator and interpreter of the action. An example is the emphatic track-in on Howard's uneasy expression as Dobbs and Curtin shake hands to seal their ill-fated partnership. Howard is also the possessor of such powerfully attractive traits as wisdom, flexibility, and stoicism, most famously represented by his heroic laughter in the face of adversity at the end of the film.

By certain conventional Hollywood standards, Curtin would appear to possess the traits best suited to fill the hero position. He is the most obviously sensitive and "normal" of the three main characters. He unselfishly risks his life to save Dobbs during the cave-in and loyally refuses to participate in Dobbs's scheme to double-cross Howard. He also inherits audience sympathy by reading aloud the dead Cody's touching letter to his wife. In some respects, Curtin conforms to the type of clean-cut boyish hero played in the 1930s by actors such as Richard Cromwell, Tom Brown, and Eric Linden—a type that had become somewhat less fashionable by 1948.[6]

Curtin is also the character with the most potential for growth. In the film's allegorical configuration, Howard goes to "heaven" by living out his days in comically exaggerated Edenesque bliss with the Indians, while Dobbs goes to "hell," an association ponderously underlined by an image of the campfire blazing up in front of him after he has shot Curtin. But Curtin remains on earth, so to speak, ready to claim a place in society by annexing Cody's farm and family in the more prosaic sphere of Dallas, Texas. Curtin is the one character who is still active at the end of the film, who still has a fate to resolve and a life to live.

Despite his abundance of heroic traits, Curtin's potential central position is undercut in several ways. In visual terms, the film in no way privileges Curtin over the other characters. Curtin does not appear more prominently in the shots; he does not dominate the foreground or the center of the frame. If anything, he is more often dominated by the other two main characters, both visually and verbally. Dobbs and Howard are usually—

Curtin (Tim Holt) in *The Treasure of the Sierra Madre* is a revised version of the clean-cut, boyish hero of classic Hollywood.

although not overwhelmingly—positioned more prominently in the frame, and they speak more frequently and vividly than Curtin does. There is also the matter of casting: Humphrey Bogart and Walter Huston have far more screen presence and star power than does the less charismatic Tim Holt.

While Curtin looks on from the sidelines, editing and framing patterns in *The Treasure of the Sierra Madre* emphasize confrontations between Dobbs's jumpy paranoia and Howard's easygoing pragmatism. However, it is difficult to read this as an alter-ego configuration, in which Dobbs and Howard externalize a struggle located within Curtin's subjectivity. This dimension might be implicit in the material, but it is not strongly developed in the film itself. Curtin is too recessive a figure for his subjectivity to function as the film's central organizing principle; instead, the conflicts between Dobbs and Howard serve mainly to displace Curtin from the center of the narrative.

Curtin's heroic capacities, although broadly hinted at, remain largely latent and unrealized in the unfolding of the narrative. His first significant action—saving Dobbs from the cave-in—does not occur until over a half hour into the film. He then recedes again, retreating to the sidelines and following the other characters' leads. Curtin achieves his position of greatest prominence when he reads aloud Cody's letter and then, shortly thereafter, takes the lead in proposing that the three partners' profits be shared with Cody's widow—a suggestion with which Howard, although not Dobbs, heartily concurs.

This represents the high-water mark of Curtin's status as protagonist, but it does not last long. Almost immediately after Curtin's altruistic proposal has been settled, a machete (wielded by an offscreen Indian) appears in the extreme left foreground, undercutting Curtin's prominence. The remainder of the scene is, characteristically, keyed on two-shots of Dobbs and Howard, while Curtin virtually drops out of sight. The film's wavering center of emphasis shifts now to Howard, who emphatically takes center stage in the quasi-mystical scene in which he raises a sick Indian child from the dead.

The Indians' enforced hospitality temporarily removes Howard from the action, leaving Curtin in a direct confrontation with the disintegrating Dobbs. However, rather than definitively raising Curtin's stature, this section is largely dominated by the spectacle of Dobbs's madness, complete with stream-of-consciousness soliloquies, such as his discourse on con-

science after he shoots Curtin or his debate with himself on the advisa-
bility of burying the body.

The ordeal Curtin suffers does help to form him as a potential hero,
as well as providing him with a motive for vengeful action. But once again
he fails to sustain his position. As Curtin is heard swearing vengeance offscreen, the camera fixes on an impassive Indian woman (with an audience
of equally impassive Indians behind her), then pulls back to show Howard
calmly dressing the supine Curtin's wounds. Howard is never more admirable than in this scene, as he nonchalantly defuses Curtin's self-right-
eous thunder by observing, "Well, I reckon we can't blame him [Dobbs]
too much. I mean he's not a real killer as killers go. I think he's as honest
as the next fellow—or almost." The single-take in which the scene is shot
serves to deflate Curtin's wrathful will-to-action by absorbing it into a
broader context, which undercuts it. Contained within the same visual field
with the Indians' impassivity and Howard's nonjudgmental equanimity,
Curtin's fury begins to seem less momentous and even slightly foolish.

Despite his tantalizing credentials, Curtin is constantly blocked out of
the hero position by the more assertive presences of Dobbs and Howard.
Only when Dobbs dies and Howard retires is Curtin apparently unblocked.
Just as the film seems ready to construct a legitimate hero, it ends.

There is something to be said for each of the three main characters as
a potential hero figure, but not enough for any single one of them. Dobbs
dominates the first part of the film, but his prominence becomes intermit-
tent thereafter. He hovers between the positions of antihero and villain.
Similarly, Howard hovers between character-actor status and the types of
leading roles sometimes taken by non-matinee-idol actors such as Wallace
Beery, Lionel Barrymore, and, on occasion, Walter Huston himself.
Curtin's qualifications as a potential hero of a more straightforward sort
are made fairly apparent but remain largely latent and unrealized.

These roles are not so much defined as suspended. Curtin, Dobbs, and
Howard never quite resolve themselves into the conventional positions of
hero, villain, and supporting character actor, nor do they really function as
multiple heroes. It is less a matter of three characters sharing the heroic
center than of that center refusing to coalesce. Their positions remain in a
state of almost constant circulation and redefinition. Various configurations are suggested, but they never jell, never become solid or fixed. Huston keeps the film remarkably open in these terms. The concept of heroism
is not a given in *The Treasure of the Sierra Madre,* nor even primarily a

source of variation (e.g., multiple heroes) or anticonventionality (e.g., an antihero). It is a problem, and one that is consistently maintained rather than resolved.

## THE RED BADGE OF COURAGE

Although not as elaborately and ostentatiously unconventional as *The Treasure of the Sierra Madre* is, Huston's film of *The Red Badge of Courage* represents a different approach to the problem of the hero—in some ways, the complementary opposite of the approach taken in *The Treasure of the Sierra Madre.*

Unlike *The Treasure of the Sierra Madre, The Red Badge of Courage* presents little difficulty in discerning an evident protagonist. The narrative is clearly centered on Henry Fleming, an inexperienced Civil War recruit who bolts during his first battle but redeems himself with a subsequent outburst of valor. The major problems surrounding Henry concern not his assumption of the hero position but his suitability for it once he has arrived there. Whereas *The Treasure of the Sierra Madre* withholds the establishment of a clearly defined hero position, *The Red Badge of Courage* goes to the opposite extreme—overemphasizing a designated "hero" whose very prominence calls into question his ability to support such a position.

In the first place, it takes Henry a little while to claim his place as the protagonist. For the first three-and-a-half minutes of the film, Henry is nowhere to be seen. Brief scenes, centered on no particular character, describe the routine of drilling, marching, and camp life. Then, in the fifth scene, after a crowd of soldiers has gathered to discuss the latest battle rumor, a soldier (Henry) seen from the back in the left foreground turns toward us, the camera following him as he walks away from the group.

Henry's abrupt elevation from nonentity to extreme prominence strikes an early note of imbalance. Having been singled out from the anonymous mass, he is now thrust into the foreground. The word "thrust" is used advisedly. Henry occupies not only the foreground of the shots but what could be called the foreground of the foreground. Especially in the first part of film, Henry is often shown with his face virtually pushed against the camera lens, precariously dominating overbalanced, sharply focused frames creaking with compositional strain.

*The Red Badge of Courage:* Henry Fleming (Audie Murphy) is merely part of the group until he uneasily emerges as a hero.

Henry is ill suited to hold such a position of over-pronounced prominence, which serves mainly to underscore his discomfort and insecurity. Audie Murphy's lack of authority as an actor contributes to this aspect of the character, as does the use of long-takes, which expose his lack of assertion—the longer the shots go on, the more apparent becomes Henry's inability to sustain his position of dominance. Examples of this are the early scene in the tent where Henry's letter writing is interrupted by the entrance of his two companions, and the scene by the river where Henry, his back wedged against a tree trunk, sourly casts aspersions on the bluster of fellow soldier Tom Wilson. In instances such as these, Henry seems oppressed by his salience; placed on the spot, he sweats, grimaces, fidgets, squirms self-consciously, and generally acts as if he were longing to bolt from the foreground and melt back into the anonymous background.

In terms of presentation, Henry Fleming makes a very unsteady pivot for the film's narrative, but, in terms of traits, he at first appears to fall more clearly within the domain of antiheroism: His insecurity, self-consciousness, and surliness are, by virtue of their unconventionality, the very foundations of identification and attention. However, Henry proceeds to squander much of his antiheroic capital by completely reversing field in the second half of the film. After establishing a basis for identification derived from his cowardice, alienation, and all-too-human failings, Henry turns into a hero of a more straightforward, Errol Flynn sort, exhibiting superhuman bravery, stridently exhorting his less intrepid comrades, and becoming something of an officers' pet.

A similar pattern can be found in Huston's first film, *The Maltese Falcon*. After eliciting admiration for his cynical flouting of law-abiding morality, Sam Spade does a complete about-face. In the final reel of the film, this erstwhile charming rascal becomes a staunch upholder of establishment values, rejecting the seductive amorality of Kasper Gutman, embracing the rigidly uncompromising moralism of his former archnemesis, Lieutenant Dundee, and "sending over" his duplicitous lover, Brigid O'Shaughnessy, to long-term incarceration and possible execution.

Henry Fleming's too-abrupt reversal, occurring earlier in the film, has an even more alienating effect in *The Red Badge of Courage*. The character does not cohere at the level of a heroic reading, calling instead for two conflicting and contradictory responses. In effect, he asks to be identified with both as an antihero and as a more conventional battlefield hero in the John Wayne-Errol Flynn tradition. These two disparate approaches to the heroic do not support each other and instead tend more to cancel each other out.

*The Red Badge of Courage* employs another strategy to undercut Henry's heroic stature: Rather than presenting the hero as a remarkable or extraordinary figure, the film works more to demonstrate how he is a duplicable and interchangeable cog in an inevitable, unending cycle. In this context, it might be useful to recall Huston's war documentaries, which brought a distinctively less heroic, less rhetorical tone to the war documentary form, most clearly in *The Battle of San Pietro* (1945).

A key stylistic element in *The Battle of San Pietro* is what might be called the catalogue sequence: a series of shots showing the same basic action being performed repeatedly by different people. Rather than seeing one soldier's corpse being bagged, we see five or ten, one after another. Similar configurations are used to show wounded soldiers carried on stretchers and Italian children emerging from the rubble. Showing different consecutive examples of the same action has the function of generalizing and deindividualizing those actions, authenticating them by virtue of their typicality and universality: This is what happens in a battle all the time, everywhere. The film concludes with a reminder that there is nothing unusual or special about this particular battle, and, after it is over, the soldiers are going to fight an almost identical battle five miles down the road.

*The Red Badge of Courage* also uses the catalogue device, although not as extensively or centrally as *The Battle of San Pietro* does. In several instances, images of Henry are sandwiched among images of other soldiers performing the same action: loading their muskets, listening to shellfire, waiting for the enemy to appear. However, it soon becomes apparent that Henry is linked with one other soldier in particular: Tom Wilson.

On several occasions, Wilson is established as Henry's double: echoing Henry's dialogue, trading places with him in the shot, figuring in symmetrical shot patterns as if he were Henry's mirror image (e.g., the series of reverse-angles when Henry first returns to camp after being wounded). However, it is important not to read Wilson as a conventional alter-ego figure who serves to reinforce the hero and externalize some of the hero's inner feelings. More crucial is the idea (similar to that of the catalogue sequences) that Wilson is interchangeable with Henry and thereby deflates Henry's specialness by duplicating his experiences.[7] Near the end of the film, Henry and Tom exchange their former positions, with the blustery Henry now in the background and the nervous Tom uncomfortably holding the foreground. It is finally revealed that Tom has had almost the same exact experience as Henry's: boasting, running away, then returning to action, where he and Henry carry flags alongside each other.

This same pattern is repeated on the macrocosmic level. Just as Henry's personal experience is found to be not extraordinary but typical of other soldiers who have had and will have experiences like his, the battle itself, we learn, was not extraordinary. In a characteristic Hustonian irony, the soldiers in Henry's unit discover that they were not even fighting the main part of the battle and that another unit is going to get the credit for the victory. Then, much as in *The Battle of San Pietro*, they march off at the end to fight another battle, which will be presumably be much like this one, and will be followed by another battle and another, each one more unremarkable than the last.

Huston's films at times give the impression that they could go belly-up, dropping the nominal hero and replacing him with another, submerged, perhaps more suitable protagonist: Gutman in *The Maltese Falcon*, Doc

Riedenschneider in *The Asphalt Jungle,* Wilson in *The Red Badge of Courage,* Lucero in *Fat City.* This works not only to diminish the stature and uniqueness of the putative hero but also to suggest the arbitrariness of the entire notion of heroism.

On the other hand, Huston does not sentimentalize or glorify the averageness of the "average man" in the manner of populist directors such as Frank Capra or (more complexly and ironically) King Vidor. Huston's conception of heroism is generally more minimal, less comforting, based more on existential notions of perseverance in the absence of expectations.

*The Red Badge of Courage* demonstrates Huston's tendency toward a context-poor style—especially though not exclusively in those films made before 1952. The establishment of setting in his films tends to be perfunctory, recessive, hermetic, abstract, lacking in specificity and richness of detail. This tendency is already strongly marked in his first film. Outside of the opening stock-footage shots and the use of some familiar street names, *The Maltese Falcon* gives virtually no concrete sense of the city of San Francisco, in which it is set—the characters seem to exist in a nebulous limbo of isolated rooms and dark, nondescript streets.

Although considerable trouble was taken to shoot *The Treasure of the Sierra Madre* on location (a rarity in Hollywood films of that period), the settings are relatively unexceptional. The early scenes convey a generalized impression of any Mexican city, rather than a tangible sense of a particular city, Tampico. Backgrounds are soft, recessive, and indefinite, without a strong sense of specific details.[8] The emphasis falls on foregrounds, which are cluttered (mostly with the heads and bodies of the actors) but not especially evocative.

The shift to desert and mountain exteriors in the latter part of the film does not significantly alter these stylistic patterns. The wide-open spaces appear remarkably confining and unpicturesque in Huston's images. Again, the emphasis falls on big heads in the foregrounds.[9] Landscapes are not strongly or actively related to the characters. There is little sense of gradation or of a fully articulated foreground-to-background continuum in the shots. The overall effect is less one of characters *within* an environment than of characters *in front of* an environment.[10]

Although the sense of environment is less vaguely and statically articulated than it is in *The Maltese Falcon* and *The Treasure of the Sierra Madre, The Red Badge of Courage* displays some of the same general tendencies. Compositions are again predominantly stacked toward the foregrounds, cluttered with large heads and figures that leave the backgrounds blocked from view or just barely squeezed in around the edges of the shot. Some scenes effectively describe the characters' penetration of the environment, notably Henry's headlong flight through the woods, where an active, constantly shifting interplay of camera movement and character movement interweaves Henry with the tangle of smoke, shadow, and foliage around him. But, for the most part, the frequent cutting between extreme close-ups of the characters and extreme long shots of the landscapes tends to weaken the sense of spatial continuum, of characters within an environment. In more medium-range shots, characters are often shot in low angle from a relatively high camera position, causing much of the surrounding background detail to drop out of the frame—a device that once again diminishes a sense of the specific context around the main characters.

It might be supposed that visual operations such as these serve to enhance the hero position by giving it more exclusive prominence, privileging it with more concentration and fewer distractions. Such an assumption, however, fails to take into account some of the central strategies of classical Hollywood style. As noted above, a key development in the history of American narrative filmmaking centers on the linking of the subjective and objective dimensions. By diminishing the sense of context around the characters, Huston's films weaken one of the most important props of classical narrative filmmaking. His context-poor style throws increased weight onto the central character(s) but also inhibits that subtle rapport between character and environment that is at the heart of the semiexpressionism of Hollywood style. Huston's style works to create a more neutral and detached and even hostile frame around the characters. Again, this can contribute to the destabilization of the hero position because the environment offers less support to the potential hero.

Huston's style often works to undermine the point-of-view configurations and semiexpressionistic mise en scène elements that are commonly used in mainstream cinema to reinforce a sliding collusion between audience identification, character subjectivity, and the fictional universe. His style is weighted more toward objectivity and an emphasis on power struggles and battles for position within the frame. At times, this works against the creation of a stable platform for a dominant point of view within the narrative. I do not mean to imply that Huston does not make use of conventional point-of-view structures in his films, but that he to a certain extent destabilizes those structures, opens up an area of erosion within them. In Huston's films, we do not so much look *through* characters looking from a dominant position as we look *at* characters struggling to obtain or struggling to maintain that dominant position. As described above, *The Treasure of the Sierra Madre* emphasizes the first type of struggle, while *The Red Badge of Courage* emphasizes the second.

This all suggests a possible logic to the apparent limitations of Huston's style by linking them to a reconception of the conventional hero in more existential terms. Less supported by the fictional universe, stuck out on a compositional limb—*"abandoned* in the world," to use Sartre's phrase—the hero position in Huston's films can be a highly uncertain and provisional one. As stated above, heroism becomes no longer a given but a problem, which has to be continually defined and redefined, and which is liable to vanish or transform itself at any moment.

Huston's style lacks the rigor and consistency that defines a more effectively minimal aesthetic. Nevertheless, this cultivation of a problematized and weakly contextualized hero position remains one of the most distinctive aspects of his tantalizingly problematic oeuvre. Erratically but adventurously, Huston's films project an invigorating skepticism toward the conventionally heroic that at times approaches the ceaseless negation and redefinition of authentic existentialism.

## NOTES

1. It should be noted that these developments were not without precedent before 1940. The work of Erich von Stroheim in the silent era and the gangster-film cycle of the early 1930s are just two examples of significant deviations from the heroic norm. It is also important to avoid oversimplifying or falsely primitivizing the earlier classical style in a way that promotes a simplistically idealistic conception of the inevitable maturation of the American cinema, and an automatic favoring of alternative modes over those modes against which the alternative is measured. Even outside of its more deviant fringes, the American cinema of the 1920s and 1930s is built upon a complex system of tensions in this aspect (as in most others). The process of deconventionalization, then, involves the elements of these tensions being to certain extent realigned and made more conspicuous, rather than an additive process leading relentlessly toward ever greater "maturity" and "sophistication."

2. The interlude is represented by the films of such directors as Robert Altman *(The Long Goodbye, McCabe and Mrs. Miller),* John Cassavetes *(Faces, Hus-*

*bands)*, Monte Hellman *(The Shooting, Two-Lane Blacktop)*, Dennis Hopper *(Easy Rider, The Last Movie)*, Stanley Kubrick *(2001: A Space Odyssey, A Clockwork Orange)*, Frank Perry *(Last Summer, Doc)*, Bob Rafelson *(Five Easy Pieces, The King of Marvin Gardens)*, Michael Ritchie *(Downhill Racer, The Candidate)*, and Martin Scorsese *(Who's That Knocking at My Door?, Mean Streets)*. Also worth noting are the earlier contributions in this area by Robert Aldrich *(Kiss Me Deadly, Attack, Whatever Happened to Baby Jane?)*, whose major films often take an aggressive attitude toward exploding heroic assumptions, combined with a considerably more adventurous and high-powered visual style than Huston's.

3. Roland Barthes, *S/Z* (New York: Hill and Wang, 1974), 8, 197–98.

4. Barthes, *S/Z*, 67–68. For example, in terms of traits, the most heroic character in Huston's *Fat City* is the defeated Mexican boxer, Armando Lucero. Lucero appears in the film for less than ten minutes and speaks only one line of dialogue. But it is he who incarnates most fully the ideal of existential, Hemingwayesque stoicism that is only fitfully approached by the more prominent characters, Billy Tully and Ernie Munger.

5. An example of this approach is Douglas Sirk's subversive melodrama *Written on the Wind* (1956), where the flamboyant antihero, Kyle Hadley (Robert Stack), is played off the paler-by-comparison conventional hero, Mitch Wayne (Rock Hudson). Other films with similar configurations include *The Roaring Twenties* (Walsh, 1939), *Duel in the Sun* (Vidor, 1947), *Touch of Evil* (Welles, 1958), and *Black Widow* (Rafelson, 1986).

6. However, Curtin's boy-scout image is somewhat tarnished when he casts the swing vote in the trio's decision to execute Cody in cold blood.

7. Similarly, in *Fat City*, Ernie duplicates Tully's past—just as Tully represents Ernie's future—in the inevitable cycle of pipe dreams and aging.

8. Alternatively, the scene will stress one isolated, overweighted detail: the dangling pair of shoes in the flophouse, the mannequins in the bridal shop window, the ornate clock in the cantina, the imprisoning metal gate swinging across the foreground as the oil workers return to town. It is this tendency that contributed to Huston's reputation for ponderousness in the eyes of revisionist critics such as Manny Farber and Andrew Sarris.

9. This is presumably the sort of thing that Manny Farber had in mind when he observed of the film, "Huge men seem nailed in front of mountains." Farber, *Negative Space* (New York: Praeger, 1971), 34.

10. An illuminating cross-reference to *The Treasure of the Sierra Madre* is provided by Anthony Mann's 1953 Western, *The Naked Spur*. Although more firmly located within a generic framework than *Treasure* is, *The Naked Spur* has many similar ingredients: an isolated microcosm of characters in the wilderness; a life-or-death power struggle motivated by greed. In Mann's film, however, there is a much more active and resonant interplay between the settings and the characters.

Wide-angle compositions, panning shots, and layered dissolves link the characters strongly to the environment and wrap it tangibly around them. Rather than serving as just a backdrop or static frame, the landscape becomes an almost living force that has to be struggled through and that enters into a dynamic, reciprocal interaction with the characters, shaping them and also being shaped by them, defining them and also enabling them to define themselves. A similar (though not quite as neat) contrast could be drawn between the use of setting in *The Red Badge of Courage* and in Mann's environmentally dense Korean War film, *Men in War* (1957).

# Mastery through Masterpieces: American Culture, the Male Body, and Huston's *Moulin Rouge*

## VIRGINIA WRIGHT WEXMAN

Know *Celia,* (since thou art so proud,)
'Twas I that gave thee thy renowne:
Thou hadst, in the forgotten crowd
Of common beauties, liv'd unknowne,
Had not my verse exhal'd thy name,
And with it, ympt the wings of fame.
—Thomas Carew

The American tradition of myths about male prowess, established by canonical writers and artists such as James Fenimore Cooper, Herman Melville, and Frederic Remington and perpetuated by filmmakers such as Howard Hawks and John Ford, plays a prominent role in John Huston's oeuvre. James Naremore has pointed to the director's "admiration for a male world" and his predilection for themes of adventure and testing oneself against formidable obstacles.[1] As Richard Slotkin observed in his *Regeneration through Violence,* such an aesthetic is founded on a frontier mentality that sees violence as a necessary component of heroic action. In describing the evolution of the American frontier myth, Slotkin explores the different directions in which legends of the New World were developed in Europe and America. While the Europeans saw the frontier hero as a husbandman, taming the land as an expression of civilized values, the American saw him as a hunter, defining himself by means of confrontations with nature.

"Acceptance of the hunter as the archetypal American hero," writes Slotkin, "meant adopting the hunter's anti-intellectualism, his pursuit of the material and the ephemeral, and his love of exploit and violence for the sake of their blood-stirring excitement—a love akin to the insatiable incontinence dreaded by Puritans."[2]

The popular genres with which Huston has been associated have been closely tied to this American ideology of self-definition through violence. He can be said to have initiated the cycles of two such genres with films that defined their tough-guy motifs and style: *The Maltese Falcon* (1941) set the pattern for hard-boiled detective films, and *The Asphalt Jungle* (1950) began the cycle of caper movies. Huston also showed a predilection toward other genres that depict violence in a male world, such as the gangster film (*Key Largo* [1948], *Prizzi's Honor* [1985]), the war documentary (*The Battle of San Pietro* [1945], *Let There Be Light* [1946]), the spy thriller (*The Kremlin Letter* [1970], *The Mackintosh Man* [1973]), and the Western (*The Unforgiven* [1960], *The Life and Times of Judge Roy Bean* [1972]).

Huston's well-publicized adventures in exotic and sometimes dangerous locales also contributed to his identification with the motif of male prowess. In his study of Carl Dreyer, David Bordwell has commented on the way in which the reception of an artistic work can be influenced by the biographical legend surrounding its creator. Huston cultivated such a legend throughout his life, most conspicuously with regard to the ideal of masculine toughness, which is celebrated in his films. A recent best-selling book about the Huston family, for example, sees John as its charismatic central figure. A *New York Times* review of the book by Nora Johnson describes him as "one of those figures dear to the American imagination: the larger-than-life artist-genius who breaks the lives of others. [He was a s]portsman, gambler, boozer, professional Irishman." The director's stature as a legendary figure was recently further enhanced by Clint Eastwood's decision to play the lead in his film version of Peter Viertel's novel *White Hunter, Black Heart,* a character widely understood to be based on Huston.

Hollywood filmmaking has traditionally associated violent heroism with representations of the male body. Sylvester Stallone's *Rambo* cycle is perhaps the most extreme manifestation of this convention. The spectacle of Stallone's overdeveloped physique engaging in heroic exploits on foreign soil to "redeem" the denizens of Third World societies in the name of American freedom suggests the degree to which American power is understood as male muscle.[3]

More sophisticated American directors whose work is associated with action genres, such as Raoul Walsh, Don Siegel, and Anthony Mann, have also favored the commanding, though not so grossly muscular, figures of stars such as Robert Mitchum, Clint Eastwood, and James Stewart as leading men in their films. Undoubtedly the most well-known personification of American prowess is John Wayne, whose very height and bulk appear to justify his claim to the American frontier in Westerns and to world dominance in war films. Huston's participation in this tradition of masculine presence is most obviously apparent in his work as an actor in films such as *The Cardinal* (Otto Preminger, 1963), *The Bible* (Huston, 1966) and *Chinatown* (Roman Polanski, 1974), where his six-foot three-inch frame and aura of easy authority readily establish dominance. In his role as director, he has shown an inclination toward rangy actors with bodies like his own, such as Sterling Hayden, Michael Caine, and Gregory Peck. Huston, who enjoyed a brief career as a professional boxer before becoming a filmmaker, identifies strength of character with physical brutality. His many films with Humphrey Bogart, whose body could appear almost frail, typically involved violent confrontations that testified to the hidden power underlying the star's unprepossessing exterior.

Such portrayals of dominant American males in the films of Hollywood tough-guy directors such as Huston did not necessarily require a contrasting female other against which the heroes' masculine virtues were defined. Instead, the other was often depicted in ethnic terms or even represented as the forces of a hostile nature over which the powerful hero repeatedly triumphed.[4] But Hollywood's preoccupation with the creation of the couple puts pressure on filmmakers to include women in their stories. Hawks and Ford responded to this dilemma by combining their male-centered aesthetic with stories of romantic love. Huston's films, following the more uncompromising tradition represented by tough-guy writers such as Ernest Hemingway (to whom the director is often compared), are less likely to make such accommodations and often conclude not with the promise of heterosexual bonding but rather with its failure.[5] Relationships established between males on the basis of the shared values of toughness typically prove to be far stronger than the bonds of romantic love. The films typically presume a world in which savagery reigns supreme (the title of

*The Asphalt Jungle* is telling). Thus in Huston's oeuvre women are often rendered irrelevant.

Leslie Fiedler has characterized such male-oriented tendencies in American culture as latently homosexual. More recently, this issue has begun to be framed in more complex terms by Eve Kosofsky Sedgwick, who distinguishes homosexuality from what she terms homosociality. Sedgwick observes that a homosocial emphasis on male bonding is typically accompanied by homophobia. In Huston's case, a homophobic tendency is evident in his first film, *The Maltese Falcon,* where the vicious attacks mounted by Sam Spade (Humphrey Bogart) on the dandified Joel Cairo (Peter Lorre) and the "gunsel" Wilmer (Elisha Cook, Jr.) are depicted with considerable relish.[6] Later, in *Reflections in a Golden Eye* (1967), the portrayal of homosexuality is overtly more sympathetic, but the humiliation of Maj. Weldon Penderton (Marlon Brando) by his wife, Leonora (Elizabeth Taylor), is again depicted with a certain gusto. In both films the contrast between heterosexuality and homosexuality is rendered by means of fetishized representations of the male body: Cairo's curls, perfume, and suggestively phallic cane; Wilmer's small size; Penderton's "prissy" mannerisms. In each case the less obtrusive performance styles of the other characters highlight the "aberrance" of the homosexual. In both films masculinity is represented in opposition not so much to femininity as to effeminacy, and it is made clear that an uncomplicated masculine presence confers power.[7]

In the context of such a preoccupation with male prowess and the power it is understood to confer, Huston's decision in 1952 to make a film about the crippled painter Henri de la Toulouse-Lautrec seems on its face incongruous. But complex personal and cultural factors formed the background of his decision. Most significantly, Toulouse-Lautrec's disability presented Huston with the opportunity to extend the theme of male heroism by freeing it from its association with the superiority of the masculine body. The vocation of painting itself implies male dominance; like film directing, it has traditionally served as a stronghold of male expression.[8] But the power Toulouse-Lautrec achieves through his art alters the terms set in the adventure films. In *Moulin Rouge* it is not physical prowess but professional prowess that empowers the hero. In place of a male body, which signifies power in and of itself, *Moulin Rouge* depicts a male body that, though it lacks prowess in the conventional sense, achieves dominance through its association with an ideology of cultural mastery. The film's love plot portrays this mastery in terms of power over women.

As adapted by Huston and Anthony Weiller from a popular novel of the day by Pierre La Mure, *Moulin Rouge* changes the facts of Toulouse-Lautrec's life in significant ways. Though we learn next to nothing about aspects of the painter's life such as his role in the artistic community or his financial affairs, we are offered elaborate fictions about his romantic attachments. Huston himself has repeatedly attributed his decision to give the movie a romantic slant to censorship considerations.[9] Such rationalizations invite critics to overlook aspects of the director's work he brackets as the result of crassly commercial interests that must be served to clear space for more "legitimate" creative expression. Similarly self-justificatory statements are frequently offered by Hollywood filmmakers as a way of defining themselves as artists—alienated individuals whose impulses are at odds with the constraints imposed by a highly capitalized and bureaucratized industry.[10] However, an alternative critical perspective would approach both personal creativity and institutionalized commercialism as part of the same impulse: to present a view of the world through forms of representation. Such a perspective allows the romance plot in *Moulin Rouge* to be seen as crucial in shaping the viewer's understanding of Toulouse-Lautrec and his art.

The film's opening scene at the Moulin Rouge cabaret presents a world of intense sexuality in which physical attraction appears to be the only value. In the Moulin Rouge, the world is divided between performers, who exhibit their bodies in various ways, and voyeurs, who take pleasure in such display. Men are measured against a physical ideal. The first words spoken in the film are by a woman: "They talk as though they were Herculeses, all of them," she scoffs, speaking of her male dancing partners. "Then, after a few turns, they pant, they wheeze." Later, the cabaret's star performer, Jane Avril (Zsa Zsa Gabor), comments on a male she notices in the audience. "He is so beautiful," she exclaims. "Look at these shoulders!" If men's bodies are admired at the Moulin Rouge, women's bodies are even more conspicuously on display. When the can-can dancers appear, only men's reactions are recorded. The monocles of two staid-looking gentlemen pop out as they gaze at the ruffled pantaloons exhibited for their pleasure. There is, in addition, a ridiculous-looking fat man, who cheers, applauds, and makes ineffectual grasping motions as the dancers perform their contortions. Thus described, the scene constitutes a variation of a familiar Huston strategy.

The conclusion of this scene of sexual innuendo and provocation departs from Huston's previous pattern by revealing that the film's hero must renounce any role based on the adulation of the human form. When the performers and the audience have left, Georges Auric's musical score reaches a crescendo as Toulouse-Lautrec (José Ferrer) rises from his chair to display his misshapen body. Viewers with knowledge of Toulouse-Lautrec's disability have watched the previous exhibitions of physical agility with this irony in mind and have awaited the revelation of his dwarfed condition. Toulouse-Lautrec's slow progress across the dance floor, recorded by a high-angle long shot that further diminishes his physical stature, is observable only by charwomen, who do not even look up to mark his passage.

The subsequent scenes, in which Huston introduces flashbacks of Toulouse-Lautrec's life before his traumatic accident, associate the protagonist's prominent role within the French aristocracy with his physical capabilities: We see him riding, and—in a pointed comparison to the earlier scene in the Moulin Rouge—dancing. His subsequent injury denies him this "normal" role in social relations, and this denial is dramatized in the film by the rejection of his marriage proposal by a young girl with whom we had earlier seen him dancing. As a cripple he is denied access to the courtship rituals in which his class and position would otherwise entitle him to participate.

Despite his handicap, however, Huston's Toulouse-Lautrec has two love affairs: the first with Marie Charlet, a cruelly rejecting prostitute (Colette Marchand); and the second with Myriamme Hayen, a fashion model who discounts Toulouse-Lautrec's body and admires his paintings (Suzanne Flon). Though Marie Charlet continually taunts her lover about his handicap, the more "civilized" Myriamme insists that "looks aren't everything." Each of these romances is associated with a celebrated art work, and both of these works depict women's bodies.

The painter's early infatuation with Marie Charlet is linked to the Mona Lisa. After Marie has treated him in an especially callous manner, Toulouse-Lautrec discusses the Leonardo da Vinci portrait with a group of fellow painters. Irascibly he asks, "How do you know it's a masterpiece?" One of the other painters replies, "Because of her smile; she smiles with her eyes." Toulouse-Lautrec then inquires, "How do you know it's by Leonardo?" and receives the response, "Every brushstroke bears his signature." The film appears to accept these critical comments as authoritative. Shortly thereafter, Toulouse-Lautrec and Marie Charlet discuss Leonardo's achievement as Toulouse-Lautrec paints Marie's own portrait. "What did [Leonardo] get out of [the painting]?" Marie inquires, to which Toulouse-Lautrec responds, "He got the satisfaction of having painted it." By painting this masterpiece Leonardo has ensured that a woman's desiring gaze is recorded for all posterity—and that, through his distinctive style, his own position as the recipient of this desiring gaze will never be forgotten.[11] The nature of the artist's "satisfaction," as defined in the previous conversation among the artists, resides in its ability to articulate a position of dominance over women. By painting Marie Charlet, Toulouse-Lautrec, like Leonardo, uses his art to appropriate the physical presence of his female subject, who thereby becomes the object of his cultural mastery. Such a conception of mastery far transcends the ephemeral sexual byplay at the Moulin Rouge.

Unlike Mona Lisa, Marie Charlet does not "smile with her eyes." In her portrait, the eyes are cold. When Myriamme Hayen eventually buys the painting, she explains, "It was her eyes. Her eyes made me realize there were worse things than poverty, hunger, and loneliness." As interpreted by Myriamme, this coldness comments not on the relationship between Marie Charlet and the artist who has represented her but on her own character, which has been shaped by "worse things than poverty, hunger, and loneliness." If Marie Charlet does not desire Toulouse-Lautrec, he can record her coldness for posterity, and he can recreate this coldness as not simply a rejection of him but as a judgment on herself.

Toulouse-Lautrec's romance with Myriamme is also associated with a classic artwork portraying a woman: the Venus de Milo. The painter and the model visit this famous statue in the Louvre. "She is so beautiful we forget that she is so old," the painter comments. Here Toulouse-Lautrec points to the power of art not to appropriate the female body but to idealize and preserve it. Unlike more conventional lovers, Toulouse-Lautrec can celebrate a woman's desirability by immortalizing her image. But the art work in question here portrays not a subjectivity that has been mastered, as with the portraits of the Mona Lisa and Marie Charlet, but a subjectivity that is totally denied: the woman as pure body. Thus the immortalization offered is the immortalization of a woman's image that is completely objectified and completely exposed. Considerations such as these, however, are not brought forward in the film.[12]

As an established and sought-after artist, Toulouse-Lautrec has by this time acquired a more potent presence than that of any ordinary lover. The progress of his romance with Myriamme is punctuated by evidence of this potency. Just before their initial meeting, the narrative is interrupted so that we may see a montage of the artist's work. The montage focuses on scenes of the Moulin Rouge that are familiar to us from the film's first sequence. The characters from the cabaret, however, have now become creations of the painter. Soon after Toulouse-Lautrec has launched his romance with the model, another montage displays his many portraits of women. This second montage sees the power inherent in Toulouse-Lautrec's ability to recreate the world in his own image as residing specifically in his ability to recreate the female body.

In the film's concluding scene, of Toulouse-Lautrec's death, the painter once again witnesses—this time in fantasy—the physical exuberance of the performers at the Moulin Rouge. Again, the ridiculous fat man is part of the scene, watching and clapping his hands in an ecstasy of impotent desire. Now, however, the painter simply smiles at the spectacle; for he, unlike the fat man, has succeeded in transcending the humiliating position in which his unattractive body had previously placed him. His status as an object has been superseded by his ability to create objects. He has succeeded in attaining an austere and unassailable dominance over his world—and particularly over the women who populate this world—through aesthetic mastery.

The striking visual style of *Moulin Rouge,* which attempts to reproduce some of the effects of Toulouse-Lautrec's paintings in the film's mise en scène, marked a turning point in Huston's directorial image.[13] Previously he had cultivated an invisible style, which critics such as James Agee had praised as "virile" and "masculine." After *Moulin Rouge,* however, Huston's technique developed more overtly experimental tendencies (for example, the desaturated color used in the initial-release version of *Reflections in a Golden Eye* and the fantasy-like dream sequences in *Freud* [1962]). The unorthodox style of *Moulin Rouge,* which initiated this shift, was received enthusiastically. Reviewers tended to dismiss the movie's plot as sentimentalization,[14] but almost all singled out the visual effects for special praise. The film won Academy Awards for art direction (Paul Sheriff and Marcel Vertes) and costume design (Marcel Vertes) and was nominated for Oscars in four other major categories, including best picture and best director. It was also awarded a Silver Lion at the Venice Film Festival the following year.

The new stylistic direction Huston initiated in *Moulin Rouge* coincided with a new direction in his authorial legend, one less associated with the heroic adventure of the American frontier than with the cultural power of the European artist. After completing the film he moved to Europe and shot many of his films there. Huston's new image built on aspects of his background that earlier discourses surrounding his authorial legend had tended to marginalize. He had at one time aspired to be a painter, and he owned a number of Toulouse-Lautrec's works. Throughout his life he cultivated the bohemian image associated with artists, most conspicuously through his eccentric style of dress, which many observers have commented on. Kaminsky reports that on the set of *Moulin Rouge* the director invariably appeared in "a burgundy waistcoat, a pink shirt, and an enormous green cap."[15] And Huston was fond of repeating a rumor that Pablo Picasso had surreptitiously watched him shooting the film.

*Moulin Rouge* provided Huston with an opportunity to appropriate Toulouse-Lautrec's power, or what Pierre Bourdieu would term his cultural capital. In elaborating his vision of art as mastery, the director poses the mise en scène of his film as an analogue to the Toulouse-Lautrec paintings it describes, thereby suggesting his own position as a "master." Huston does not merely identify with the film's leading character but supplants him as the movie's hero. As Mimi White has observed, Huston's nonnaturalistic mise en scène represents the director as an artist and Toulouse-Lautrec, the subject of the film, as merely a draftsman whose art reproduced in "realistic" terms what had already been created by the film's director. White writes: "Lautrec's 'genius' . . . ultimately becomes a fiction or effect of filmic mastery. In relation to the mise-en-scene, the art produced by the Toulouse-Lautrec character appears to be a realistic representational style; the paintings he creates look like the diegetic world of the film (in terms of color, composition, scale, lighting, and so forth)."[16] Huston initiates this strategy of creative appropriation during the film's credit sequence by "signing" his name as director in the typographic style of a Toulouse-Lautrec poster, over the image of a Toulouse-Lautrec painting.

The "artistic" cinematography of *Moulin Rouge* is especially notable for its innovative use of color. Huston later wrote about the film, "I was going to try to use color on the screen as Lautrec had used it in his paintings. Our idea was to flatten the color, render it in planes of solid hues, do away with the highlights and the illusion of the third dimension which modeling introduced."[17] This strategy was a highly complex undertaking in which cinematographer Oswald Morris, aided by color consultant Eliot Elisofon, executed technological processes never before attempted in commercial filmmaking. Huston underlined the innovative quality of their experiments by focusing on the difficulties they had with the Technicolor laboratory, which was initially skeptical about the results they could expect to obtain.[18] This project finds an echo in the film itself when Toulouse-Lautrec, embarking on his first attempt at printmaking, is told by the printer that the colors he desires do not exist. Like Huston, the artist in the film takes up the implied challenge, replying, "Then I'll make my own colors." The innovative use of color in Huston's film not only associates him more strongly with the creative genius of Toulouse-Lautrec but also speaks to the significance of technological innovation in defining American industrial might. In a study of Hollywood's appropriation of color, Edward Branigan points to the etymology of the term "technique," which ties artistic style to technological power and thereby endows technological innovation with the aura of artistic expressivity. Huston's unconventional use of color in *Moulin Rouge* allowed his film to be seen in the context of a tradition of modern vanguard art in which innovation was associated with masculine sexuality. In an essay analyzing this phenomenon, Carol Duncan has noted "the expectation that significant and vital content in *all* art presupposes the presence of male erotic energy."[19] Duncan investigates the forms this erotic energy takes in early twentieth-century European paintings of women, in which "the artist makes visible his own claim as a sexually dominating presence, even if he himself does not appear in the picture."[20] Duncan observes that critics have consistently construed this celebration of male mastery as a celebration of individual freedom.

> One idea in particular is always emphasized: that avant-garde art consists of so many moments of individual artistic freedom, a freedom evidenced in the artist's capacity for innovation. . . . The presence of innovation makes a work ideologically useful because it demonstrates the artist's individual freedom as an artist; and *that* freedom implies and comes to stand for human freedom in general. By celebrating artistic freedom, our cultural institutions "prove" that ours is a society in which all freedom is cherished and protected, since, in our society, all freedom is conceived as individual free-

dom. Thus vanguard painting, as celebrated instances of freedom, functions as icons of individualism, objects that silently turn the abstractions of liberal ideology into visible and concrete experience.[21]

Duncan locates this aesthetic of freedom defined as virile self-expression within a tradition of European cultural production. By creating *Moulin Rouge* in a self-consciously vanguard style, Huston positions himself as an inheritor of this tradition, and by incorporating it within the conventions of Hollywood cinema, he appropriates it as part of an American aesthetic rather than a European one.

Art's significant role in American foreign policy following World War II is documented in Serge Guilbaut's book, *How New York Stole the Idea of Modern Art*. Guilbaut traces the process by which the development of abstract expressionism allowed the United States to assume the position of world dominance as a center of art that had previously been held by Paris. A Hollywood biography of a great European painter could accomplish still more than this because it spoke of the past as well as the present. Despite the high reputation of abstract expressionism, the great European canon still presented itself to many Americans as an object of envy and veneration. Guilbaut quotes from President Harry S. Truman's diary:

> Took a walk at 10 A. M. Went to the Mellon Gallery and succeeded in getting the watchman on duty to let me in. Looked at the Old Masters found in salt mine in Germany. Some very well-known paintings by Holbein, Franz Hals, Rubens, Rembrandt and others. It is a pleasure to look at perfection and then think of the lazy, nutty moderns. It is like comparing Christ with Lenin. May there be another awakening. We need an Isaiah, John the Baptist, Martin Luther—may he come soon.[22]

*Moulin Rouge* indirectly responded to Truman's plea by representing the United States as a cultural power and recreating history as a story of the progression from the canonic arts of Europe to the more technologically sophisticated art of Hollywood, an art that could reproduce the effects of European painting and tell a story as well. That Truman recognized that a conspicuously creative Hollywood could represent the United States to the world as both an artistic and a technological leader is confirmed by a high-ranking official of one of the film industry's overseeing bodies, who stated in 1950: "Many times I have talked to President Truman about the influence of American films abroad and he has said he regards American films as 'Ambassadors of good will.'"[23]

The production of *Moulin Rouge* symbolized in many ways Holly-wood's new relation with Europe and the rest of the world following World War II. The film was financed with British money, which gave Huston more power over the production while allowing its British investors to gain an access to the American market that was otherwise unobtainable.[24] Its European subject, along with its Parisian locales and "writerly" style, gave it some of the aura of a foreign art film. Foreign films had just begun to infiltrate the U.S. market as a prestigious alternative to the newest entertainment technology, television, with productions such as *Children of Paradise* (Marcel Carné, 1945), *Bicycle Thieves* (Vittorio De Sica, 1948), and *Rashomon* (Akira Kurosawa, 1950). *Moulin Rouge* countered this trend by helping to forge a path for a newly international mode of Hollywood production. As Thomas Guback has amply demonstrated, this new mode did not so much weaken the power of the American film industry as make it more difficult to pin down. American values and American profits remained the driving forces of such productions.

Huston's own relationship to this American multinationalism is suggested by yet another feature of his authorial legend, his receipt of the One World Award in 1949. In the words of the presenter, Huston received the award because he had "advanced the cause of freedom and . . . founded his motion pictures on the firm basis of the dignity of the human being regardless of race and station."[25] In his acceptance speech, Huston pledged to go around the world "to fashion a portrait, as true a likeness as I can, of man in the aggregate, his thoughts, desires, frustrations, and fulfillments."[26] The emphasis on internationalism, the use of the word "freedom" by the presenter, and the assumption that an American could depict "man" from a disinterested position make this occasion a reenactment in miniature of the course pursued by the American film industry as a whole during this period.

Huston's attempt in *Moulin Rouge* to reframe Toulouse-Lautrec's European art in American terms is evident in the emphasis he gives to certain aspects of the painter's life. Toulouse-Lautrec's dwarfism is attributed in part to the weakness caused by the aristocratic custom of intermarriage between close relatives. Thus the historic structures of European society are tacitly criticized. At the same time American democratic principles are celebrated when Toulouse-Lautrec confers fame and respectability on the common people by popularizing and immortalizing the Moulin Rouge cabaret. Huston's American chauvinism extends even to his choice of actors, for the women in the film are Europeans who speak with distinct French accents, while the painter-protagonist is a well-known American who has no accent at all.[27] This strategy followed standard Hollywood practice, whereby films set outside the United States were cast with American stars in leading roles supported by "exotic" European character actors. In this way Hollywood tacitly defined the heroes of such films as American. Huston also conformed to Hollywood convention in casting the Hungarian actress Zsa Zsa Gabor as Jane Avril, thereby conflating her accent with the French accents of the other female characters and, in effect, lumping them all together as "foreigners." Thus, like the film's artistic reproductions of the female body, its women characters, besides being rendered as objects of an all-encompassing patriarchal domination, are more specifically identified with a tradition of European culture, which must be mastered by the patriarchal power represented by American cold war ideology.

That Huston was personally concerned about the issue of declaring American dominance over the European cultural tradition is explicitly suggested in his autobiography, where his discussion of the production of *Moulin Rouge* is interrupted by a curious digression in which the director tells of the strenuous effort he made to create a place in French horse racing for Billy Pearson, an American jockey friend of his. He describes how he gathered together a group of American friends to cheer for Pearson at French races. As a result of Huston's machinations, both he and Pearson were able to win formidable sums of money betting on European races by acting on tips they received from European jockeys and trainers. Huston describes how the two spent their winnings in London: "Billy and I, in addition to ordering shoes and boots from Maxwells, and suits and riding clothes from the tailors Tautz, invested in Benin bronzes and other *objets d'art*."[28] This story, which begins by celebrating the achievement of enabling an American to compete in a European arena and concludes by describing the way in which this achievement opens the door for Americans to appropriate icons of European culture, can be read as an analogue for Huston's role as director of *Moulin Rouge*.

Huston's appropriation of the European tradition of vanguard painting into the quintessentially American art form of Hollywood cinema can thus be viewed as an attempt to usurp the cultural capital represented by European art by depicting a more technologically potent mode of creative prowess.

If *Rambo* can be said to speak for the right of America to dominate the world by means of a heroic depiction of the male body, *Moulin Rouge* can be said to argue for a similar dominance—not because of the superior ability of American brute force to vanquish enemies but because of the superior ability of American technology to create cinematic masterpieces. Huston's achievement was followed by other Hollywood biopics about canonical European artists, most notably Vincente Minnelli's *Lust for Life* (1956), based on the career of Vincent van Gogh, and Carol Reed's *The Agony and the Ecstasy* (1965), which deals with the life of Michelangelo. Both of these later productions follow Huston's lead by featuring lavish production values, enhancing their aura of visual splendor through the use of sumptuous set designs and expansive wide-screen processes. Like *Moulin Rouge,* these films simultaneously showcase the European tradition of high art and make a place for themselves as heirs to that tradition.

*Lust for Life* and *The Agony and the Ecstasy* also repeat the strategies of *Moulin Rouge* by relating their depictions of aesthetic mastery to the physically traumatized or compromised male body. *Lust for Life* builds its climax around the severing of van Gogh's ear, while *The Agony and the Ecstasy* emphasizes the pain Michelangelo endured as he lay on his back to paint the Sistine ceiling. Further, both films use love stories to suggest that the art works produced by their painter-heroes have granted them mastery over women's bodies. Thus, Huston, whose career was primarily devoted to stories of heroic adventure glorifying tough-guy heroes, initiated in *Moulin Rouge* a new strategy for representing patriarchal power by posing male dominance in terms of an aesthetic mastery that could transcend a physically compromised body. In this revised fantasy, the traditional view of America as a frontier conquered through heroic acts of violence is supplanted by a vision of America as a nation possessing unrivaled creative and technological prowess. Not surprisingly, American men are the heroes of this new myth, just as they were of the old one.

## NOTES

1. James Naremore, "John Huston and *The Maltese Falcon*," *Literature/Film Quarterly* 1, no. 3 (July 1973): 242. Reprinted in this volume.
2. Richard Slotkin, *Regeneration through Violence: The Mythology of the American Frontier, 1600–1860* (Middleton, Conn.: Wesleyan University Press, 1973),

130. Though not an issue in my own discussion, the pursuit of material wealth referred to in Slotkin's formulation is often seen as a central theme in Huston's oeuvre, another aspect of his position as a representative American artist. Critics such as Manny Farber, Pauline Kael, and Peter Barnes have cited Huston films such as *The Maltese Falcon* and *The Treasure of the Sierra Madre* as evidence for this view.

3. Mark Fasteau's essay "Vietnam and the Cult of Toughness in Foreign Policy," in *The American Man,* ed. Elizabeth H. Pleck and Joseph H. Pleck (Englewood Cliffs, N.J.: Prentice-Hall, 1988), argues that American foreign policy, which is centered on the need to dominate and win in every situation, is based on a male-identified ideal of toughness.

4. Theoretically oriented studies of cinematic representations of the male body have only recently begun to emerge, but they have tended to follow the model posed by many feminist studies of the image of the female body and have focused on issues of sexuality and gender difference. These studies include Richard Dyer's essay on male pin-ups, "Don't Look Now," *Screen* 23, no. 4 (Sept.–Oct. 1982): 61–73, which emphasizes the significance of hardness and muscularity in erotic depictions of the male; and Steve Neale's article "Masculinity as Spectacle," *Screen* 24, no. 6 (Nov.–Dec. 1983): 2–17, which claims that when the male is presented as the object of the viewer's gaze, his body is feminized. Peter Lehman's study *"American Gigolo*: The Male Body Makes an Appearance, of Sorts," in *Gender: Literary and Cinematic Representations,* ed. Jeanne Ruppert (Tallahassee, Fla.: Florida State University Press, 1989), focuses on the problems engendered when the male body is explicitly sexualized. My own interest in Huston's representations of the male body frames the issue in somewhat different terms by concentrating on strategies of power that transcend an exclusive focus on sexuality as the sole measure of gender identity. This approach makes room for discriminations based on ethnicity, class, and other factors, which a reliance on the broad categories of sexual difference alone often obscures.

5. This point is developed specifically in relation to Huston's and Humphrey Bogart's representation of the male body in my essay "Kinesics and Film Acting: Humphrey Bogart in *The Maltese Falcon* and *The Big Sleep," Journal of Popular Film and Television* 7, no. 1 (1979): 42–55.

6. Parker Tyler reports that the original German meaning of the word "gunsel," which is also employed in Dashiell Hammett's novel, implies homosexuality.

7. For critical appraisals of both of these films' rendering of homosexuality, see Vito Russo, *The Celluloid Closet: Homosexuality in the Movies* (New York: Harper & Row, 1981), 46–47, 166; and Richard Dyer, "Homosexuality in Film Noir," *Jump/Cut* 16 (1977): 18–21.

David F. Greenberg observes in his book *The Construction of Homosexuality* (Chicago: University of Chicago Press, 1988) that Freud characterized homophobia as a reaction formation in response to a fear of homosexual tendencies within the self. Paul Willemen, "Anthony Mann: Looking at the Male," *Framework* 15/16/17 (Summer 1981): 16; Robin Wood, "Cat and Dog: Lewis Teague's Stephen King Movies," *CineAction* 2 (Fall 1985): 39–45; and Robert Lang, "Looking for the 'Great Whatzit': *Kiss Me Deadly* and Film Noir," *Cinema Journal* 27, no. 3 (Spring 1988): 32–44, have applied this insight to cinematic representations, arguing that the violence in American male action films is often the result of homosexual anxiety. As stated by Wood: "Masculine violence in our culture (the construction of the male as violent) must be read as the result of the repression of bisexuality. Violence against women: the woman represents the threat of the man's repressed femininity. Violence against other men: the man represents the threat of the arousal of homosexual desire." Wood, "Cat and Dog," 41.

8. The complex and thoroughgoing process by which women have been excluded from the realms of "master" painters is explored in Linda Nochlin's much-cited essay, "Why Have There Been No Great Women Artists?" in *Women, Art and Power* (New York: Harper & Row, 1988).

9. John Huston, *An Open Book* (New York: Alfred A. Knopf, 1980), 206; Stuart Kaminsky, *John Huston: Maker of Magic* (Boston: Houghton-Mifflin, 1978), 96–97; Gerald Pratley, *The Cinema of John Huston* (New York: A. S. Barnes, 1977), 94.

10. Similar explanations are frequently offered by creatively ambitious filmmakers working within the Hollywood system, who often scapegoat the industry's fondness for "boy-meets-girl" plots as the cause of the shortcomings of their films. See, for example, Budd Schulberg's statements regarding his reluctance to include "love interest" in *On the Waterfront* (Carbondale: Southern Illinois University Press, 1980), 145, 147.

11. John Berger's now classic study of representations of women's bodies traces this tendency throughout Western art. *Ways of Seeing* (Hammondsmith, England: Penguin, 1972).

12. Peter Brooks's essay "Storied Bodies, or Nana at Last Unveil'd," *Critical Inquiry* 16, no. 1 (Autumn 1989): 1–32, explores many of the difficulties and contradictions posed for realistic narrative and painting by the portrayal of the nude female body, which is both desired and feared by the male artist. In particular, he notes the tendency of artists to model these kinds of works on classical sources to provide an acceptable motivation for their interest in creating such images. Huston's film similarly presumes that viewers will not consciously concern themselves with the subject of the sculpture beyond seeing it as a classic work of art celebrating female beauty.

13. Huston's strategy may have been inspired by Vincente Minnelli's much admired "artistic" mise en scène in the climactic dance sequence of *An American in*

*Paris,* released the previous year and filmed at MGM when Huston was on the lot making *The Asphalt Jungle* and *The Red Badge of Courage* (1951).

14. Some representative comments: "glib and misleading," Gavin Lambert, *"Moulin Rouge," Sight and Sound* 22, no. 4 (Apr.–June, 1953): 194; "appalling vulgarity," Peter Barnes, "The Director on Horseback," *Quarterly Review of Film, Radio and Television* 10, no. 2 (Winter 1955): 285; "a dim-witted tearjerker," Raymond Durgnat, *"The List of Adrian Messenger," Films and Filming* 9, no. 10 (July 1963): 25.

15. Kaminsky, *John Huston,* 93.

16. Mimi White, "An Extra-Body of Reference: History in Cinematic Narrative," Ph.D. diss., University of Iowa, 1981, 49.

17. Huston, *An Open Book,* 210. V. F. Perkins has argued that Huston's experiments with color in *Moulin Rouge* fail not because they reject the prevailing realist standard of three-dimensionality but because the world he presents does not follow consistent rules. Perkins argues that the impressionist atmosphere the film established "could [not] tolerate a room that changed colour in sympathy with its occupant's moods. When the director characterized his hero's jealousy by flooding the set with, in the film's own terms, inexplicable green light, he broke down the essential structure of the film's relationships and thus destroyed the world within which his hero existed." *Film as Film* (Baltimore: Penguin, 1972), 122–23.

18. Morris and Eliofson also went on record to stress the innovative character of their work on the film. Quoted in B. P. Marple, *"Moulin Rouge," Films in Review* 43 (Mar. 1953): 143–48. Important issues were at stake in Huston's experiments with the Technicolor process, for at the time *Moulin Rouge* was being made the Technicolor company was struggling to maintain its dominance in the face of a threat from the much larger company, Eastman-Kodak, which had introduced Eastmancolor, a battle it eventually lost. Technicolor's brief reign as Hollywood's preferred color system was based on its claim to be able to create a look of realism that conformed to Hollywood's classical norms. In particular, the company promoted its process as a means of attaining a greater illusion of three-dimensionality through modeling. It was this standard, in particular, that Huston's use of color in *Moulin Rouge* challenged.

Following some disastrous experiences with the application of its process by incompetent technicians in the early 1930s, Technicolor, for its own protection, monitored all productions with which it was involved. This practice included the requirement that all Technicolor films use color consultants approved by the company. Thus Huston's often-repeated boast about the commitment to quality he showed by hiring Eliofson appears to have been something of a self-serving fiction, since Technicolor would have forced him to employ some such person in any event.

The failure of the Motion Picture Academy to nominate Oswald Morris for an Academy Award for his work on Huston's film was possibly a response to its prior decision to honor Minnelli's *American in Paris*, which had won an Oscar for cinematography the year before. Given the dominant Hollywood aesthetic regarding the "proper" use of color (as set forth in the standards Technicolor had developed), for the academy to have honored Huston's similarly "artistic" use of color in *Moulin Rouge* the following year might have made for a certain feeling of discomfort in the industry. Accordingly, in 1952 the Academy Award for color cinematography was given to John Ford's *The Quiet Man*, which represented a conventionally realistic use of the new technology.

For more extensive discussions of the issues raised by the Technicolor process, see Fred Basten, *Glorious Technicolor* (New York: A. S. Barnes, 1980); David Bordwell, "Technicolor," in *The Classical Hollywood Cinema: Film Style and Mode of Production to 1960*, by David Bordwell, Janet Staiger, and Kristin Thompson (New York: Columbia University Press, 1985); Edward Branigan, "Color and Cinema: Problems in the Writing of History," in *Movies and Methods*, vol. 2, ed. Bill Nichols (Berkeley: University of California Press, 1985); Steve Neale, "Colour," *Cinema and Technology: Image, Sound, Colour* (Bloomington: Indiana University Press, 1985); and Roderick T. Ryan, *A History of Motion Picture Color Technology* (New York: Focal P, 1977).

19. Carol Duncan, "Virility and Domination in Early Twentieth Century Vanguard Painting," in *Feminism and Art History: Questioning the Litany*, ed. Norma Broude and Mary D. Garrard (New York: Harper & Row, 1982), 306.

20. Ibid., 292.

21. Ibid., 294.

22. Serge Guilbaut, *How New York Stole the Idea of Modern Art*, trans. Arthur Goldhammer (Chicago: University of Chicago Press, 1983), 4.

23. Thomas Guback, "Hollywood's International Market," in *The American Film Industry*, ed. Tino Balio (Madison: University of Wisconsin Press, 1985), 413.

24. *Moulin Rouge* was produced by Romulus Films under the auspices of United Artists, which was then undergoing reorganization under Arthur B. Krim and Robert S. Benjamin. As Tino Balio describes the situation, this arrangement became a prototype for the wave of independent production that began during the 1950s, which gave Hollywood star actors and directors far greater independence and vastly increased their incomes.

25. There were widespread rumors that the process of choosing the recipient of the award had been rigged by Columbia Pictures to publicize their film *We Were Strangers*, which was directed by Huston.

26. Kaminsky, *John Huston*, 66.

27. Though Huston was forced to hire José Ferrer, who owned the rights to

Pierre La Mure's novel, *Moulin Rouge* (1950), the decision to highlight Ferrer's American identity by casting French actresses opposite him was the director's. Though Ferrer was actually of Puerto Rican descent, his public image during the 1950s deemphasized this fact.

28. Huston, *An Open Book*, 21. This series of events is related somewhat differently by Stuart Kaminsky, who evidently interviewed Pearson about them. Kaminsky reports that Huston bought a horse in Europe for Pearson to ride and lost heavily by betting on it. Pearson was subsequently forced to loan the director money to tide him over until his next advance arrived for *Moulin Rouge*. If Kaminsky's version is correct, Huston's rendering could be seen as an attempt to shape his authorial legend by fictionalizing his own biography, just as he had fictionalized Toulouse-Lautrec's life in *Moulin Rouge*.

# Shadowboxing: *Fat City* and the Malaise of Masculinity

GAYLYN STUDLAR

I n 1910, Ernest Thompson Seton, a founder of the Boy Scouts of America, declared, "I do not know that I have met a boy that would not rather be John L. Sullivan than Darwin or Tolstoi. Therefore, I accept the fact and seek to keep in view an ideal that is physical."[1] However, by 1910, the boxer who supposedly was every boy's ideal, no longer climbed into the ring to make good on his famous challenge: "My name is John L. Sullivan, and I can lick any son-of-a-bitch alive." At age fifty-one, the former heavyweight champion was an old man. The million dollars he had won prizefighting were gone. The body of the bellicose StrongBoy of Boston was in ruins. Grossly overweight, he was plagued by illnesses attributable both to the debilitating punishment he took in the ring and to the debauching alcoholism that ruled his public and private life for some thirty-five years.[2]

In spite of the fact that the champion's raucous life had countered virtually every self-proclaimed value of his age—self-discipline, sobriety, temperance, religiosity, and monogamous domesticity—the image of John L. Sullivan and the sport of boxing continued to dominate the imagination of American men and boys well into the twentieth century. This, in spite of the fact, too, that when Sullivan first began brawling his way to celebrity in the 1880s, prizefighting was illegal in all thirty-eight states. Professional boxing was regularly denounced as promoting criminality, especially when the fledgling motion picture medium began to bring "obscene pictures" of actual matches or faked versions of famous pugilistic battles to every American city and hamlet.[3] A cycle of boxing films produced by a variety of film companies between 1900 and 1915 achieved enormous national popularity despite a pattern of confiscation, censorship, and public denunciation by progressive reformers.[4] The brutality of the sport as mass entertainment and the controversy surrounding Sullivan's life could not dim boxing's importance to a changing concept of American masculinity, one inextricably linked to the "cult of the body."

In the 1890s, body building, football, and boxing, and the concomitant hero worship of the lower-class athlete, emerged as a part of a discourse on masculinity aimed at revalidating male identity in the face of a perceived "feminization" of American culture.[5] A new emphasis on physical prowess in leisure sports served as the middle-class means of redefining a masculinity that was perceived as being eroded by an increasingly industrialized, bureaucratic, and sedentary culture equated with the feminine.[6] While earlier generations of Americans had contrasted masculinity with "childishness" rather than femininity, now gender difference became irrefutably inscribed as oppositional values.[7] Because of this polarized hierarchy of gender values, the male body became the last refuge of manliness when traditional institutional supports for defining masculinity appeared to collapse the distinctions between the masculine and the nonmasculine, now defined as "feminine."[8]

Within this cult of the body, amateur boxing was sanctioned as gentlemanly training for the strenuous life promoted by many men of the bourgeoisie, including President Theodore Roosevelt. In the words of the *North American Review,* boxing was "distinctly a man's game—helping to stave off effeminacy that is one of the dangers of nations that grow old and soft and unwilling to endure hardships."[9] Professional boxing became the ultimate spectacle of manliness, with half-nude, lower-class men confirming the energy, brute power, and instinctive decisiveness that middle-class men were terrified of losing in the modern world.[10] The ethos of violent physical superiority that underscored boxing also spread into the arena of international relations as bully America enforced its phallic superiority with TR's ubiquitous "big stick."

A similar investment in the male body as symbol of anxious masculinity and the same trajectory of American success and apparent self-destruction exemplified by John L. Sullivan's life are also evident in John Huston's 1972 boxing film, *Fat City*. That Huston would finally make a boxing film is not surprising. His interest in the sport dated back at least to the 1920s when, as a teenager, he became a ranking lightweight as a club boxer in California.[11] However, his desire to become a professional artist prevailed over his wish to become a fighter. Huston was unsuccessful in his attempt to become a painter, so, logically, as the son of a successful journalist, Rhea Huston, he turned to writing to make money. Two of his early short stories, drawing directly from his adolescent experiences in boxing, appeared in H. L. Mencken's prestigious *American Mercury*. In "Fool" and "Figures of Fighting Men," Huston describes a world of lower-class camaraderie, where the ethnic and racial divisions so emphasized in prizefighting promotion are not as immutable as the difference between good fighters and bad. Within this milieu, the young can momentarily sustain the belief that "all paths led to love and physical supremacy," but the older fighters know the tragic ironies of a "sport" based on physically beating your opponent into submission. In such an unforgiving arena of ritual violence, a good fighter, who was once "as hard to hit as smoke," usually ends up as a human punching bag.[12]

As both author and filmmaker, Huston's depiction of this world of boxing reflects the influence of contemporary discourses on masculinity that circulated in his youth and coincided with boxing's rise to a symbolic if controversial status in the American cultural scene. Considering Huston's youthful attachment to boxing, one might expect *Fat City* to be an old man's nostalgic homage to the sport as a spectacle of uncomplicated masculinity and youthful physical prowess. Instead, the film can be read as holding a complicated ideological position toward its subject, both exposing and evidencing a certain complicity with the ideological contradictions in an American ideal of masculinity defined through competitive violence and fetishistic consumption. Showing the meager comforts to be derived from male camaraderie, *Fat City* refuses to celebrate a male world and refuses to glamorize the male body's potential for aggressive power. Instead, the film's disturbing tensions suggest the very impossibility of the ideal

*Fat City* takes a complicated ideological position on the issue of masculinity and physical prowess.

based on the cult of the body even as it reveals the pernicious force still exerted by that necessarily aggressive ideal on economically marginalized, white working-class and minority men in late twentieth-century America. Even as the early cycle of American boxing films frequently depicted interracial bouts and reflected the racial anxieties of the time, Huston's film suggests the racial ideology of the time in which *Fat City* was produced, an era dominated by the problem of America's Vietnam experience and that war's exploitation of lower-class white males and minorities in an effort to prove America's manhood in a symbolic struggle for international dominance.

In this respect, *Fat City* deviates in important ways from the formula of the classical Hollywood boxing films popular in the 1930s and 1940s. These films traditionally utilize the male body as the means of melodramatically revalidating American myths of aggressive masculinity. For example, in *Body and Soul* (1949), John Garfield's prizefighting keeps his mother off welfare during the depression. The film makes it clear that any "kid who can fight" attracts money, and money attracts crooks, so that Garfield's final victory with his fists must be a moral victory. In the ring he reasserts the integrity of violence to regain symbolic dominance over the forces of corruption that threaten to make him a loser—the guy who takes a fall to ensure the profits of others.

More recent boxing films continue to validate the cult of the body. The phenomenally successful *Rocky* series of Sylvester Stallone most obviously attests to this fact. But "revisionist" boxing films like Martin Scorsese's *Raging Bull* (1981), even when appearing to question the moral power of violence, continue to glorify the raw power of the male body. In keeping with earlier boxing films such as *Body and Soul, Raging Bull* and its protagonist, Jake LaMotta (Robert DeNiro), reaffirm the myths surrounding immigrant success based on masculine physical prowess. In the words of Pam Cook, "The film itself looks back nostalgically to a time when pure animal energy formed the basis of resistance to oppression and exploitation, identifying that energy with masculine virility."[13] According to Cook, the viewer is seduced into identifying with and enjoying the violent power exercised by the "beautiful body" of the hero. LaMotta is ultimately punished for his violence, but only because he cannot keep it contained within the ring.[14] Nevertheless, in step with the cult of the body, *Raging Bull* entices the audience into agreeing that the decisive blow—the knockout punch—represents masculine truth in its most satisfying essence. Spectatorial pleasure is centered on the male body in its production of meaningful masculine violence.

While *Raging Bull* is committed to the same fundamental myths of lower-class male success as the classical boxing film, *Fat City* undermines these very same myths of bourgeois ideology. Not only does the film reject a melodramatic polarization of good and evil, but it denies the dramatic role of decisive male violence. As a consequence, the film undermines the myths of contemporary American masculinity that depend on the specific instrumentality of the male body. I wish to caution that *Fat City* does not postulate a radically subversive alternative to these myths; its fascination with masculinity is tempered, however, with evidence of a certain ironic distanciation, one that might be traced (at least in part) to its director. This distanciation produces a textual ambiguity that suggests, from an auteurist perspective, Huston's troubled and unresolved fascination with masculine behavioral norms defined by qualities of physical toughness, stoicism, aggressiveness, and a commitment to "success" as commonly defined in American culture for men.

This ambiguity has been overlooked in most considerations of Huston that equate the mere presence of a Hemingwayesque "bachelor subculture" in his films with an automatic valorization of manliness based on physical toughness (see Wexman in this volume). In the tendency to lump all directors of male genre films together as purveyors of the same misogynistic subjectivity, Huston's distinctively ironic stance toward the relationship between masculinity, violence, and American success has been insufficiently addressed. Also overlooked is the relevance of his films' self-evident fascination with failed masculinity to a theoretical consideration of the spectatorial pleasures to be derived from Hollywood's representation of men.

One unexpected clue pointing to the inscription of a certain skepticism in Huston's films regarding the ideals of masculinity enshrined by the cult of the body is suggested by the reaction of the auteur critics to Huston's work. In the 1960s, the exclusively male auteur critics embraced directors such as John Ford, Howard Hawks, Budd Boetticher, Robert Aldrich, and Raoul Walsh. The transparent masculinist streak in their criticism led Pauline Kael to write a scathing rebuttal to the dean of American auteurists, Andrew Sarris. Kael dismissed the auteurist championing of Hawks's *Only Angels Have Wings* (1939) as nothing more than a confirmation of the appeal of "sex and glamour and fantasies of the high-school boys' universe."[15] Sarris's lavish praise for Raoul Walsh's *Every Night at Eight* (1935) demonstrated, in Kael's opinion, "narrow notions of virility," while his rejection of John Huston was obvious proof of the auteur theory's inept critical standards.[16]

Sarris's notorious ranking of directors in *The American Cinema: Directors and Directions* relegated Huston to directorial purgatory: the rank of "Less than Meets the Eye." Huston's lack of visual style was cited as one reason for his lack of auteur status, but Sarris's remarks also suggest that Huston did not present a sufficiently positive model of masculinity compared to other specialists of homosocial Hollywood cinema such as Hawks and Walsh. According to Sarris, not only were Hustonian heroes unable to express emotion, but, unlike Hawks, Huston did "not believe sufficiently in the action ethos to enjoy action for its own sake."[17] The director "overloaded the physical" with the moral. More disturbingly, "His protagonists almost invariably fail at what they set out to do, generally through no fault or flaw of their own." Sarris concluded: "Unfortunately, Huston is less a pessimist than a defeatist and his characters manage to be unlucky without the world being particularly out of joint."[18]

In the defeatism that Sarris found so inexplicable, we can locate *Fat City*'s uncomfortable revelation of some of the ideological contradictions in a specific model of American masculinity. Perhaps Huston's "defeatism" is so disturbing because one of the director's primary thematic preoccupations—the quest for material success—is at the problematic heart of the ideological construction of American male identity in the twentieth century—capitalism. Unlike the films of Hawks, Huston's are not obsessed with the man who must pass a test of self-integrity to achieve success measured by the heroic ideals of his male peer group. Huston's films offer a much more anxious vision of masculinity. His characters most often appear to operate according to pure self-interest. For example, in *The Maltese Falcon,* Sam Spade is not interested in avenging the murder of his partner, Miles Archer, but in preserving the reputation of his successful detective agency. As Spade says, to let his partner's killer get away would be bad for business. He abides by his masculine "code," but the film makes it abundantly clear that adherence to that code may be less a free choice than Spade's neurotic mechanism for survival in a world he does not trust or really like.

Although not presented as muscle-bound Adonises, Huston's heroes are often exemplars of the cult of the body in that physical risk-taking and prowess are central to their masculine identity. In films such as *The Man Who Would Be King* and *The Asphalt Jungle,* the robust, manly quest for material success is exposed as a dubious grail, leading, at best, to amused self-knowledge and temporary riches, at worst, to disillusionment and death. The bodies of Huston's heroes become the inadequate tools with which they attempt to validate a masculinity ultimately dependent on money as the sign of their achievement (and identity). Ironically, where Huston's protagonists, such as Fred C. Dobbs in *The Treasure of the Sierra Madre,* often actually meet with momentary success in their individualistic quest for wealth, they fail afterwards in the test of living with themselves and the system in which they operate so uncomfortably. Even when they are not American by nationality, Huston's male protagonists tend to operate within a peculiarly aggressive American model of masculinity. Although they may momentarily delude themselves otherwise, an American predilection for possession guides their risk-taking. However, like Fred C. Dobbs, and like Dix Handley in *The Asphalt Jungle,* Huston's heroes frequently discover too late the malaise involved in clinging to an aggressive, greedy ideal of masculine success.

The obsessive playing out of this pattern in a number of Huston films, including *The Treasure of the Sierra Madre, The Man Who Would Be King, The Asphalt Jungle,* and with variation in *The Misfits* and *The Maltese Falcon,* show Huston's ambiguous attitude toward one model of twentieth-century American masculinity, a model he appeared to attempt to live, but which was always threatened by his status as an "artist"— writer, filmmaker, actor—and also threatened by his background of privilege, which marked him as different from many of those with whom he found male companionship (boxers, gamblers, sportsmen, etc.). Consequently, what Sarris found to be so upsetting about Huston's films—their defeatism—raises fundamental questions about how *Fat City* constructs masculinity, and about the relationship between fascination with masculine failure and the kinds of pleasure that film spectators might derive from Huston's films.

*Fat City* opens with a roving montage sequence, which offers a fluid, impressionistic view of the seedy side of Stockton, California. From skid row missions to urban "renewal" (demolition of existing structures), images of environmental change merge with those of human stasis. Men in groups, men with little to do, men of every color who make the street their meeting place and home document a separate male subculture, which has

184

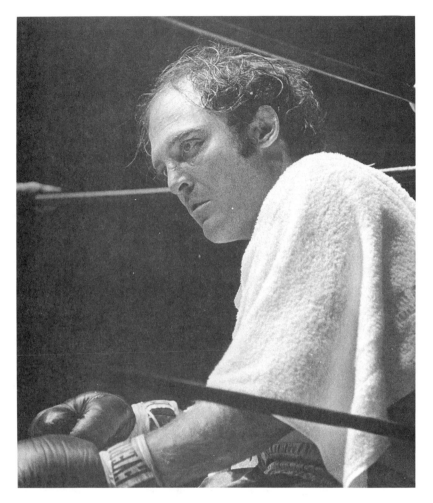

*Fat City:* the malaise involved in clinging to an aggressive masculinity.

passed from most of the American scene.[19] A middle-aged Hispanic man squats on the sidewalk, myopically surveying the changing urban land-scape. A group of older black men gather on a street corner to argue and boast. Old, wine-soaked white men stand on the sidewalk, dissipated, but clinging to their fragile dignity in dingy, ill-fitting suits.

Finally, the camera focuses on a large skid-row hotel. A dissolve takes us to an interior shot of a hotel room, where Billy Tully lies in his underwear, sprawled on the bed. At twenty-nine, Tully (Stacy Keach) is a has-been, a boxer washed up in booze and failed dreams. He gets up and looks in vain for a match to light his cigarette. He pulls on his pants to venture outside. After a few seconds of shadowboxing in front of the hotel, he returns to his room to pick up a gym bag. Tully walks to the YMCA, where he sees a teenager working out on the suspended punching bag. Tully shadowboxes, then asks the kid if he wants to spar a little. The kid is vaguely reluctant: he asks Tully if he is a pro. The response is, "I used to be." They spar. Tully pronounces the teenager a "natural" and tells him to go see his old manager, Ruben Luna (Nicholas Colosantos). Although he has only thought of boxing as "fooling around" in the gym, the kid, Ernie Munger (Jeff Bridges), follows Tully's advice. The film then develops its narrative by cutting between Ernie's dubious rise from the status of a novice into the lower ranks of professional boxing and Tully's fitful attempt to make a comeback in the ring. At first, Tully's days are spent in the fields of the San Joaquin Valley, where he works as a day laborer. His nights are spent drinking alone in skid-row bars until he meets Oma (Susan Tyrell), a sherry-drinking "juicehead." When Earle (Curtis Cokes), Oma's black lover, is jailed for assault, Tully moves in with Oma. In the meantime, Ernie is confronted with the pregnancy of his girlfriend, Faye (Candy Clark). Reluctantly, he marries her. Once he is seriously training and sober, Tully can no longer tolerate Oma. He leaves her. He wins his first fight but goes back to the bottle and unsuccessfully attempts to reconcile with Oma. Ernie's nose is broken in his initial match (the same thing happened to Huston as a club boxer). He is knocked senseless in the first few seconds of another but chooses to continue a career in which his wins are achieved mainly by decision rather than the decisive knockout. Months later, Tully is back on the street, panhandling a match for his cigarette. He happens to see Ernie getting into his car. Ernie tries to get away from his former mentor, but his car won't start. He agrees to sit down with Tully for a cup of coffee in a local game room. The film ends as the two sit wordlessly sipping their coffee.

The first two scenes of *Fat City* typify the film's representation of the male body. Spread-eagle on his bed in his T-shirt and jockey shorts, Tully is displayed for the spectator's curious gaze (to borrow from Laura Mulvey),[20] but the bedframe discretely blocks our view of his genitals. Unlike *Raging Bull*, *Fat City* does not offer a "beautiful body as an object for contemplation" as Pam Cook asserts.[21] There are no fetishizing close-ups of taut muscularity to promise the power and excitement of physical action. Tully's listless form is not an erotic spectacle or a cult ideal, but the object of the camera's detached, distanced, almost clinical gaze. Tully's face is barely visible in the opening scene, but his eyes stare at the ceiling with a kind of emptiness that will reoccur at unexpected moments in the film. His weariness is reiterated in the movement of the camera as it slowly follows him around the small space of his room. At his bureau dresser, the camera does not hold on Tully's face but fixes level on the top of the dresser with its clutter of empty liquor bottles. The bottles and the image of Tully's distended belly immediately convey the boxer's deteriorated physical condition and its apparent cause. When Tully sits down and looks out the window, the diffused white light filtering through the dirty window pane prevents a view of what lies outside this tiny room. The feeling of claustrophobia is intensified by Tully's movement around the room. He remains within a confined circle. As the film unfolds, its narrative will duplicate this circular movement as the penultimate scene of *Fat City* brings the film back to its beginning: We find Tully destitute and once again hunting for a match.

In the next scene, Ernie Munger is introduced at the YMCA. His is no glistening physique either, and his physical presence is minimized by the distanced camera, which makes him appear insignificant against the large scale of the gym's open space. Although Huston often prefers static two-shots to shot-reverse shot patterns, here the shot-reverse shot, which might serve to bind the spectator into identification with the characters, is mediated by the camera's extreme detachment. Long shots initially make Tully a tiny figure in the background; a reverse places Ernie in a similar position. A measure of intimacy is achieved when, at the end of the scene, Tully praises Ernie's abilities. He warns him: "Don't waste your good years." Medium close-ups are exchanged between the two characters as Tully asks Ernie if he ever saw him fight. The monotone reply, "Once." Tully asks, "Did I win? " Ernie replies, "No." Tully philosophically accepts this reminder of his past failures with a vague shrug.

The even, anticlimactic tone of this scene, characteristic of the entire film, and the detached camera style extend the stylistic tendencies in many of Huston's other films. Frequently, Huston's visual style has been faulted as one that remains detached from the struggles of his characters. Referring to *The Treasure of the Sierra Madre,* the director himself admitted that his camera was "impersonal, it just looks on and lets them stew in their own juice."[22] This visual detachment may have contributed to Sarris's assertion that Huston lacked a commitment to the action ethos. Pauline Kael has suggested that the detached camera of *The Man Who Would Be King* limits its "levels" of meaning. She remarks that Huston "just sits back; he seems to be watching the events happen instead of shaping them. . . . The camera now seems to be passively recording . . . without the sudden, detonating effects of participation."[23]

Kael also links the detachment of Huston's camera work to the director's sense of irony. It should be remembered that irony is a technique sometimes associated with an author's need to distance him/her self from material that may be too close to his/her own feelings. Following contemporary psychoanalytic film theory, the detachment of Huston's camera might be seen as a defensive strategy against the dangers of objectifying the male body. Does Huston's clinically "objective" camera/eye work to avoid turning the camera into an instrument of the desiring gaze, of a homoerotic voyeurism that patriarchal homosociality cannot openly tolerate if its structures of power are to remain intact? Or does it have other psychological or social functions?

Drawing on the theoretical work of Paul Willemen, Steven Neale has argued that the male spectator's look at the cinematic representation of other men is filled with sexual anxiety. The violence of male genres, the presence of "mutilation and sadism," says Neale, are "marks both of the repression [of desire] involved and of a means by which the male body may be disqualified, so to speak as an object of erotic contemplation and desire."[24] Because male homosexuality must be repressed to maintain the gendered order of patriarchal relations, says Neale, the male spectator's gaze at the bodies of men must be "heavily mediated by the looks of the characters involved" to "disavow any explicitly erotic look at the male body."[25] Violence against the cinematic male body serves as a displacement of homoerotic desire. With the "erotic component" of men looking at men repressed by "mutilation and sadism," the viewer's pleasure is taken in a "narcissistic" identification with male figures, even those who may be doomed within the context of the narrative.[26]

If we follow Neale's argument, then the violence commonly exercised by and against Huston's protagonists might be read as evidence of an unconscious (and commonly held) attempt to "disqualify" the male body as an object of desire within films dominated by the depiction of the male body, male camaraderie, and concerns often stereotypically labeled as masculine. Both Neale and Laura Mulvey have claimed that Hollywood films use male protagonists as central figures with whom the camera aligns its vision and in whom the audience, therefore, invests emotion.[27] In the instance of *Fat City,* one might expect Huston to use Tully and Ernie as central relays of identificatory looking, anchors who guide the camera's look so that the viewer could avoid an objectification or even "fetishization" of the male as an erotic object. Instead, Huston's camera rarely aligns itself with their point of view. Not only is male subjectivity rarely inscribed through point-of-view shots, but it is lacking in other possible cinematic structures: voice-over narration, flashbacks, dreams, or fantasy sequences. Only in the very last scene of the film is this pattern decisively altered. Until this disturbing moment (which I will discuss later), the men are watched by the camera as despecularized figures who are engrossed in contemplation. They do not control the narrational agency through their alignment with the camera's eye. They are objects of the camera's inquiry rather than controlling subjects of its presence.

As a consequence of these patterns, we must consider whether the detachment of Huston's camera in *Fat City* has ideological functions that are not adequately explained by Neale's psychosexual theory. Does the camera's implication in the creation of *Fat City*'s ironic tone suggest a strategy of distanciation meant to prevent too close an identification with failed masculinity—both for the director and for spectators? Or is it indicative of a critically conscious, objectively distanced inquiry into the contradictions of patriarchal masculinity?

Perhaps *Fat City* is best understood as participating in both these possibilities: The film projects common cultural fascination and fear surrounding masculine failure even as it openly explores the ideological limitations inherent in a physically based concept of American masculinity. Taken from the perspective of Huston's apparent fascination with losers, the film is illuminated by some comments made in his autobiography, in which he described a recurring dream. In the dream, he feels "weak, dissolute, and shiftless" because he is broke and must go to his father for money.[28] This dream scenario cuts to the heart of American masculinity and a culture that defines masculine success in largely monetary terms.

Huston goes on to dismiss his dream's significance by saying that it "doesn't match up with anything," but it certainly does match up with the trends apparent throughout his film oeuvre. Rather than projecting these masculine anxieties onto a "bad object" (the villain) in the classic psychological pattern of refusing to recognize something about oneself, *Fat City* offers a complex representation of masculine failure achieved through sympathetic characters but mediated through an ironic narrational agency. Huston's often hyperbolized camera distance and the refusal to align the camera with character point of view prevents a close identification with characters such as Ernie and Tully, who act out, perhaps, Huston's unresolved fascination with masculine failure, and, in deeper terms, with the inability of the male body to prevent that failure.

In telling a story in which working-class men turn to boxing as a way out of poverty, *Fat City* resists the spectacle of the male body and constantly refuses to celebrate violence as a pleasurable ritual. Ernie's matches are presented in a few, telling seconds, and Tully's important return to the ring becomes the film's only protracted fight sequence. In the latter, Huston's clinically detached camera prevents a close identification with the ostensible protagonist, Tully. We do get a close-up of Tully's eyes as he sits in his corner, but his emotions are unreadable, his face a blank mask that registers, perhaps, nothing more than the neurological damage that his behavior throughout the film implies. Curiously, the fight lacks suspense, for the audience already knows enough to harbor little hope that this violent encounter will actually mean anything to anyone. Only Tully still holds to the dream that this match has any meaning. When he discovers he has made only a hundred dollars from the fight, he argues bitterly with his manager. He is plunged into despair that his "sweat and blood" is worth so little. He goes back to the bottle.

Although the camera's studied distanciation may prevent our sense of immediate involvement, another means of preventing sympathetic identification with Tully occurs when the film wordlessly sketches out a telling portrait of Tully's Mexican opponent. Echoing Tully's own ill-fated trip to Panama, in which the absence of his manager led to disaster in the ring, Armando Lucero arrives by himself on the bus from Mexico City. Neatly attired in slacks, sport jacket, tie, and hat, he steps off the bus with businesslike precision and walks to an "international" (i.e., Hispanic) hotel above a pharmacy. In his room, he downs pills and holds his stomach. He goes to the bathroom, where he passes blood. At the fight, Lucero never hints that he is ill. Tully notices that his opponent is "weak below" and goes after him, but Lucero is a puncher who refuses to give up.[29] Tully is declared the winner of the bout, but he is so dazed that he thinks he must have been knocked out. Just as he achieves no pleasure through violence, the spectator may be placed in a similar situation.

Ascertaining how violence is read by male or female spectators is a complicated task, but film theory has often been quick to regard filmic violence as an inducement to spectatorial sadism directed against one or both of the participants. For example, in reference to *Raging Bull,* Pam Cook suggests that Jake LaMotta is brought low to evoke the spectator's sadistic pleasure.[30] Her remarks are the predictable result of psychoanalytic film theory's conflation of "aggression" and "sadism" and its tendency to ignore the possibility that the representation of violence (and the pleasure it evokes) might not always be "sadomasochistic."

Jean Laplanche reminds us in *Life and Death in Psychoanalysis* of the original conflation in Freud's work of "aggression" and "sadism," the latter having a sexual aim that the former does not.[31] Freud never resolved the contradictions in his theory of sadism. He finally resorted to an asocial notion of the "death drive" or "Thanatos" as an explanation for the genesis of the urge to destroy. In an effort to clarify the distinction between sadism and aggression, Laplanche notes that aggressiveness is a primary instinct "that is directed outward but not sexual." It is, says Laplanche, a demonstration of "the tendency to make oneself the master of one's fellow being in order to achieve one's ends, but without that action—which could be characterized as entirely instrumental—implying any sexual pleasure in itself."[32] In contrast to sadism, the pain of the other does not matter in aggression, "and even less the pleasure discovered in the other's pain," because aggression, says Laplanche, is an exercise of pure destruction.[33]

Laplanche's discussion opens the possibility of distinguishing between sadism and aggression in both their psychoanalytic and social dimensions. In light of his remarks, the articulation of violence within *Fat City* challenges the theoretical assumption that violence necessarily creates "sadomasochistic" pleasure for film spectators (male or female). The film also reminds us that we should distinguish more carefully between many types and depictions of violence (the ritualized, the vengeful, the impersonal) and consider the different pleasures available from these various modes of violence. Pam Cook claims that the fight scenes of *Raging Bull* are pleasurable (even to women) because they give the spectator the illusion of being in the midst of the action and afford the "real turn-on" of experiencing "the risk involved" in boxing.[34] However, in *Fat City* the spectacle of boxing's ritualized violence is either elided, truncated, or offered through a detached camera style that precludes identification with violence as a meaningful or pleasurably essential element of masculinity.

*Fat City* foregrounds the function of violence in the social construction of masculinity and its determination by specific historical and ideological circumstances. In the late Victorian cult of the body, the violence of boxing was ideologically complicit in defining American masculinity according to a physical model previously limited to the lower class. While violence was linked to the middle-class demand for masculine redefinition, it was publicly articulated through working-class combatants who often saw their own participation in practical social terms: as the chance for success within a system that offered few and sometimes brutal opportunities for advancement.

Rather than "an essential component of masculinity" that leads the hero into the ring as a path of social resistance,[35] violence in *Fat City* exists as part of a repressive social system. *Fat City* repudiates the myth of the lower-class hero whose own aggressive desires lead him into the ring. Tully and Ernie are not depicted as being aggressive by nature, but as being drawn into the game to succeed with the only frail commodity they have—their bodies, confirming late nineteenth-century commentary on boxing that compared the sport to prostitution.[36] The ritualized violence of the ring is merely another way to commodify the bodies of lower-class, predominantly minority males. When Ruben attempts to get Tully a match, the fight promoter asks him, "Who's pay to see Tully in a tune-up fight?" The only way to exploit Tully as a commodity is to play up the racial, ethnic angle and pair him with a Mexican boxer, to increase the dramatic tension of the fight in a racially divided society.[37] Similarly, Ruben's enthusiasm for Ernie is partially based on the fact that he has "a good pair of legs" and a long reach, but he invests in him as a prospect primarily because Ernie is "white . . . a real clean, good-looking kid." Ruben tells his wife, "Anglos don't want to pay to see two colored guys fight. They want to see a white guy fight. He'll draw crowds someday."

For those men, black, brown, or white, who operate on a physically based concept of masculinity, athletic success in the ring leads to temporary acquisitions defined in traditionally consumerist (and masculinist) terms rather than to social power. While working at picking walnuts, Tully nostalgically recalls what boxing success once brought him: a new house, a new car, and a sexy blond wife. They are all gone. As Ruben tells it, Tully's wife ran off when he began losing, but Tully still clings to her as the symbol of his success. He tells Ernie why he has to return to boxing: "I get the fight, I get the money, and I send for my wife. I can do it. You should have seen the things we had."

Through such scenes, boxing is represented less as a celebration of the symbolic phallic power of the male body than as the last desperate strategy for blue-collar survival. Like the young Huston, who briefly (and unsuccessfully) returned to boxing when he could no longer support his new family,[38] Tully returns to boxing because his other choices run out. When he's on the bottle, Tully is hired as a day laborer in the farms and orchards surrounding Stockton. In predawn darkness he joins the other men waiting for these jobs, mostly black and Hispanic, or old white men who respond to the field boss's cry: "Who wants to go to work?" Because of the combination of his youth and color, Tully seems out of place: An old man asks why he doesn't have a "proper job." The hiring boss promises a decent wage to any man who wants to work, but the reality is that many earn only five dollars a day after deductions. As the bus pulls out into the darkness, the camera point of view takes approximately a central place among the workers. In spite of sharing a visual field with the men, our identification with them is carefully delimited. They remain faceless. Only their voices are heard as they comment on their hopeless financial situation. "Good God," says one man, "what am I doing back here?"

If the body wears out in the field, it wears out even faster in the ring. Hands, eyes, backs, and brains are ruined. Tully and Oma go out for drinks with a Hispanic boxer whose hands are gnarled into rigid stumps. Tully explains: "He hit too hard." Within this stratum of society, bodies are made to be exploited.

For eighteen-year-old Ernie, the process of physical debilitation begins quickly. In his first pro bout, he is felled in seconds. When revived, he doesn't know where he is. The doctor enters the ring, holds up five fingers, and pronounces him fit. Ruben's assistant, Babe (Art Aragon), later tells his boss that he thinks Ernie's sudden elopement with Faye is a reaction to the experience of being knocked out. Babe recalls how scared he was when he first passed blood, and adds, "What bothers me is getting my throat ruined." He asks Ruben: "How's your nose? Can you breathe?" Ruben replies, "Yeah, can't you?" Babe says, "Not on a wet day." Their tone is matter of fact, without rancor, and marked by a detachment that matches the tone of Huston's strategies of film narration.

In spite of the distancing of the narrational agency of the film from its many characters representing failure, Huston qualifies what might be re-

193

garded as their shame with a sense of the dignity with which these men face inevitable hardship. We might be tempted to regard their problems as individual, subjective, or psychological. The day after he first makes love to his girlfriend, Ernie tells another young fighter, Buford, "I hope I didn't leave my fight in the bedroom." Buford dismisses such talk as nonsense. "It's all in your mind," he replies. "Hoping never done nothing, it's wanting to do it." Buford affirms the American success myth that tells men that to be successful they must first have "character" and be in psychological command of themselves. Buford berates Ernie: "You don't want to kick ass. You want to get your own ass wupped."

Buford's blunt words give voice to the audience's suspicions regarding both Ernie and Tully, that they are responsible for their own failures. Ruben claims that Tully was "on his way to the top," the best fighter he had ever handled. He blames Tully's wife for destroying the boxer's "peace of mind." However, Huston refuses to make the truth of such judgments self-evident, for Buford's aggressive, hypermasculine attitude proves inadequate to ensure his ability to "kick ass," and Ruben's statements are qualified by Tully's story of how he lost a crucial fight in Panama because Ruben was too cheap to send someone to second him.[39] Society offers these men chances for success that are really little more than disguised opportunities for failure.

The last scene of *Fat City* offers textual ambiguity triumphing even over narrational irony. For the first time, the camera's protective distanciation from the characters collapses. Drunk and dirty, Tully panhandles for a match to light his cigarette. He sees Ernie at his car and hails him. Ernie tries to leave, but is caught in conversation with Tully. Where he once praised Ernie as "a natural who comes along once in a million," Tully now says that the first time they met he said to himself, "There's a guy that is soft in the center." His verbal reduction of Ernie to the "feminine" by aligning him with softness may be motivated by jealousy, for Tully then tells him, "Forget it. You got everything going for you. . . . You got a wife and a kid." Of course, these were acquisitions that Ernie desperately attempted to avoid. Ernie refuses Tully's offer of a drink but agrees to have a cup of coffee. They enter a huge game hall and order at the food counter. Tully stares at the aged oriental waiter who slowly shuffles to them with their coffee. "How'd you like to wake up in the morning and be him? What a waste." Ernie wonders out loud if the old man was ever young. Tully is polite, almost gallantly tender in thanking the old man for the coffee. "Maybe he's happy," Ernie says. "Maybe we're all happy," retorts Tully. He then turns around on his counter stool and stares at the middle-aged black men playing cards at the tables. From Tully's subjectivized point of view, the frame freezes, then a pan moves the field of vision from one table of men to another. The camera then reverses through a cut to an extreme close-up of Tully's blank eyes. In close-up, Tully turns to face Ernie in a two-shot. Another cut brings the camera into a position across the axis line that reverses screen direction. Through this reverse, Ernie and Tully are placed in the positions each formerly held in the frame. Ernie attempts to leave, but Billy asks him to stay and "talk a while." In a frontal two-shot, they sit in silence, sipping coffee, as the sound track concludes with the instrumental version of the theme song heard in the film's opening scene, Kris Kristofferson's "Help Me Make It through the Night."

This final, disturbing scene is extremely perplexing. The camera breaks its pattern of distanciation, but while visual intimacy of a sort is achieved, the characters appear incapable of either self-disclosure or self-knowledge. It remains unclear whether Tully fully recognizes the connection between his life and that of the old Chinese waiter, but he philosophizes, "Before your life gets started, it makes a beeline for the drain." The black men who are depicted in the subjectivized shots of the card tables appear unreal. Like the men on the field buses, they have no faces. We see only their backs, and we hear nothing of their conversations (the sound track drops out). Their representation through the hypertechnical intervention of the combination freeze frame/pans is open to multiple interpretations. The shots may register Tully's isolation, his loneliness, his realization that this world of male ritual play is as meaningless as the violent "play" that has dominated and depleted his own life. Perhaps Huston is attempting to provide the audience with a visual indicator of Tully's alcoholism, his neurological as well as psychological distress. We cannot be certain of any of these interpretations.

Tully is desperate not to be left alone during this moment of altered vision, but he and Ernie remain in what amounts to little more than a parody of intimacy (reflecting the "norm" of male "intimacy"?). The sudden reversal of screen direction that switches their placement on the screen may signify that Huston wants us to draw comparisons between Ernie and Tully, for if Tully fails to see how the old Chinese man represents his future, Ernie also fails to see how Tully's debilitated condition likely represents his own future in the inevitable cycle of boxing "success." If Ernie

The aging fighter (Stacy Keach) and the younger man (Jeff Bridges) can only shadowbox the male image in *Fat City*.

and Tully are alike, then they are alike in being defeated by more than their own minds. They are defeated by a society in which their "pursuit of happiness" will inevitably be unhappy. Failing to fulfill their dreams of success, they are left to rationalize working-class lives that cannot measure up to impossible cultural ideals. They are left to shadowbox with the myths of American masculinity.

## NOTES

1. Joseph and Elizabeth Pleck, eds., *The American Man* (Englewood Cliffs, N.J.: Prentice-Hall, 1980), 2.

2. In retirement, Sullivan was certainly not destitute, but his alcoholism led to ugly public incidents, often involving the police, and resulting in bad press. In

1905, he suddenly stopped drinking—for good—and enthusiastically took up the cause of temperance. See Michael T. Isenberg, *John L. Sullivan and His America* (Urbana: University of Illinois Press, 1988), 354–74.

3. Dan Streible, "A History of the Boxing Film, 1894–1915," *Film History* 3 (1989): 239.

4. See Streible, "History of the Boxing Film," and Charles Musser, *The Emergence of Cinema: The American Screen to 1907* (New York: Charles Scribner, 1990), 194–208.

5. See Pleck and Pleck, *American Man,* 26, and Joe Dubert, "Progressivism and the Masculinity Crisis," in Pleck and Pleck, *American Man,* 304–9.

6. Dubert, "Progressivism," 308–9, and Jeffrey Hantover, "The Boy Scouts and the Validation of Masculinity," in Pleck and Pleck, *American Man,* 285.

7. Edward Anthony Rotundo, "Manhood in America: The Northern Middle Class, 1770–1920," Ph.D. diss., Brandeis University, 1982, 441–46.

8. Hantover, "Boy Scouts," 288.

9. Isenberg, *John L. Sullivan,* 63.

10. Elliott G. Gorn, *The Manly Art: Bare Knuckle Prize Fighting in America* (Ithaca: Cornell University Press, 1986), 227.

11. John Huston, *An Open Book* (New York: Alfred A. Knopf, 1980), 26.

12. See John Huston, "Fools" and "Figures of Fighting Men," in Part III of this volume.

13. Pam Cook, "Masculinity in Crisis?" *Screen* 23 (Sept.–Oct. 1982): 43.

14. Ibid.

15. Pauline Kael, "Circles and Squares," repr. in *Film Theory and Criticism,* 3d ed., ed. Gerald Mast and Marshall Cohen (New York: Oxford University Press, 1979), 677.

16. Ibid., 667, 672–77.

17. Andrew Sarris, *The American Cinema: Directors and Directions, 1927–1968* (New York: Dutton, 1968), 158.

18. Ibid., 157.

19. Pleck and Pleck suggest in *The American Man* that intimate male-to-male relationships may be the norm for American adolescents, but the separate male culture that was once an integral part of immigrant and working-class culture has "become peripheral to men's daily lives." See p. 35.

20. Laura Mulvey, "Visual Pleasure and Narrative Cinema," *Screen* 16 (Autumn 1975): 6–18.

21. Cook, "Masculinity in Crisis?" 43.

22. James Agee, "Undirectable Director," in *Agee on Film* (New York: McDowell Obolensky, 1958), 327.

23. Pauline Kael, "Brotherhood Is Powerful," *New Yorker* 90, no. 45 (Jan. 5, 1976): 109.

24. Steven Neale, "Masculinity as Spectacle," *Screen* 24, no. 6 (Nov.–Dec. 1983): 8.

25. Ibid., 14.

26. Ibid., 8, 10.

27. Ibid., 5, and Mulvey, "Visual Pleasure," 12.

28. Huston, *An Open Book,* 147.

29. Both Martin Rubin (see this volume) and Stuart Kaminsky, *John Huston: Maker of Magic* (Boston: Houghton-Mifflin, 1978), 191, see Lucero as representative of Huston's ideal. Nevertheless, the question remains, why does Huston devote a few minutes to Lucero and two hours to Tully and Ernie?

30. Cook, "Masculinity in Crisis?" 42, 46.

31. Jean Laplanche, *Life and Death in Psychoanalysis* (Baltimore: Johns Hopkins Press, 1976), 89.

32. Ibid., 90.

33. Ibid.

34. Cook, "Masculinity in Crisis?" 42.

35. Ibid., 39.

36. See Musser, *Emergence of Cinema.*

37. See Streible, "History of the Boxing Film," 242–43, for a discussion of interracial bouts in the early cycle of fight films.

38. Huston, *An Open Book,* 8.

39. The novel on which the film is based underscores the manager's responsibility by having Ruben repeat his actions with Ernie. He sends Ernie alone to a fight in Salt Lake City. Ruben's excuse is, again, lack of money. Leonard Gardner, *Fat City* (New York: Farrar, Straus, and Giroux, 1969), 171.

# Part Three

DOCUMENTS

# John Huston:
# A Biographical Sketch

DAVID DESSER

I n the fall of 1990, director Clint
Eastwood released a film adaptation of Peter Viertel's 1953 *roman
à clef, White Hunter, Black Heart.* In this thinly disguised story surrounding John Huston's making of his film classic *The African Queen,* superstar
Eastwood does a creditable imitation of Huston's breathless speech. He
also captures something of Huston's legendary savoir faire combined with
his very American sense of mischievousness. Huston's macho posturings
and genuine courage are also neatly captured by the talented directing and
acting of Eastwood. Missing from this enjoyable and perceptive film, however, is a sense of Huston's commitment to his craft. The making of the
film within this behind-the-scenes tale is not simply deemphasized in favor
of a look at male camaraderie and the "fictional" protagonist-director's
near-mystical desire to shoot an elephant, but positively repressed. Yet, it
is hard to believe that *The African Queen,* one of the world's most beloved
films, was made simply as an excuse to go on safari in Africa; hard to

believe also that John Huston, whatever his sense of sport (and it was by all accounts considerable), did not take his filmmaking equally seriously.

This is not to fault Eastwood's film, nor the novel upon which it is based. Instead we might note that John Huston is surely one of the few film directors whose life could, and did, inspire novels and films in its own right. In point of fact, Huston's filmmaking, too, inspired a handful of books. Nonfiction accounts of the production of *The Red Badge of Courage, The African Queen,* and *The Misfits* provide insights not only into Huston's working methods, but into a changing Hollywood.[1] Yet it is Huston's life, his mercurial, ever-youthful personality, and his towering intellect and range of interests that to some extent pervade these accounts, and others, of the director's films and filmmaking.

An earlier generation of film critics, inspired by French auteurism, undervalued Huston's cinema as the product primarily of a *metteur en scène.* In this interpretation, he was a director who merely "placed in the scene," and whose filmmaking was subordinate to the screenplay, itself typically derived from a work of literature. It is the work of many of the articles in this anthology to refine the implications of, or perhaps even refute, this notion. Furthermore, auteur criticism itself has been subjected to numerous forces over the last twenty years so as to question the notion of cinematic authorship advanced by auteurism and its critical emphasis on a personal sense of style that allegedly must be extracted from the manifest content of the film.

A glance at Huston's life, moreover, reveals that questions of cinematic authorship aside, there is a genuinely autobiographical cast to much of Huston's cinema even, often especially, apparent in those films based on works of literature. That Huston's great-grandfather, William P. Richardson, was a hero of the Civil War who lost an arm at Chancellorsville lends more poignancy to the tale of courage and cowardice that is at the center of Huston's *The Red Badge of Courage.* A love of painting, which motivated Huston's own experiments in the art all his life, and to which he turned with great seriousness near its end, surely explains the fascination with Toulouse-Lautrec and the formal visual experimentations of *Moulin Rouge,* Huston's film version of Toulouse-Lautrec's life. That an early interest in painting overcame Huston's desire to become a welterweight champion in the boxing ring surely attests to the sympathy accorded the athletic milieu in *Fat City,* one of Hollywood's most perceptive films on the fight game. And that Huston's grandfather, John Gore, became the magistrate of a town he helped found during the opening of Oklahoma Territory in 1889, gives the historically inflected whimsy of *The Life and Times of Judge Roy Bean* an obvious personal stake.

Lest we are guilty of fanciful eulogizing, like the columnist for the *New York Post* who claimed in an obituary for Walter Huston, John's father, that he was "a very American figure" despite the fact that the actor was born and raised in Canada,[2] we might say of John Huston that there was something very American about him, even essentially American. That he adapted *Moby-Dick,* the most archetypally American novel, to the screen is only one index of this. His fascination for typically American characters, from world-weary yet romantic Sam Spade of *The Maltese Falcon,* to the even more world-weary and cynical American prospectors of *The Treasure of the Sierra Madre,* to the conniving criminals in *The Asphalt Jungle,* to the lost wayfarers of *The Misfits, Fat City, Wise Blood,* and *Under the Volcano* reveals a spirit deeply in tune with the cultural convolutions of the American soul. The very parameters of his life reveal something profound and profoundly paradoxical about the American spirit, not the least of which is Huston's apparent rejection of his homeland, first for the green fields of Ireland and later for the desert and beaches of Mexico. That all-American spirit of wanderlust may be seen in Huston's peripatetic filmmaking habits, shooting movies quite literally all around the world, from the habitable pleasures of Ireland, Italy, Paris, and Japan, to the more primitive pleasures of Mexico and Africa, to the rather forbidding environment of the Moroccan desert. This wanderlust also expressed itself through five marriages and a number of long-term relationships with women to whom he could or would not stay either faithful or married. More particularly, there was something essentially American about Huston in his attempts constantly to remake, to reimagine, himself. Becoming master of the hounds at his Irish estate, or the old gringo in a ramshackle Mexican adobe are less rejections of America, perhaps, than obvious attempts to recreate himself in his own bold imaginary image of a certain kind of man. In light of this, it is no surprise that among the books that Huston adapted to the screen was the Bible!

It should not be forgotten also that John Huston was one of the rare directors of Hollywood's Golden Age to approach film directing via screenwriting. It was in Hollywood that he found his first real success in the world of work. Previous to 1932, he pursued less than successful stints as an actor in New York, a boxer in California, and an artist (painting in Paris among other locales). His talent for screenwriting may explain his penchant for adaptations as a director, for the screenwriter in the film factories of the old studio system was in some sense always an adapter, a craftsman fashioning movie scripts from novels, short stories, magazine and newspaper articles, even from other screenplays.

Yet the necessity of earning a living did not define Huston's relationship to writing. Huston came by his love of and respect for the written word honestly. His maternal grandparents were pioneer stock and newspaper people. His mother, Rhea Gore, with whom he lived and traveled as a youth, was a well-known free-lance journalist. Indeed, she met John's father while she was a journalist in St. Louis covering the local theater where Walter Huston had a role with a traveling company in *The Sign of the Cross*. In fact, along his circuitous route to Hollywood screenwriting, John tried his hand at journalism and short-story writing (two of his stories appear in part 3 of this volume), as well as playwrighting. While his credited and uncredited screenwriting contributions to an impressive group of studio films (produced primarily at Warner Brothers) deserve attention, Huston will always be best remembered as the director of nearly three dozen feature films, a handful of which are among the best-loved and fondly remembered films ever produced in the American cinema.

Huston's directing debut came in 1941 with *The Maltese Falcon*, as assured a directorial debut as one could hope for. Besides some lean years in the late 1970s, Huston's feature films came thereafter at an almost yearly interval, interrupted only by the war years of 1943–1945, and in this interim he made three of the most memorable documentaries in American film history. While several articles in this anthology put the war in critical perspective, it is worth remembering that Huston himself conceived of it as his dominant influence.

Almost immediately after the attack on Pearl Harbor that plunged the United States into the war, Huston volunteered for the Signal Corps. In May of 1942, he reported for duty as a lieutenant and was immediately assigned to make a documentary in Los Angeles detailing the process of making B-25 bombers. When, in September of 1942, he was ordered to the Aleutian Islands to make a film about building an air base in the desolate wastes of the frozen north, something profound changed, not only in the history of documentary filmmaking, but in John Huston's life. We can only speculate that it was the life-and-death danger Huston experienced in the air over the Aleutians and in the ground war in once-bucolic Italy that finds reflection, in part, in *The Battle of San Pietro;* or perhaps the change was bound up with Huston's participation in the camaraderie experienced by men in battle as an inevitable and inevitably complex part of war. It may also be related to what Huston claimed was "the closest thing he ever had to a religious experience," that is, when he "submerged himself in the mental disorders of the patients at Mason General" hospital for the making of *Let There Be Light.*[3] Whatever the exact nature of Huston's wartime experience, he returned from the war a changed man.

The war changed Huston as it changed America. Huston's rather naive desire to get away from studio shooting through his enlistment had resulted in experiences that gave him a deeper understanding of the complexities of human behavior. After the war, there was virtually no major Hollywood genre in which he did not work (science fiction seems the only exception), though his affinity with the "masculine" genres such as the gangster film, detective story, adventure film, and Western seem clear. In this respect, Huston's films reflect and participate in a dominant tradition of American arts and letters, a tradition of masculine adventure that extends easily as far back as the novels of James Fenimore Cooper, through Herman Melville, Mark Twain, and Ernest Hemingway (with whom Huston struck up a friendship beginning in 1948, and whose short story, *The Killers,* Huston helped adapt into film in 1946).

This male-centered perspective, which links Huston to many of the most significant filmmakers of his generation (John Ford, Howard Hawks), as well as a generation that followed and was influenced by him (Don Siegel, Robert Aldrich, Sam Peckinpah, Walter Hill, among others), is sifted not only through his biographical experiences and his own considerable artistic imagination, but also through one of the transcendent experiences of Huston's and the nation's life, the Second World War. And if the war made Huston take a more nuanced and ambiguous stance toward his vision of the American male, it also forced him to see his native country in a more ambivalent light and search more deeply into human relationships. Thus, it only added to the richness and complexity of a film career that would be unique in world cinema by the time that John Huston died a few days after his eighty-first birthday in the summer of 1987.

## NOTES

1. On the making of *The Red Badge of Courage*, see Lillian Ross, *Picture* (New York: Rinehart and Co., 1952); on *The African Queen,* see Katharine Hepburn, *The Making of "The African Queen" : Or How I Went to Africa with Bogart, Bacall and Huston and Almost Lost My Mind* (New York: Alfred A. Knopf, 1987); on *The Misfits,* see James Goode, *The Making of "The Misfits"* (New York: Bobbs-Merrill, 1963).

2. Quoted in Lawrence Grobel, *The Hustons* (New York: Charles Scribner's Sons, 1989), 352.

3. Ibid., 271.

# Encounter with Rui Nogueira and Bertrand Tavernier

TRANSLATED BY RUTH A. HOTTELL

It seems to us that you added a lot of humor into your adaptation of "Reflections in a Golden Eye"?

I believe that the humor is already present in the book, although in an implicit way . . . But when you see it, you recognize it better. The colonel for example, his despondency after the death of his wife, his refusal to sleep with his friend's wife, it's all in the book . . . But when you see it, you laugh. There's possibly a little more humor in the Brando character in the film.

The two classes that he gives are not in the book and are very important . . .

Yes, that's true. I added them. Carson McCullers came to see me a short time before her death. She was very, very sick you know. She had not been out of bed for three years. I went to see her at her home in New York and we talked about Ireland. She told me that one of her dreams was to visit the country. I answered: "You can come as soon as you feel better." That became an obsession: to see Ireland. She decided to pass a weekend at the Plaza to see if she could hold up. She was brought to the Plaza in an ambulance and all went well, so she decided to take the trip. I had arranged everything: ambulances at the airports, stretchers in the plane . . . She spent a month at my house in Ireland, without ever getting out of bed . . . I even thought she was going to die one day . . . Then she returned to America and she died one or two months later! It was a remarkable experience and I'm happy it worked out. Suddenly she no longer had the impression of being a prisoner: doors were opening in front of her. We made plans together: to go to Greece by boat, the sort of miracle which never occurs. And we talked about the scenario that she had read. She gave her complete approval. She thought it was a marvelous scenario and even told me she would have liked to put certain details which I had added into her book . . . She was marvelous! I sincerely believe *Reflections in a Golden Eye* is a profound film. You cannot imagine how happy I am you liked it. As for me, I love it . . .

**We get the impression that you got along very well with Brando and that, together, you enjoyed creating a character who is an enormous caricature, who renders the army and society ridiculous . . .**

It was a pleasure to work with Brando. I had been told that he was very difficult. On the contrary, he was great. He spent his time perfecting his character, trying to find little touches which would reinforce the meaning of the film. It would take hours for me to tell you all the qualities I find in him. I think he's the best actor I've ever worked with.

**Who is Chapman Mortimer, the cowriter of the script?**

Chapman Mortimer is an excellent English novelist who never broke through. He was never famous or even known. I've read his novels throughout the years. They are very odd . . . I don't know which works to compare with them . . . They are very carefully written books, very mysterious, but their mystery is now created by the dramatic situation. In three novels, Father Goose and two other characters are speaking and you don't know who Father Goose is: it is God! As for the two others, we don't know who they are and they talk about the situation, go to bed, wake up, argue. And they talk about a very real situation. For example, in one of the novels, we see a Spanish peasant who comes from the mountains and attends a fair. His brother was murdered. He wants to avenge his brother; he doesn't know who killed him. His detective work takes place on a purely instinctive level, both stupefying and incomprehensible. At the end, he discovers the murderer and kills him before returning toward the hills. His clues are always little emotional clues. He solves the enigma and finds the murderer by spelling out each letter . . . During this time, in a boat far from the bank, the three characters talk and argue, discussing what is taking place and actions that they don't see . . . As you can see, it is rather eccentric and I don't know with whom to compare Mortimer . . .

**Chesterton?**

No, no. He's stranger than Chesterton. He's more French, although I can't think of any French writer who resembles him. He wrote a script which was rather good. I think that he'll write well for film, but in this case he was too conscious of writing a scenario: He sought images, symbols, as all novelists do when they start to write scenarios. Gladys Hill, who was my secretary, reworked the scenario. We sat down and we wrote it . . .

**There are practically no symbols in the film.**

No, that's true. Except perhaps for what I call "conscious symbols" like the stolen spoon, but that's not even a symbol. Just an occurrence. It's not a psychoanalytic film . . . If you treat homosexuality, the critics think you're making a psychoanalytic work. There is no explanation. Only occurrences!

**The center of interest in the book was the young boy. You moved it toward the Brando character. Why?**

The film centers around two accidents: The young soldier sees a nude woman and the captain discovers the existence of the young soldier. The entire film is dependent on these two "chance happenings." A series of implacable events will result from these two meetings. The internal logic of the film is constructed from these two occurrences, which both refer to the captain and to the young boy who thus become the two poles of the story, a story where everybody watches everybody. Myself, I do the same as all my characters, I watch. I don't judge. I limit myself to watching. That was one of the very important points of the books, this absence of judgment. It is a detached look. I don't have to say: "X is bad or rotten." That puts the public in the position of God, in the situation of God. In appearance, there is no message and that bothers spectators, they are obliged to take the responsibility. The simple act of looking makes you an accomplice of what is happening in front of you. That's what I wanted people to feel while watching the film.

**It was a little strange to choose Brian Keith to play the role of the major . . .**

He is such a good actor . . . You know, he's great. He is one of those modest actors who knows how to portray a number of incredible things. Physically, he's a handsome man, but his attractiveness can be a little absurd due to its massive, muscular side . . . That's a facade, or rather, he has the talent to make that felt. And behind this facade, this physique, there is a gentle side. There is a soul somewhere inside Brian Keith: It's hard to find, but it exists. I had only seen it in one film, *Nevada Smith,* and I liked it very much. I decided to try him in the role and he's perfect. You remember the moment when he decided to send his wife to an asylum: you feel that a sort of sorrow invades him and that he is completely lost. It is a sorrow halfway between pain and numbness.

**It seems that "Freud" marked a turning point in your work. You are more interested in the interior struggle of characters.**

I don't do that consciously. It is certain that *Freud* was a turning point . . . But I am not conscious of the change. One of the last films I made is everything but interior. It's *Sinful Davey.* It's nothing, but it's funny. It's the story of a young Scot, based on a journal or rather, on the real memoirs of a young man who was hanged at twenty-six years old. The scriptwriter made Davey the son of this man who tries to surpass his father in crime and looting. It is the classic theme of rivalry between father and son. He wants to do better than his father in all domains. It's a very relaxed and I think very amusing story.

**The music for "Reflections" is superb . . .**

It was done by a Japanese composer, the same who did *The Bible.* A few years ago I heard some of his records. I didn't know him, but

somebody had sent me his records. I sent for him because I was imme-
diately fascinated by his compositions. I think that what he did in
*Reflections* goes incredibly well with the film. There is not the first
Southern theme, not the first Stephen Forster [sic] tune.

**Where did you get this fascinating noise: the groaning of the wound-
ed horse?**
All the sounds in the film are natural. I had sent a team to record everything that happened in a stable. For the scene you're talking about, we
simply drugged the horse. That's the normal sound he makes while
sleeping. It went very well. And the breathing we recorded, we put it as
it was in the film, without adding any effects.

**Why all those pan shots at the end?**
I'm not going to go into an intellectual explanation . . . I wanted to give
the impression that everything stopped, everything froze at the same
time. Another way of obtaining this result would have been to stop the
image, but I thought that by moving the camera I would get this same
feeling of immobility, this absolute freeze of feelings and duration . . .
You know, several things surprised me about the film's reception
among American critics: that nobody mentions or even notices the humor, the derisory absurdity of certain sequences or certain characters.
And I regret the fact that practically nobody saw the original version
with the colors! It was so beautiful! Ingmar Bergman wrote me to tell
me that he had been so impressed by the colors that he wanted to use
the same process in an adaptation he planned to make of *Peer Gynt.*

**Why did you give up on "The Madwoman of Chaillot"?**
The producer and I had differing views from the beginning. I agreed after having read the script, which was a good script. I had seen the play
in New York right after the war and I decided to read it again. And I
discovered that the play was better than the scenario, far better. In the
scenario, they had (they being the producer) what he believed to be
contemporary elements: helicopters, computers. It was an attempt at
modernizing the play. And it didn't work well. Then, I got a literal
translation of the play and this translation was much better than the text
they had staged in New York. The literal translation was wonderful.
And Giraudoux's intentions were so clear and radically different from

the producer's ambitions. It really was a choice: Either we adapted Giraudoux or the producer *(laugh)*. I chose Giraudoux. The producer didn't like Giraudoux, not really. The important part of Giraudoux's play was these men with no face who recognized each other in spite of the anonymity: financiers, capitalists from the world over. It had nothing to do with hippies, computers, LSD. It was about "Men of Money" with gray faces, who wanted to destroy Beauty and Personality. You couldn't mix the two styles.

**At first you were an actor in a Sherwood Anderson play, "The Triumph of the Egg."**
You know that story? No? That was a beautiful story which has been dramatized. I was visiting my father in New York when Kenneth Mc-Gowan, for some strange reason, asked me to read the play, then to play a role: that of the old man, well, that of a man my age now ... I never seriously regarded myself as an actor. I always thought that my father sought this activity for the whole family. It was a very interesting little play which could be taken up again today.

**Then you wrote "Frankie and Johnny"?**
I knew a girl who had a puppet theater and I wrote that for her. It was staged with a rather big success. It was based on the song. George Gershwin was one of my friends and one day at a party at his house, they showed the play with the puppets and he improvised some music for the play. Then he spoke to me about doing an opera. We never did it, but the text was published.

**You played Lincoln in "Abe Lincoln in Illinois" by Robert Sherwood ...**
Not by *Sherwood,* by Howard Koch ... And it wasn't called *Abe Lincoln in Illinois,* but *The Lonely Man.* I never played in the Sherwood play!

**You collaborated numerous times with Howard Koch ...**
Yes. I met him in New York; he had written that play and I met him thanks to Robert Milton, a stage director who wanted to put Koch's play on. They were able to stage it in Chicago and I only accepted be-

cause he was a very good friend . . . It's an interesting play. It has some good moments, but on the whole isn't excellent. It became too sentimental in places. That's always the danger when you take Abraham Lincoln and contrast him with a modern political situation. Koch was a very good writer and a wonderful man. After that experience, we had the idea of doing a play of *Woodrow Wilson,* which became *In Time to Come.* We wrote this play about Wilson, then I went to Hollywood and gave Howard Koch's name as somebody who could become an excellent scriptwriter. They had him come to Hollywood and Warner Brothers put him under contract. He became a first-rate scriptwriter. It was during that period that our play on Wilson became *In Time to Come,* which was staged by Preminger. I didn't see his staging. The play was well received and won the Critics' Award for the best play of the year. It was a critical success, but not a public one. Alexander Knox played the role of Wilson. He later played it in the film.

Earlier, you had directed a play, "A Passenger to Bali."

It was a very interesting play, but I would never have directed it without my father. He was playing one of the roles and declared that he would play only if I directed it. There were a lot of good things about this show, but it was not a success. It should have worked because it was very good.

You started in cinema by playing in three films by Wyler: "Shakedown," "Hell's Heroes," and "The Storm."

No, that's an error! It was Sam Goldwyn who brought me to Hollywood. The director Herman Shumlin was one of my friends and he gave my name to Goldwyn and recommended me as a writer. I had only written short stories. Nothing happened with Sam Goldwyn. They didn't give me anything to do. So I found a job at Universal. Goldwyn loaned me to Universal and I wrote a scenario. They took my father to act; it was called *A House Divided,* which was directed in 1931 by Wyler. That's when I met Wyler for the first time, but I never played in any of his films. *A House Divided* was an acceptable film, not better than acceptable. It was a melodrama which took place in a Vermont fishing village. A man and his son became rivals. They fell in love with the same girl . . . It had a certain charm.

You collaborated on a film people have called excellent, "Law and Order," by Edward L. Cain.

There is a great writer in the U.S., who wrote a lot of remarkable books: W. R. Burnett. He wrote a book called *St. Johnson* which I have always found excellent. It was about a real person from the West who was still alive and who had become a legend. The studio was afraid to make the film, fearing a suit. They had bought the rights on my advice. It was truly a great book, as many of Burnett's books are. Try to find it and read it. As a matter of fact, it was about Wyatt Earp and Wyatt Earp was still alive. I wrote a scenario based on the book. But it didn't have anything to do with Burnett, it wasn't faithful to the book. It was a very conventional Western, but with added elements: humor and a precise sense of the period. There was also an idea behind it: to show that this handful of men who had arrived in this little town were merely satellites of this living legend. They lived in his shadow, doing the same work and, like him, shooting their guns to clean up a town. At first, they were heroes to the inhabitants. Then they discovered that everything was not so obvious: Their motivations were multiple and divergent and the town slowly turned against these men . . . The staging was rather good. The direction of the actors also. The photography wasn't very good and the work overall could have been better. The parts didn't mesh well together. I wanted to do a remake, with no success . . . I was told that Ford had left this film to do *My Darling Clementine*. Yes, really, *Law and Order* had qualities.

You collaborated on "Murders in the Rue Morgue" by Florey . . .

Yes, I saw a bit of it again on television not long ago. It was okay. There again, there were some things that worked well. It wasn't faithful to the Edgar Allan Poe short story. The short story is so condensed, so pure. We stretched it a little. We added a love story. But it had its qualities. Some scenes turned out well.

Bogart called "The Amazing Dr. Clitterhouse," by Litvak, "The Strange Dr. Clitoris" . . . (laughter).

I think that's true . . . It's quite possible! *(laughter).* I was only a scriptwriter under contract with Warner and some scenarios needed work (doctoring). I was considered a possible doctor who could fix them. It wasn't a very good film, but Edward G. Robinson was funny. Bogart was in it? I had forgotten that Bogie played in the film . . .

As a scriptwriter under contract, could you write about original subjects or only work on scenarios already written?

Both. It was a wonderful experience. Between the time when I worked at Universal and when I was hired by Warner, the average level of films rose sharply. And when I went to work at Warner, I had a good reputation. They bought a story I wrote with Howard Koch, *Three Strangers,* then I worked a little on *Jezebel* by Wyler and on two films by Dieterle: *Juarez* and *Dr. Ehrlich's Magic Bullet.* Those two scenarios were very good and I was a little disappointed by the films. I worked for almost a year on *Juarez* with two other people. Aeneas McKenzie and Wolfgang Reinhardt, who had contributed a lot. There was a lot of truth, an ideal, and some very well-written scenes. Aeneas McKenzie worked at Warner in the history research department. I took him away from that and he became a very good scriptwriter and an excellent collaborator. That was the good side of Warner. They supported us and left us entirely free. I'd like to take advantage of this time to praise the conception of cinema that the big studios had (and especially Warner, which was the best of all) and to say something in their favor . . . People have said so many bad things about the big companies . . . They need a lawyer . . . But when I saw the film, I noticed that they had a made a lot of changes because of Paul Muni. It wasn't nearly as good as the scenario.

Did Dieterle collaborate on the scenario?

No! And when I saw the film, I said to myself: "I never want to write again, to spend a year and be disappointed by the result." I broke my contract to become a director. Muni messed up *Juarez.* He was a good actor, which doesn't necessarily mean that you possess the slightest degree of intelligence.

At that time, Warner films had a certain style . . .

That was due to a number of things. First, there was Darryl Zanuck, who was young at the time, and wanted to draw scenarios from the front page of the newspapers. Then, there were several excellent producers: first, Henry Blanke who produced *Pasteur* and *Dr. Ehrlich* and

*Juarez.* Robert Lord also was very good. Finally, there was a whole group of writers and scriptwriters. Warner gave great importance to the scriptwriter and that didn't exist at the other studios, except maybe at MGM, but in a completely different way. At Metro, they had to write for stars. At Warner, the scriptwriter came first and it was the story which counted because of the politics of this little group of men. First and foremost Zanuck, then Blanke and Lord. Hal Wallis succeeded Zanuck. He was a very intelligent man. I said that I was going to defend the system of the old studios. It was good at least for the scriptwriter. When you're paid by the week, it doesn't matter how much time you spend on a scenario. Whereas if you are paid for each scenario, you hurry to finish it so you can start another.

**And at Warner, the directors were freer, especially regarding editing, and had access to actual exterior sets, as opposed to those at MGM . . .**

That's true. In this regard, Warner was truly an extraordinary studio, and I have nothing but praise for it. But it was the studio system which was good. A film never started before the scenario seemed perfect; but once it was finished, they didn't like for the director to get involved in rewriting it. They wanted him to follow the scenario. For example, at that time, I had no contact with the director. Scriptwriters didn't go on the set. They worked for the producer. The producer gave the script to the director. Sometimes the director had ideas or suggestions and they were communicated to the scriptwriter through the intermediary, the producer. You had to be a very well-known scriptwriter to talk to the director.

**Were your scenarios cut technically?**

Yes, I have technical indications, but the director paid no attention!

**What do you think of "High Sierra"?**

I like it a lot. Yes, a lot . . . Walsh really had . . . He had "something": an incredible instinct. Burnett's book was remarkable. He wrote a great deal of excellent books which were massacred on the screen and that should be redone: *The Iron Man,* for example . . . People have said *High Sierra* was influenced by the Fritz Lang film *You Only Live Once,* but I think it was a coincidence. I am very proud of this film, and that's how I would have filmed it.

216

*Have you worked on scenarios without being mentioned in the credits?*

That only happened to me once. With Anthony Veiller, I wrote the scenario for *The Killers,* by Robert Siodmak from the Hemingway work. I was in the service at the time and I didn't want my name on the film: I didn't want to be part of these men in uniform who filled the credits of films then. But I didn't work with Brooks on the film. It was Tony Veiller and I who wrote the scenario.

*What was your role on "Sergeant York"?*

It was Lasky who had chosen the story and who had brought it to Jack Warner with Hawks. I don't know how I got involved . . . I don't remember any more if it was through Lasky or Hawks. I worked quite a bit with Hawks, especially on the dialogues. He is a remarkable director and the film was well done.

*Your admirers often reproach you for this film, which they consider militaristic.*

The first thing you can say is that it's a true story. It is a raw news item. And this news item is extraordinary. You know, it took place almost exactly as it was shown in the film. He was an aggressive mountain man who liked to drink a lot. One day lightning struck near him and he took that as a sign from God, particularly because his rifle had melted. He believed that God was showing that violence should be forbidden through this sign. When he was called up for service, he refused to use a weapon. It was only after a time and then with a heavy heart that he gave in. That's when the extraordinary episode in the trenches occurred, when he fired on the Germans. I talked to York about it on several occasions and he told me, and this is what is fascinating, that he was convinced that he was saving hundreds of lives by acting in this way. He said to himself: "If I destroy this machine gun, I am saving thousands of people." He still believed it when we discussed it!

*What do you think of this character?*

First, that he is very funny. You know, York was a very amusing man and I tried to make that felt in the film. I tried to show his comic side. And then, dramatically, he is a fascinating individual. I don't think that the film presented a very profound or politically involved message. If there was a moral, it was a little like that of all the war films of the period, including those written by the Communists, like John Howard Lawson. But it was above all an incredible story. We didn't want to do *All Quiet on the Western Front*. There's a film that intended to show the First World War with all its horror in order to strike the spectator harder, to convince him that we mustn't start up again . . . As for us, we chose to treat the story of an individual, of a particular case. It is completely childish and absurd to try to find a general moral in it. I think that Hawks, who is a great director, is a reactionary man, in life at least. It doesn't show, either in the films he makes or when you work with him!

It has been said that you played a big role in "Three Strangers."
No, that's not true. I had written the original story, then a scenario that was rewritten by Howard Koch who changed a lot of things. I based my story on an actual event—something that had happened to me in London. There were three of us in a room and we bought a ticket for the Great National [Lottery]. I was going through a difficult period and we did it for fun. In fact, at that time, I didn't even have a place to sleep and I wandered around between the docks and Hyde Park. Our ticket won and my share was around a hundred pounds. Those hundred pounds represented the greatest sum I had ever received! I based *Three Strangers* around that.

It's also the beginning of "Sierra Madre."
Yes, that's true, even though the lottery ticket is also in the book by Traven, the mysterious author. Everybody thinks that Traven was the man who claimed to be Traven's secretary but I don't agree. I believe that for a very precise reason: I saw that man a lot and he never gave the slightest hint of possessing the least creative ability. And Traven must have had almost boundless creativity. To be honest, I should say that I know somebody else, Ray Bradbury, for whom the corner café is the planet Jupiter. And he will never take a plane! He has a lucid style, filled with marvelous poetic images, and his conversation . . . I think he is the dullest man I have ever known! Every time he opens his mouth, clichés come out. He is walking banality! However, he writes wonderful stories.

218

**Have you worked with Dashiell Hammett?**

No, but I knew him well. He is one of the most extraordinary men I have ever known! He had great personal elegance: He always wore gloves and used a cane. His appearance had nothing to do with fashion. He had a handsome face, the face of an intellectual, of an ascetic. Aside from that, he was the biggest alcoholic I ever met! And the most dangerous! He had a gift for getting involved in scandalous situations. He was always in the midst of people trying to kill each other with knives or, in the best of circumstances, of knocking each other on the head with broken bottles. And suddenly you would see Dash take his cane and his coat and disappear! He was a delightful man. He had no instinct of self-preservation. I heard a story about Dash which took place during the time he worked as a detective for Pinkerton. His calf was cut by a razor. It happened during a raid and they were evacuating the place. Dash's leg had been deeply sliced, so deeply that the skin was hanging out of his pants' leg. Somebody said to Dash: "Good God, pick that up and hold it, at least for a minute," and Dash did it, at least for a minute. Then he forgot and left!

Dash was a gentleman, a true gentleman. I'll never forget the night when he called me. I had just come back to Hollywood after being away awhile and Dash invited me to a party . . . We were still in the midst of Prohibition. It took place in a private club in the country. And Dash, who loved jazz, invited the band to join him in the suite he had in the Knickerbocker Hotel. And the band played on until three o'clock in the morning. The telephone rang constantly. I had been there five minutes when somebody knocked violently at the door and Dash, who had been pouring a drink, went to open it, a bottle in his hand. He closed the door back and returned to the room. It was rather strange: He hadn't been gone long enough to talk to anybody. I went to open the door and I saw a man lying unconscious on the floor in front of the door. Dash had opened the door, struck him with a bottle and closed the door!

He was a lucid artist and a cultivated man. A very great stylist who knew what he was doing. He was also Lillian Hellman's mentor and a very involved writer, politically speaking. During the war, I spent some time in the Aleutian Islands. It was an out-of-the-way, godforsaken spot. Dash had volunteered for service because he was past the normal draft age. They sent him to the Aleutian Islands as a sergeant and from there he edited and directed the *Aleutians,* the soldiers' newspaper. Nobody stayed there long, otherwise you would go mad. Dash refused to leave. He had to be given precise, strict orders before he would leave his post. He didn't want to go back to America. After the war, he lived in a little cottage owned by Lillian Hellman near a lake. There, he pampered himself and took care of the house . . . I visited him. The walls were covered with photos, drawings, reproductions, all representing the human eye. He studied the human eye constantly. That's where he was picked up by the Committee on Un-American Activities.

Is that what destroyed him?

No, not him. Anybody else, but not him. I was abroad at the time, but Lillian Hellman visited him regularly. He was totally happy and couldn't have cared less about being in prison. And you remember what he told them, the senators and the members of Congress who were questioning him and who said: "Did you know that by refusing to answer, you are in contempt of court?"—"There are no words to express the contempt I feel for this court!"

In *The Maltese Falcon,* I tried to be as faithful as possible to the dialogues he had written. He was an extraordinary novelist! I simply translated the novel into images. It was a joy to make this film. During that time, given the politics of the big studios, the actors knew their lines. They didn't arrive on the set unprepared. Take Peter Lorre for example . . . He was a man with a very subtle humor and a refined actor. When I filmed a scene with him, I never had the impression that it was particularly good. And when I saw it on the screen, it was a discovery: It was ten times better than I thought.

We have never seen "In This Our Life" . . .

It wasn't a very good film. You haven't missed anything . . . To thank me for having done so well with *The Maltese Falcon,* they gave me this film with a prestigious cast . . . Only big names! I was flattered that they gave me a production of this importance for my second film. Howard Koch had written the scenario and there was an interesting side: the racial theme. It was the first time, I believe, that a black was presented in a serious manner in an American film. It was the only worthwhile point of the film along with the circular structure, which was due to Koch.

*"Across the Pacific"* is a very amusing film which deserves better than its reputation . . .

There were some very amusing moments: The scenes in the boat are full of humor and derision. I guess you know what happened? Since I knew I was going to be drafted, I arranged it so that I left the film when Bogart was in an inextricable situation, surrounded by hundreds of enemies, menaced by machine guns . . . And Vince Sherman had a tough time getting Bogart out of the mess. It was absolutely impossible . . . All the critics said the end was not nearly as good as the rest of the film. I didn't dare come back for four years!

What do you think of your documentaries, like *"Battle of San Pietro"*?

I like them a lot. *Report from the Aleutians* wasn't bad. As for *Battle of San Pietro,* the people from Staff Headquarters didn't like it, not at all. They didn't want it to be shown. General Marshall saw it, and said: "Have this film shown." He liked it and it was he and he alone who permitted the release of the film. There were at least two versions of this film. But even in its long version, there are cuts. I think however that they were right for I had gone overboard. I had made interviews with young soldiers. I didn't keep the questions in the final editing. And in these interviews, they talked about the meaning the war had for them, what they felt, the role they had played and quite a few of the answers were very touching, very profound. I had made twenty-five or thirty of these interviews. Then, among these young soldiers, several were killed. I put the text they had said when they were still alive over the images of the cadavers. It was too heartrending, too unbearable. And think of the families seeing that . . . So it was cut. I still wonder if it was right to cut them . . . I don't know . . . On the one hand, it was too . . .

And *"Let There Be Light"* was never shown . . .

No, it was banned and still is . . .

That's where you got the idea to make *"Freud"*?

Yes, my interest in Freud dates from that experience. I swear to you, I don't know what got hold of them to make them ban it. It isn't a shocking film. They thought, I suppose, that to see the effect war can have on minds is more frightening that the sight of mutilated bodies. You can stand to see an operation or a man without a leg, but not a brain, a deranged, unhinged mind. In fact the film tells of the readaptation of these men, how they are brought back and set on their feet. It was almost a religious experience to see them evolve mentally and to witness psychiatric experiments. The film ends at a baseball game: One of the soldiers who couldn't speak is the announcer for the game, another who was paralyzed is running form one base to another, a third whose entire body trembled dreadfully plays the batter. And nothing was planned in advance. I simply put these men on a baseball field . . . They were, I wouldn't say healed, but back on their feet. They felt as well as when they entered the army. People have tried for years to have this film released, with no success. Every month, somebody calls me from one country or another, requesting this film. And I know that the War Department was contacted several times and the answer was always negative. Only doctors under special circumstances have been able to see it.

**Some people have claimed that Bogart's death in "Sierra Madre" was filmed by another director.**
That's absolutely false. In fact, it was the first time that a director in Hollywood filmed a fight or action sequence himself. Usually, this type of scene was entrusted to a stuntman, who prepared the whole sequence. In *Sierra Madre,* the stuntman started and I stopped him in order to shoot it myself . . .

**Key Largo seems rather theatrical now.**
I am certain of it. It comes out theatrical and a bit old-fashioned!

**The end bears some resemblance to Hemingway's book, "To Have and Have Not."**
I never thought of that, but now that you mention it . . . It is quite possible that I was influenced in an unconscious way by Hemingway's book. [Richard] Brooks must not have thought of it either. He was a very good scriptwriter, excellent for everything concerning dramatic art. He has a lot of strength and vitality and works very hard. He is a very disciplined writer and a good director. I think that *Elmer Gantry* was a phenomenally well-made film and very fascinating . . . I don't know *The Last Hunt* . . .

"We Were Strangers" marked your first collaboration with Peter Viertel . . .

Ah, yes, the film that takes place in Cuba . . . There were interesting things in it, but it wasn't a very good film. I felt the opposite at the time and then, one day, I saw it again, several years later, and I found it very disappointing. It was a little ersatz . . . The theme wasn't treated very well, the moral wasn't clear and it was too sentimental. You always felt you were dealing with actors. When you see them get deeper into the characters, it isn't realistic at all. There are several good scenes: when the little man arrives and teaches them to make the bomb, the funeral that they change, things like that, but on the whole it is very disappointing. That said, when I made it, they called me a Communist. They accused me of making a film which showed people what to do to overthrow the American government.

You were never called in front of the Committee on Un-American Activities?

No, I didn't hide what I thought of that committee and of its practices. During the interrogations, I led a group of people in Washington to protest against Parnell Thomas. The American Legion picketed the premiere of *Moulin Rouge,* marching with signs accusing me of being a Communist. But I wasn't a Communist and everybody knew it. In fact, I was and am anti-Communist . . . Philosophically, I can't accept communism, but they had the right to express themselves and to say what they wanted to say . . . It was a violation of constitutional rights. Parnell Thomas and McCarthy destroyed one of the democratic waves of this country, which has never really gotten over it. Part of the events happening today are due to the fear those abominable individuals caused . . .

Your company produced "The Prowler" by Losey?

Exactly, but I had nothing to do with the film. Spiegel took care of the production. It's a good film.

Was it after your trip to Washington that Bogart changed his mind?

Yes, he said that he had been ill-advised . . . It's sad, but I have to say that the pressures were terrible. And the result was not only the destruction of some individuals, but what is worse, these pressures created an atmosphere of fear which paralyzed the whole country and prevented it from coming to the aid of the few people who were fighting to save democracy. When they spoke of a black list, you would have thought that the people of the U.S.A. would stand up and say: "No, stop this," but nothing happened. It took a long time for anybody to attack this oppressive system: Ed Murrow was the first, but a long time afterward. New York and California were devoured by fear. People were afraid of losing their jobs. I'll never forget the night when I was part of a Directors Guild meeting. And there was this absurd thing of making people raise their hands to prove, to swear that they weren't Communist. It was stupid and the sole purpose it served was to take the liberals' voices away. A motion was made, stipulating that the oath be spoken. Then an amendment was added dealing with whether the oath would be written or through a show of hands. The rumor was circulated that all those who were against a show of hands were pro-Communist. And everybody supported the hand vote, except for me and Billy Wilder, who was seated next to me. There were two of us against one hundred and there were whispers in the room. We were Communists. That was the last Directors Guild meeting I attended . . . The sad part of this story is that the accusers didn't cause a great deal of harm to other people. They caused it to themselves and they dirtied the soul of America. A lot of the informants came about as a sort of agreement: "You denounced me and I'll denounce you." It was a deal of sorts . . .

**"Asphalt Jungle" is one of your best films.**
I love it . . . I saw Hayden the other day . . . He denounced people too, but afterward, he declared: "I'm ashamed of having done that," and I take my hat off to him. He wrote a beautiful book which is dedicated to the man he betrayed, the Yugoslav who introduced him to the Communist Party. He is an anarchist, a solitary wolf . . . And I was very proud of him when he publicly declared: "I behaved shamefully." It's a shame he doesn't appear in more films. He has tremendous style, an admirable face and my God! He is taller than I am . . . He never mixes in with the crowd . . . He's not a fake.

**"Asphalt Jungle" has been imitated a lot.**
Yes, but the directors always make an enormous error. They give utmost importance to the hold-up, to the crime, and forget the characters.

In my film, the hold-up was secondary. The motivations for the hold-up were much more important. A lot of people found the film immoral, because you are forced to sympathize with the criminals . . . Obviously, to treat a subject, a character, you first understand it/him and in understanding it, you identify a little with the subject or the character. Those people were afraid of what the film awakened in them. They felt like criminals in understanding the state of mind of the criminals. Burnett has a very deep and very strong approach for this state of mind. He is an extremely subtle observer.

**The end was inspired . . .**

We wanted to convey something very precise: this man must have been raised among horses, but he was too tall to ride horses and not intelligent enough to become a trainer. He began to bet and that caught him up in the system. And suddenly there was this terrible need to return home and he fell in the field. And if you fall in a field, you will see the horses coming near to look at you, whoever you are. His true home was with these horses . . .

**People have reproached Burnett for being sentimental toward his gangster characters . . .**

That's false. He isn't sentimental. But he knows this type of character so well that he is taken by friendship for them. You know, you can't beat Burnett when it comes to the Underworld . . . Burnett's genius, what strikes me each time I read one of his books, one of his good books, is the fantastic way in which he conveys the reality of characters and objects. Few writers know how to bring such a degree of reality into their works with the exception sometimes of Hemingway . . . He isn't the sentimental type, quite the contrary. He likes his heroes, secretly. I read one of his last books . . . He had sent me the manuscript . . . It's impossible to make a film of it because he did something he shouldn't have. It's about a criminal who finds the daughter he never knew twenty years later. The meeting is so fortuitous, but the man's character is superb . . . Burnett can introduce you into the interior of the thought system not only of a criminal, but of a marginal individual. You should read his Westerns and especially *St. Johnson!* In *Asphalt Jungle,* there was a very well-written character who was superbly portrayed: James Whitmore's character [Gus Minissi]. [Whitmore is] an incredible actor who brings a quality, a dignity, to everything he does . . . Later, they wanted to set him up as the new Tracy, which was a mistake. He wasn't Tracy, he was Whitmore. There was a whole philosophy to his acting.

**It's been said that Andrew Marton played an important role in the battle sequence of Red Badge . . .**
Let me think . . . We rehearsed the stunts with several experts and then we rehearsed the entire film which was filmed in record time: six weeks I think. Marton was there. He's a great person for this kind of scene. In the case of *Red Badge,* he didn't direct himself. He followed my instructions. Practically speaking, there was no second string work. Marton helped me plan the battle strategy and set it up . . .

**In an interview done by Mary Blum, Audie Murphy made some statements running counter to "his character" and coming closer to the moral of your film . . .**
You know, Audie is a fascinating guy! Very intelligent. He has a sort of genius: When he is possessed by violence, he moves about as if he were an angel . . . He has moments of depression. I have sometimes thought, and that bothered me a lot because I love Audie, that he was going to commit suicide. One time in particular, I thought that he was going to do it. He didn't say anything, but I knew that he was turning the idea over in his mind . . .

**You chose him because he was the most decorated soldier.**
Oh no, not at all . . . I chose him for himself, not for what he represented. I think that he was great in the film. We met in Italy during the war. And after the war, I got to know him better and we became very good friends. Audie was very frank and very courageous from the political point of view. And for obvious reasons, nobody dared accused him of being anti-American or Communist. He wasn't a politician or a politically active artist, no more than I was I might add, but we had the same opinions . . . He was a very sensitive individual and he could have become a good director. But Audie is a gambler, an obsessed gambler. He puts all his money on horses and he's the unluckiest gambler I have ever known! I never saw him win anything at all in any game . . . He

was forced to work to pay his taxes and his debts . . . I have a theory about Audie . . . I think he used up all his potential for luck during the war in staying alive. He doesn't have any left for dice or the track. It seems that I have always attracted individuals deprived of any instinct of self-preservation. Take James Agee for example . . . He was a wonderful man and a marvelous writer. He died two years after *African Queen,* but he had his first heart attack while we were working together. He almost died. He was lying there stretched out on a bed and nobody knew if he would be still be breathing in five minutes. I went into the room, forgetting to put out my cigarette and suddenly I realized. Too late. He opened his eyes and said to me: "John give me a puff."—"But it's going to kill you . . . "—"It doesn't matter." Afterward, I tried several times to reason with him, to get him to change his life-style. He would look at me, smile and continue . . . He died very young.

### Where did you get the idea for "Beat the Devil"?

It was thanks to one of my friends who live in Ireland. He traveled all over the world as a correspondent for the *London Times.* He became a Communist and founded a paper called *The Week.* It was read as much by bankers as by journalists. It was a cooperative political paper. During the war, he had to stop his paper and come to live in Ireland. He went through a very dismal period. He is a very funny guy, very brilliant, who wrote quite a few books, including a fascinating autobiography. He wrote a book called *Beat the Devil.* It was a little amusing book, full of ideas. Since he needed money, I was able to convince Bogart to buy it for his production company, which also made films without Bogart. One day, Bogart called me: "You made me buy a book that I can't get free from. The only way to be rid of it is to make a film with me in the principal role. So, it's up to you to get me out of this." Peter Viertel and Tony Veiller wrote a scenario and it wasn't very good. It was even rather bad. But we had to go ahead and make the film. I arrived in Rome and met Bogart and we hired a few actors. We still didn't have a script . . . I remember saying to Bogie: "We can cancel everything and I'll split the costs with you." Bogart wasn't much of a big spender, I might even say that he was rather a skinflint, but he answered: "I don't give a damn, we're doing it." It was his money . . . Capote was in Rome. I knew him only through his stories, but he was a writer and he was in Rome. I needed somebody to work with . . . We only had two weeks before beginning to shoot. We started to write, but hadn't made much progress when we had to start shooting . . . We went to Ravello, the place chosen for the film, by car with Bogart. We were on the road to Naples and that's where we got the idea . . . The driver hesitated between which one of the two roads to take and suddenly he slammed the car into a brick wall. Bogie was sleeping in the back seat . . . I was awake and unharmed. After impact, I got up and looked around: no Bogie . . . Suddenly, he got out and a sonorous pulp escaped from his mouth: "Wheeeeeeerre aaaam I?" and his front teeth were gone. And I was laughing while he was spewing out incomprehensible sounds *(outburst of laughter as Huston imitates Bogart)*. We had to send him to the hospital and we lost a little more than a week. They had to order new teeth from the States. Luckily, most of those he had lost were false. We started writing, but production soon caught up with us and we had to write the scenario day by day. But we had found a style . . . Nobody knew what we were doing, ourselves included, but we had a style . . .

You have practiced very rewarding "miscasting" . . .
Yes, especially with Lollobrigida. It was very funny.

Cukor, who was supposed to do "Lady L" with her, thought that she was the worst actress in the world and the stupidest.
Let's say that she is not Katharine Hepburn, but she has a certain form of talent . . .

The line: "Those men are gangsters because they didn't look at my legs." Was that yours or Capote's?
It was in the book, I think. That was a great line. The fascist Major character was also partially in the book. We had a ball doing this film and everybody collaborated. With Morley and Lorre, I did a pastiche of my own work: They were the couple from the *Maltese Falcon,* but not at all dangerous.

Certain critics, like Luc Moullet, have claimed that the film was shot in color and printed in black and white.
No, that's false. The film was shot in black and white.

**Weren't you tempted by the role of Ahab?**

Yes, of course, but I like Peck's performance very much. It is very underestimated. He was hampered by the image people had of him and they were very hard on him about his acting (in *Moby Dick*) which was superb. He had a dignity, a depth, an O'Neill side. It was Peck who added the O'Neillesque side . . . The film itself was a blasphemy, an extraordinary blasphemy. I don't think any critic has ever written the word blasphemy. And it is nevertheless the central subject of the film. I was so happy with Peck that I wanted to do *Typee* with him. But we had to give up the idea. *Moby Dick* was not a success except on the critical side. It has become a success now. But at the time I would have expected the film to be better received by the public. I've never known box office triumphs and what is certain is that my favorite films are not those that made the most money. I am rather indifferent about *Moulin Rouge,* for example, except for color studies. I have a particular tenderness for *African Queen,* even though it is a work which is foreign to me. I don't feel like it is one of *my* films. It is in another vein . . .

**We prefer "Heaven Knows, Mr. Allison" to "African Queen"** . . .

*Heaven Knows* is a completely under-appreciated film, critically speaking at least. Critics approached it with a preconceived notion: They thought they were going to see a little sexual play about the relationship between a marine and a nun. I did the opposite. I wanted to obtain a pure, virginal, extremely sensitive rapport. These two characters had to be very sensitive. Somebody, I think it was in *Time,* wrote that it was a voyeuristic spectacle! An imbecile! I have always liked this film. The book was very bad and changes the moral, the relationship, everything. It was disgusting, humorless. I got along very well with John Lee Mahin, the remarkable scriptwriter, but it is untrue that Ring Lardner, Jr., collaborated on the film.

**How do you interpret the end?**

She will continue to be a nun. She doesn't throw away her veil. Everything will continue as before. I didn't mean to say anything else.

**Did you get along well with Mitchum?**

He is one of the most incredible characters in the world today. An unbelievable guy! And an admirable actor. He is one of the people I prefer. Do you remember when he crawls through the grass to reach the Japanese tent? We shot the scene once and I asked for a second take, then a third. And each time, he had to go where the grass had not been trampled down. We could have kept the first take. I said: "That's good, it's a take," and he turned around. I noticed that his body was covered with blood. I hadn't seen it before because he kept his back to me. The grass was not only incredibly sharp (it was the most fearsome kind), but it was poisonous. It was worse than crawling over razor blades. And he had turned his back to me so I wouldn't see the blood and so he would be ready to crawl again if I asked . . . That's the kind of man Mitchum is. And at the same time he is the most sensitive individual who exists. He is a true anarchist and under the gruff exterior, a cultured guy and a good musician . . . He doesn't take himself too seriously, which is a quality in this day and time. You can't imagine how happy I am that you say you like this film. I had such a good time making it . . . You remember Mitchum's raids on the Japanese camp, the troops landing on the island. And Deborah Kerr, she was wonderful!

Flynn liked "Roots of Heaven" a lot . . .

He was very good in that film and I liked him a lot. But the film is bad. It's sad. It could have been a very good film and I take complete responsibility for the failure . . .

They said that you killed elephants during the filming.

That's false. I didn't kill any . . . I chased some, but didn't kill any.

But you tried.

Yes, I tried . . . but it didn't work. I never found one with tusks big enough to allow us to commit this sin . . . During the filming, Flynn was dying. He also had a fascinating style, a side beyond control. In the past we had some very strange dealings. It was at a party a long time ago. He had said something bad about somebody, we argued and finally we decided to fight. Without being seen, we went to the far end of the garden and fought for a very long time. We had to stop when the lights from the departing cars suddenly shone on us. I had been on the ground at least ten times. Flynn had high and low moments . . . They had to put us in two different hospitals and the next day he called me to see how I was doing. Then we lost track of each other and it was Zanuck, who knew about the story, who suggested his name for the role. In Africa, I got to know him and to like him. He was an admirable man. He knew that he was dying and didn't care. He often stayed up at night, a bottle of vodka in his hand, and we talked. He drank a bottle a night and the minute there was the slightest delay, he got dead drunk and we'd need drugs to get him back on his feet. He was a very touching man and an underrated actor! One day I wanted to organize a little hunting expedition and, to avoid being bothered, I kept the departure date secret. But Flynn guessed the truth and left with me. The heat was horrible and you had to be in incredible physical condition. And he held up . . . Of course he didn't walk as much as we did, but he got along incredibly well without a drop of alcohol. All of a sudden, he was alive again, he was another man. He spent some wonderful days there and I was very happy that he had come with me. Several months later he died . . . He was another person who had no instinct for self-preservation. There was something mysterious about him . . . I am sure that there was a secret hidden in his life . . . Something must have happened in his past, with his family, with his mother . . . I don't know . . . But there was a mystery.

**One gets the impression in "The Unforgiven" that John Saxon's character is not complete . . .**

It was demolished! It don't think it was a very good film. There were some interesting things. They'd had a preview with great results. Wonderful reactions, particularly concerning John Saxon's character which was very good in the film, let me say that in passing. And I don't know what happened. I left and they cut the film for mysterious reasons. There was a scene where he came to warn the whites that they were going to be attacked even though he didn't like them. He didn't like Lancaster. Then after warning them, he left. They saw him fall from his horse and he was dead. He had been wounded, coming to warn them, by the Indians. Nobody liked him and he didn't like anybody.

**He was somewhat the mirror of the character played by Audrey Hepburn.**

Yes. He was a little bit in the same situation except he wasn't an Indian. Everybody thought he was but he was Portuguese . . . In cutting the role, they gave the film an ambiguous moral, even a racist one. He was the key character.

**How was the book by Alan Le May?**

Interesting; not great, but interesting, especially for literature on Westerns. Ben Maddow did great work. The way in which the Joseph Wiseman character was written . . . It was at once strong and realistic. There were a lot of eccentric types in the West at that period. And I wanted to make a film about the different types of fanaticism. Religious, racial, familial fanaticism. And also to show how the Indians had been treated. Worse yet than blacks. The crime committed by the United States against the Indians is much greater than all that has been done to blacks. My grandmother believed that the only good Indian was a dead Indian. What we did to them was one of the greatest disgraces of history.

**But the piano scene can be interpreted as a victory of white civilization over barbaric music.**

My sympathies were with the Indians, but, on the other hand, the whites were the ones who were attacked. That happened often at the time. And I wanted to show that there was no victor. The piano was one of the means of defense . . . They used it as if it were magic.

**Yes, but it covers the Indian music and at the end, Lancaster fires on the Indians first and the public identifies with him.**

I would have preferred that the public not identify with Lancaster, but it's implicit, you can't help it. Sometimes the action is not clear because of the cuts, but at any rate, I don't believe that it's a good film. I like the scene when John Saxon tames the horse a lot. There's a great attraction between him and Hepburn, because they are from the same mold. I chose Audie Murphy for the role of the racist brother because of his untamed side. You can get a kind of madness from him, and he's very good in the film.

**The second part of "Freud" seems much longer than the first.**

The film was much better in its long version (two hours and forty minutes). I wanted it to be projected in two parts, but they didn't believe it was the kind of film that could fare well with special ticket prices. If there were horses running in it, it might have been possible. I think that *Freud* is a well-told story, that its pace, its logic are proper. That is due in part to Sartre who worked on the original scenario. Now, certain things are no longer very clear; for example, Freud's idea that neurosis was provoked by fathers who molested their daughter. Dreams must seem as concrete as any other form of thought. They were lacking an interpretation. And they were an intimate part of Freud's theory. People have discussed and worked on these dreams, on the way of presenting them . . . Do I dream like you? In color? Maybe all our dreams resemble each other. That is what Freud says. And from a technical standpoint, I had to draw from my own dreams since I was not violating any secret. A dream is an exclusive, enormous thing. We only see the essential. Everything disappears except this lone word or mental image.

**Do you mean to say that you put some of your dreams in "Freud"?**
From the technical viewpoint only, not the content. No, I simply took the plastic side from my dreams, the images of old films where there is no contrast. We used an old film to get this effect. It looked like a silent film.

**Why did you choose Larry Parks?**
I remembered what a good actor he was. What I like in him was his conservative side, "square," intelligent, methodical. I don't know why he doesn't appear in more films. After what happened to him during McCarthyism, he gave up the cinema and got rich in business. He was happy to play this role but he makes no effort to continue.

**"The List of Adrian Messenger" was a joke?**
Yes, but it was funny. I think it was a well-told story. For me, it was a good detective story, but the film wasn't popular and I know a lot of people who hated it.

**You were supposed to direct "This Property is Condemned" . . .**
In the long run, it didn't interest me. It was adapted from a very short Tennessee Williams play and the script didn't open up to anything very interesting.

**It was sort of "in the style" of Tennessee Williams . . .**
That's it exactly, you are absolutely right.

233

What was your approach for the "Night of the Iguana"?

I wanted to make a funny film with moments of lyricism. Plus, I like the film. I like the acting.

Have you thought about [Buñuel's] "Nazarin"?

No, but maybe I should have . . . *(laughter)*. It is very close to the Tennessee Williams play. We added several scenes. Tennessee even came for a while and wrote two sequences: He is walking on broken glass; *that* was his sequence. It is very good. I like Deborah Kerr a lot in the film. There's an actress I love. Inside her is something very deep and very complex which contradicts her appearance and the type of roles she is too often given. She can be very erotic like in *From Here to Eternity* and very reserved.

You seem to never have problems with actors?

That's true. In all my career I have had problems with only two actors: Susannah York and John Wayne. With Wayne, there weren't exactly problems but we didn't like each other much. Susannah York, who is very good in the film, was a pain to direct. It was the beginning of the "hip" generation, of rebellious actors. In fact, they were catching up to Hollywood, ten years behind and snobbier: People like Brando were far ahead of them. This attitude of "angry young star" which ran rampant in England bugged me royally. This tearoom anarchism . . . But in the long run, she was good.

What interested you the most in "Night of the Iguana"?

Above all, the character Shannon, who is both funny and tragic, which is a good mixture. It's a little like Brando in *Reflections in a Golden Eye*. Burton has this same inexplicable quality, of knowing how to mix intimately, and in one movement, absurdity and depth. Think about his relations with the old maids. I like the film and I like my work in the film. There is only one scene that I think I failed with. It's the first sequence in the church, when he is speaking to the worshippers. That should have been funnier. It was too straight. It was the first scene I shot and I didn't realize it until I saw it on screen. It should have been funny: He slept with that woman. Everybody knew it . . . It isn't an illustration from the play. That provoked some problems with Tennessee, for whom I have the greatest admiration . . . maybe not the greatest, but almost. He is one of the good writers of his generation.

### He had written a short at first?

Yes, then a one-act play, then two acts, then three acts. In the play, the Ava Gardner character was different. She was the spider who catches men and imprisons them . . . You know, the old theme . . . And I couldn't manage to conceive that. The woman was at first described with love and then everything changed. Tennessee and I argued a lot about it. I accused him of hating women. And Tennessee said to me: "Maybe you're right!" *(laughter)*.

### What does the Sue Lyon character represent?

Oh! She is simply an excited, sex-hungry little girl. She's an empty character, not enigmatic at all; she is the kind of girl who brought trouble to Adam. I think that the seduction scene in the hotel is very amusing. I kept a big part of Tennessee's text and when I made changes, it was with his consent. I like the way he writes a lot. Sometimes it's a little sentimental and it's possible that his work ages quicker than that of some others. But I'll never forget *A Streetcar Named Desire* . . . He is a better short-story writer than a playwright. He doesn't have the classical rigor of Carson McCullers, who is a much more important writer and who surpasses Capote.

### Have you seen other film adaptations of Williams's work?

I have only seen *Sweet Bird of Youth,* which I didn't like much, especially because of the colors. Geraldine Page and Ed Begley were very good, but the colors bothered me. Speaking of colors, I'm sorry I can't see the original version of *Reflections* . . . I can't manage to deal with the color of the distributed copy. From the technical and production points of view I think that *Reflections* . . . is my best film.

### The car accident isn't in the book.

No, I added it for two reasons: I wanted to show that the major's thoughts were so centered around the young soldier that he wasn't aware of anything else around him. Everybody ran to see the accident and he didn't budge.

The young soldier didn't either.

There was an exchange of looks between them that wove a very strong bond. And this accident seemed trivial and unimportant to them. There were very few details in the script. For example, Brando crying in front of his students wasn't there. We added that during the shooting. There was quite a bit of improvisation.

**What direction did you give Brando when he is looking at himself in the mirror?**

That was a scene which was written. I wanted to show a man who is trying to protect the image he has of himself. And that image doesn't exist, it's a dream. He goes through a variety of feeling and states of mind: ambition, servility, satisfaction. He sees himself decorated, received by a general, promoted to an important position. He is superb in that sequence.

**It has been said that he changed his lines all the time.**

Not with me. He didn't change one line. He is the most obedient actor with whom I have worked. He is admirable in the scene with all the other officers before his wife comes back to lash him with the riding crop. He is at once present and absent, with them and not with them. He is absolutely fantastic for that kind of thing.

**A French critic wrote that Brando resembles Mussolini in the film.**

That's stupid, absolutely stupid! Brando possesses an exceptional power: He can take a small detail, appropriate it for himself, and integrate it as if it were a part of him. Look at the way he talks to the young soldier in the beginning, what he does with several lines!

**What are your favorite films?**

I think that I would put *Reflections* in first place . . . I like the film in its entirety. Then, certain sequences from *The Bible*, from *Freud, Moby Dick*. And finally *The Treasure of the Sierra Madre; Heaven Knows, Mr. Allison; The Maltese Falcon;* and *The Asphalt Jungle*. You can't know how touched I was about the way you spoke about *Reflections*. I haven't met half-a-dozen people who understood the film. I have to say that the critical level in the United States is appalling. I don't think there is a single one of them who knows how to talk about cinema. It is

236

incredibly poor. I saw a film that I was prepared to hate because "intelligent" people had told me so many bad things about it and I loved it: it was *Bonnie and Clyde*. It is an extraordinary work, steeped in the unknown and in adventure. Do you know *Twelve against the Gods?* There is a definition of the adventurer: An adventurer is somebody who begins by leaving his house and who then abandons all conventions and rules in order to seek something for its intrinsic value. Among the adventurers I can name, you have Cagliostro, Casanovo, Napoleon III, not Napoleon I. This search becomes their life and their reason for being. And all of a sudden, I felt that *Bonnie and Clyde* fit into this category: They had taken a funny way, a strange route—all those murders, robberies, assassinations—but they were succeeding in creating their own world. They were recreating their life! I thought it was incredibly well done. What Warren Beatty conveys in this film is phenomenal: this mixture of psychopathic neurosis, of exaggerated attitude and of genius, all that skillfully combined. And it was really a love story and their lives took on an immense significance. I can't praise this film enough. It's the best I've seen in years and years. And there was no false, doctored scene except for the scene with the mother, filmed through a filter. It was the only mistake and that's the sequence everybody talks about. And the violence . . . I don't like gratuitous violence, but in this case it had a meaning . . . When I think that in America they put *Bonnie and Clyde* on the same plane as *In the Heat of the Night* and *The Graduate* . . . Mike Nichols's film is well made and well casted, especially the secondary roles, but it's a bourgeois, narrow work. Whereas *Bonnie and Clyde* is pure adventure . . . It's so good that I'm surprised American critics like it!

# Fool

## JOHN HUSTON

Victor du Lara was a young Italian. He had the shape of head you often see on clever boys. You would call it conical. From a small hard jaw it widened upward to a cranium that was round like a bowl. He had a hard mouth, and his eyes were set wide apart. He was short with a strong back, so he could hold like a vise and pound in the clinches. He was a slugger with a lot of native speed. Like a nail he made his own openings, and he followed up fast, hammering like a carpenter.

Victor and myself, and a fellow named Harry who used to second for us, and a friend of Harry's, a man whose name I forget, who had just got out of the army, were all of us on the street car. We were coming away from Madison Square Garden down in Darktown.

Madison Square Garden is a Negro fight arena, named after the big Madison Square Garden in New York.

When I think about that ride I get elated. Something had happened that put me at the dirty end of the stick, I had done something terrible, I want to say that Victor and Harry and the soldier were three men of mercy. They laughed at my sin and didn't rub it in. They let it go at that. Their treatment rid my nature of a lot of rubbish.

Victor du Lara and I had gone as children to the same school, but we had not known each other. That is, we had never been friends. I was a few months younger than he, and that made a great difference. He was the crustiest boy in the school.

The neighborhood of the school was poor. Most of the students were the sons and daughters of low-class Italians and Negroes and Polacks. Besides myself, there was only one other child who could lay any claim to being well raised, and he was slightly effeminate. The Italian boys used to gang him on his way home—not from lack of nerve, for any one of them could have handled him. They only desired to share the pleasure. I envied them.

One night after school I was alone with the tormented fellow. I hoped vicariously to enjoy the companionship of the roughnecks by beating him myself. But it was a heartless effort. He made no resistance. The yard was deserted except for the effeminate boy and me. I had been awkward about starting the fight. He would resent nothing. Finally I pushed him over. When he got up I knocked him down with my fist. Then he sat in the sand, rubbing his eyes and weeping, while blood trickled out of his nose. I threw him my handkerchief and went home.

To and from school, and in the recess periods, Victor jumped rope and shadow boxed. He was the youngest in his room and he was small, but he could teach tricks to anybody in the school. Into the Negroes he put the fear of God. He called them jigaboos. I have seen him step into a group of blacks, measure the largest, and without warning slap him flat-handed. The jigaboos came to understand that any defense meant twice the punishment. Whenever they gathered there was always one posted to keep a nervous watch for Victor. When he came toward them they'd separate. He never picked on a jigaboo alone.

In those days all paths led to love and physical supremacy. They were the male and female and they embraced in constant beauty. The youth of the school were hot-blooded. Hardly any of us were graduated without physical experiences of love. At fourteen the Latin girls had swelling breasts. The eighth grade was a hotbed of romance.

Victor wore bracelets on his wrists, and rings too small for his fingers dangled on strings over his chest. The jewelry belonged to girls. It was secured by Victor's plights. He was a vowing lover.

His first professional fight was when he was sixteen. At the athletic club he had one or two starts. But he was full of contempt for the amateur. They tried to give him a bronze medal for clouting the State champion, but Victor said keep it: if he didn't get cash he wouldn't fight. His professional start was out at Monrovia, which is a little fight town about twenty-five miles away from the city. It is quite a fight center. They have several good Negro boys out there. They still have battles royal, which they wisely keep all black. They make up their main events by bringing two good boxers in. The crowds are mixed, but they are mostly white. It is a good tryout place.

Victor boxed a white man, who was getting old and going down. But he had been good in his day, and he had an awful stock of tricks. At Monrovia they like blood. They judge a card by the number of knockouts. The matchmaker out there would rather put a ham and good boy together than two evenly matched hams. The man Victor was to box had a little reputation, so the matchmaker must have thought it would be that kind of a fight. The State limit was four rounds. Victor forced the going from the first. His opponent was a general, and tried to stall by clinching. But he found that the young Italian was like a riveting machine. He could jar himself loose. Then the man got dirty. In a clinch he rolled the heel of his glove over Victor's nose, and when Victor lowered his head, he gave him his elbow and put his thumbs in his eyes.

Remember, this was Victor's first professional fight. He had boxed up at the athletic club with kids his own age. Here was something new. He'd never been up against a man like this before. What he did showed there was no dog in him. Nothing in Queensbury could help him. So he bared his teeth and caught his man by the throat. Then he hung on. That's the kind of a guy he was.

The beginning of our friendship was one day in the gymnasium he asked me to work out. It's best to be careful of a pickup. If you're known to be any good, and if he isn't afraid of you, he'll usually try and put one over for the crowd.

"All right if you'll take it easy. I only want to sweat."

We boxed nicely. Afterwards I took my rubdown. Victor asked me to be first. While I was being rubbed he talked.

"I'm no good with tall fellows like you unless I go hard. That's the only way I can fight. If you can't box you can't beat a man that won't fight. There are two kinds of fighters, offensive and defensive. What's your religion? Are you a Catholic?"

"No," I answered.

"But you believe in God."

"Yes, indeed."

We took our shower together. While the water rained down on him he stuck out his belly.

"You went to the Lincoln Heights school, didn't you?" he asked.

"Yes," I said. "I remember you. You were in the eighth grade when I was in the seventh. I only went there one year."

"Are you using your real name?"

"No." I told him what my real name was.

While we were drying he asked if I liked wine. I said that I did, and he invited me to come over to his house.

"There's no one there but my old lady."

When we got on our clothes I went with him.

His mother was a nice Italian lady, who spoke no English. She sat with me in the parlor and smiled, while Victor got wine and glasses. I do not believe she drank any, but held some in her glass, and smiled while we drank, which was her Latin breeding.

The ride on the street car that I spoke of at the start was after the night's bouts at Madison Square Garden, where Victor and I had both fought.

I want to say that an all-black crowd makes about the best audience there is. Jigaboos have a real sense of humor, no mistake. What happened that night a white audience would never have stood for.

We used to get only fifteen or twenty dollars for a fight out there. It would have been worth it if we had fought for nothing. Those blacks were a picnic. The referee was a jigaboo who had been a fighter himself. He was the most comic man I ever saw in a ring. He was a regular actor. It was worth the price of admission to see that man break up a clinch. He would knock with his knuckle on a boy's shoulder, very dignified, as though he were knocking at a door. Then when they broke he would thank them, bowing from the waist. That used to bring down the house.

The way they make up their cards out there was a scream. Two days in advance they wouldn't know who was going to fight. But the bills would have been out for a week. How they worked it was they just threw a lot of fake names on the poster. Then first come, first served. You could look over the programme, and choose for your own whichever name you liked best. Those jigaboos introduced me by six different names the times I fought.

This evening I fought an extra time to fill up a vacant spot on the bill. My first fight was the one I was matched for. It was with a big red-headed boy. They introduced me as Battling Levinsky, which is very funny, as I am neither Russian nor Jew. The first fight was no match. We were stopped in the third round. That black referee stopped more fights than any man I ever saw. Maybe it was because the matches out there were the craziest in the world. But all the boxers were not hams. Occasionally they brought in some good boys who were short on pin money, and two fine young Negroes were developed out there and got their start. Still, almost anybody could get on. At Madison Square I've seen boys fight in those Y.M.C.A. gymnasium pants, and tennis shoes.

The Irish kid whom I boxed that evening wasn't much above that class. He was heavier than I but he could never get inside my long arms. And for all his weight he wasn't even strong. Although I am not a hard hitter, they had to stop us because the Irish boy couldn't take it.

My second match you would never call a fight. It was with Victor to help him out. Everything was agreed upon beforehand. His boy did not show up, and there was no one on the card good enough to match him with. At Madison Square they never heard of a forfeit. He would either lose his twenty dollars, or we would have to pull a fake.

That fight was the funniest thing that ever went in a ring. I was a lightweight and very tall, and Victor du Lara was a welter. As I said there was an all-around understanding,—the matchmaker, the referee, even the audience.

To line us up just about as we were, I'll say that Victor was a hard hitter, a slugger with speed. He fought low, weaving his body and swinging them up from his hips, with his whole weight behind each blow. But for all that he was a very clean cut kind of boy. I was tall with long arms, and I knew how to keep them out. I was naturally a straight hitter, right from the start when I had my fights at grammar school. I developed a short jab in my left that was almost automatic. It would work without my thinking of it. The blow was not hard, you understand, but it was stinging and cutting, and it used to make them first mad and then disheartened.

We were introduced and the fight started. No two boys ever came together who could fake less convincingly. Victor with a slugger like himself, or I with the other kind of fighter, a more scientific person, might either of us have stalled it out. But the two of us together trying to bluff were the craziest pair you ever saw.

My left went out automatically, and chopped him right on the nose. I knew what I had done and I climbed into a clinch where I apologized. Victor, as he was a welter, could have killed me.

The jigaboo crowd knew what had happened. They laughed. If a white audience had been around that ring, we would have been mobbed. But jigaboos are either sillier than whites or they have a finer sense of humor. I'll leave it to you.

In the clinch Victor didn't answer me, but only pushed me off. I was frightened and puzzled. I didn't know whether he was angry or just keeping up the bluff. I broke clean and began to dance around. Then he came at me hard, or so I thought.

"I don't like to do this," I thought, "but if he is going to make a real fight of it I'll stay in as long as I can."

So I nailed him again right on the nose.

I heard the crowd yell. It was certainly a peculiar situation. Jigaboos are quick to see a thing. They could tell about my dilemma.

Victor drove in with a one-two, but I caught both blows on my forearms, and gave him back two short ones right square on his nose. I felt the bone give through the pads on my knuckles. A red clot big as a polliwog came down out of his nostril and hung over his lip. I was certainly afraid. I was worried for fear it was all a great mistake. I grabbed Victor's arm and yelled in his ear over the noise.

"Vic, did I hurt you?"

He said something back, but for the noise of those jigaboos I couldn't hear. I tried to see the expression on his face. He was so bloody I couldn't make him out. It was time. I went to my corner worse off than ever. In my corner I decided there was only one thing to do. Rather than take any chance about his meaning business, I'd leave an opening. If he wanted he could knock me cold. It would be better than my picking them off his nose that way, and he trying to do the right thing. I tried to catch his eye across the ring. I thought maybe if he could see me smile at him he might understand.

Harry, the man I spoke of, was my second. He was a friend of Victor's and friend of mine. As Harry liked us both I thought he might tell me, if he knew, what was going on.

"How does it look?" I asked.

"It looks great," answered Harry. "Nobody saw anything like it."

I was all turned around. I believed, or tried to, that Victor wasn't in earnest, that he could lay me out whenever he pleased. But there was the shade of the doubt. My mind was made up to do as I said. I'd leave a spot open; then, if he wanted, he could cut me down. Anyhow I'd know what the game was.

But that is harder to do than you'd think. Your instinct is not to drop your arms and let yourself be plugged. It was certainly nerve-wracking.

The bell had rung and I had come out. I was dancing around.

All the blacks in the house were on their feet, yelling their lungs out. The referee was making comic antics. I couldn't see humor in anything. Victor edged toward me. The Negroes pounded their feet and clapped. I never heard such a racket. The referee darted around the ring like a bird. I just danced back and forth.

I thought, "I'll have to end this."

I stepped over and made a wild swing at Victor's head. I expected him to dodge it, and maybe lay me cold on the spot. But it landed, and I never hit a punch more solid.

That almost killed those jigaboos. They laughed and laughed. I never heard such laughter in my life. I grabbed Victor and clinched. He pushed me away. I just stood there with my hands down.

He looked at me strangely, and backed off a little lowering his own hands. The referee paused in the center of the ring, and the Negroes all shut their mouths. Everything was at a standstill.

Right then was the strangest moment I ever spent. Victor didn't lead and I didn't. The whole world seemed paralyzed. I had only one thought.

I thought, "I'm a shameful fool! I'm a shameful fool!"

The bell sounded. That crowd released. I mean they let everything loose. Nobody ever heard a yell like that crowd gave. I ran to Victor and threw my arms around him.

Don't believe I'm one of those guys who kisses a boy after he's knocked him hell west and crooked. I never hugged any boy before, and I never have since. I'll leave it to you to understand.

It was only the end of the second round, but the fight was over.

"I didn't cross myself," Victor said. "It was a fake, so I didn't like to cross myself."

We climbed out of the ring and walked down the aisle. Those Negroes got up off their benches and slapped our backs. And I want to say that I never felt anything so comforting as those black hands on me.

To show you the kind of fellows those jigaboos were, when the manager and referee came back to pay us off they offered me thirty-five dollars.

"For that last fight," I said, "I don't want any money."

"You aren't getting any," the referee said. "The extra fifteen is just a present from the house."

So they made me take the money.

And I want to say right here that I never knew a guy like this Victor. He stood up there and let me break his nose like the shameful fool I was when he could have stretched me unconscious with either hand in less time than it takes to tell it here. That's what I call a man of mercy.

We got dressed and went outside and caught the street car. The soldier who had come with Harry, and Harry were along with Victor and me.

I remembered Victor as he was back in the Lincoln Heights school, when I used to stand back and envy him. Then I thought to myself,

"That same guy lets me break his nose."

Suddenly I felt happy. I stopped feeling terrible about the thing I'd done. I only felt glad I was with those three guys.

I began to talk without there being sense to anything I said. But those three fellows all listened to me as if they wouldn't miss a word. I never had such a time. I sat there with my cap in my lap, bent toward those fellows. When I had anything to say I would put my mouth to the nearest ear and shout. Harry and the soldier talked the same way. I guess we were having what you'd call the social instinct.

The soldier would speak, then Harry or I, then Victor would break in. After that long silence in the ring I certainly wanted to hear him talk.

He said: "Listen. I believe that Christ and Judas were in cahoots. I believe it was all laid out between them. Christ told Judas in private to sell Him for thirty pieces of silver, that if the Jews thought he'd been sold for that much, had suffered on the cross all for thirty pieces of silver, then they would not want to be like Judas and would want to be like Christ. It would make them good. I believe it was all fixed."

"I believe that," said Harry.

"Of course," said Victor. "He was the only one to die with his Lord-and-Master."

The soldier turned to me.

"What do you think? Do you believe that, too?"

"That was it," I said.

# Figures of Fighting Men

### JOHN HUSTON

---

### *MAXIE*

In the gymnasium a wrestler is working out with the bag. He is a deep-chested, powerful man, thirty-five or forty years old. There is a bulge of muscle on his neck at the base of his shaved skull, and he carries a hump of muscle on his back. The veins swell and stand out over his heavy arms and legs. He throws his weight against the bag, and a spray of sweat settles to the floor. Then he grunts and capers into position for another blow. The bag swings slowly upward, and there is a moment's terrific tableau before it comes rushing back.

How different the fighters, underdeveloped and spidery, look beside this big Greek wrestler. Some of them are strikingly effeminate in their grace. Their hips sway, and they teeter in their steps as though they wore high heels.

Maxie, the middleweight, is positively girlish as he skips the rope. He dances over the floor scarcely lifting his feet. Maxie is a cruel fighter. He

249

was only thirteen when he had his first professional match, and he is a past master at all the little tricks that take the heart out of a man.

He has climbed into the training ring with a red-headed young heavyweight, and he snipes away with little short jabs at his nose. In a few seconds the boy's face is bloody. The blow travels only a few inches. It is more a flick of the wrist than a clean punch. The tip of the glove brushes the end of the boy's nose. Maxie picks away. The boy's eyes are watering. He raises his guard and tries to protect his nose with his right hand. But it is no use, Maxie feints it down. It is a game. Maxie won't hit him any place but on the nose. The boy's middle is a wide open target, but Maxie only feints toward it and the boy gets another flip on the nose.

Sometimes his mark is an eye, or the ribs, or an ear. Maxie has probably heard more ears pop than any fighter in the business. An evil smile has Maxie, fleeting as his slapping, tap-dancing style of fighting. His victims have been known to weep between doses of his medicine. They never throw their arms around him after the fight.

## THE OLD TIMER

A few years ago he fought the champion of his class for the title. Now he is on the march back through the ranks of the preliminaries. Tonight he is second on the card in a small club. A dozen more matches and he will pass out of the picture.

He has taken too much punishment. His brain is getting cloudy. Head down, his misty eyes on the eyes of his man, he comes doggedly in. The younger fighter is trying to put over a knockout. His right fist is on a line with the old timer's jaw, ready to whip across. It circles slowly, like the head of a snake about to strike. There is a shock. The old timer's knees buckle. Then he shakes his head and comes forward again.

Perhaps he doesn't even know how badly he is being beaten. He doesn't hear the bell at the end of the round, and he has a hard time finding his corner. His second slaps him on the face and blows a mouthful of water over his chest. His head lolls back and he breathes with difficulty, like a horse whose wind is broken. But when the bell rings he is on his feet instantly.

There is a flurry of gloves, then a long clean blow right to the point of the old timer's jaw. He sways, half turns, and staggers across the ring, out standing up. The young fighter is after him, to finish him off. He swings all his weight into every blow, and they land without mercy, right, left, on the old boxer's bloody face. But he does not go down. Somehow he manages to hold himself up and fall into a clinch. He is not very strong. The young fighter rips away at his middle, but he hangs on and his head clears. The referee breaks them up. And now the old timer is leading again.

In the days of his youth, the old timer was a very showy boy. He fought in the young Griffo style, slipping and dodging like a ghost, and making a fool of his man. In more than a hundred fights he hadn't a knockout to his credit, but he was as hard to hit as smoke.

Then, in what amounted to no more than a training bout, a second-rater dipped his gloves in rosin and rubbed them in the old timer's eyes during a clinch. His sight was ruined, but his fighting days were not over. Now he showed them he could take it. He became a punching bag in the small clubs. His pretty boy face was knocked lop-sided. In a few months he was one of the old men of the ring.

## AIN'T IT A SHAME?

On a table in the dimly lighted dressing room a boy who has received a vicious body beating is asleep. Every now and then he wakes up and gags. He has a colored manager, and an hour or so before the fight the two of them sat down to a meal.

Whenever the boy awakens the colored man holds a bottle of water to his lips. He fills his mouth, throws back his head, gargles, and spits the water on the floor. Then he sighs and goes to sleep again.

At last he is slumbering peacefully. His manager pulls back the cover, and stands there looking at the welts and bruises over the boy's middle. He shakes his head dolefully, and repeats over and over, ever so softly, so as not to disturb the sleeper:

"Ain't it a shame? Ain't it a shame? Ain't it a shame?"

## THE KING

The Irish boy has a half-frightened look on his face. His body is tense, the muscles flexed in his big rigid arms, and his movements are short and

251

jerky. King, the colored heavy, outweighs the white boy by nearly forty pounds, but his advanced years more than make up for it. He is old enough to be the boy's father, and there is something fatherly about the way he handles him.

Old King's big brown figure, the muscles softened a little, the waist a trifle full, his black shaven head, his golden smile, and his movements, slowed down, but so purposeful, strike a rich chord. The King is an old warrior. His nature has ripened. The killer in him has been dead a long, long time.

He talks to the boy, but not in a way to frighten him. He might be giving him a boxing lesson.

Don't keep your hand down, boy. Lift it up. And shoot'em out straight, don't swing so. And don't jump around like that. You'll get wore out. What's ailing you? You ain't scairt, are you? . . . You see? I told you to keep that left hand up. That's right. Now shoot'em out straight. They ain't *no* trouble to stop when you swing that way. I just reach out and stop'em like that,—see? Don't be scairt.

As the rounds go on the Irish boy forgets his nervousness, and the pace of the fight evens out until the very sound of the blows falls into a monotonous rhythm.

## THE CHAMPION

He is trained down to several pounds below his natural weight, and his face shows the strain. He looks like a sick boy of ten or twelve. There are pin points of sweat on his pale forehead, and he shivers.

His trainer and seconds hover him while he touches gloves with the man he is about to fight, and when he listens, head bowed, to the referee's instructions. One of them slips the robe off his shoulders. How white his flesh is! He has been working out indoors, away from he sun. He has a starved, sick look.

The house goes black, a pyramid of light hangs over the ring. The bell rings. He crosses himself rapidly, and comes out of his corner. It is all over in an instant. From a shivering, sick child the champion is transfigured into a flashing wraith, elusive and beautiful as a flame, who bewilders his victim, lashes him into position for the knockout, and drops him with a blow.

*AD*

Two boys in the training ring begin to mix it up, and old Ad stares at them with ferocious intensity. His gray eyes harden, and his shapeless face takes on a keen look.

"Kill the—!" he cries, in his high, sing-song voice.

Everyone turns. The colored boxer in the ring smiles, and the white boy slows down his pace. There is a ripple of laughs. Old Ad's forehead is covered with scars chalked on in a lifetime of fighting, and his ears are like two peonies. Ad had the fighting heart. He always said he would take one to give one. Ad took one too many. He thinks he is still the champion. He has stopped in today to see the boys work out, and to make arrangements for a fight with a man who has been dead ten years. The dead man was the one who took the championship away from him.

Everybody likes Ad. He gets along by the quarters and half dollars they give him around the gym. Sometimes young fighters box a round or two with him. That is like a drink of whiskey to him. It loosens his tongue, and he tells the stories of his old fights, round by round. The fire still burns in his heart. His voice thins to a snarl and comes through his teeth with terrible energy. Slowly he works himself into a fighting rage. His tale breaks off, and a stream of curses follows. He dares any man present to raise his hands and fight him.

Then at the peak of his fury the thread snaps. His face clears, like the sky after a rain. He shakes his head, smiles, and he is back again in that dim, hazy heaven, where the boys who liked to take it spend their days.

# Undirectable Director

## JAMES AGEE

The Ant, as every sluggard knows, is a model citizen. His eye is fixed unwaveringly upon Security and Success, and he gets where he is going. The grasshopper, as every maiden ant delights in pointing out, is his reprehensible opposite number: a hedonistic jazz-baby, tangoing along primrose paths to a disreputable end. The late Walter Huston's son John, one of the ranking grasshoppers of the Western Hemisphere, is living proof of what a lot of nonsense that can be. He has beaten the ants at their own game and then some, and he has managed that blindfolded, by accident, and largely just for the hell of it. John was well into his twenties before anyone could imagine he would ever amount to more than an awfully nice guy to get drunk with. He wandered into his vocation as a writer of movie scripts to prove to a girl he wanted to marry that he amounted to more than a likeable bum. He stumbled into his still deeper vocation as a writer-director only when he got sick of seeing what the professional directors did to his scripts. But during the ten subsequent years he has won both Security aplenty (currently $3,000 a week with MGM and a partnership in Horizon Pictures with his friend Sam Spiegel) and Success aplenty (two Oscars, a One World Award and such lesser prizes as the Screen Directors' Guild quarterly award which he received last week for his *Asphalt Jungle*).

Yet these are merely incidental attainments. The first movie he directed, *The Maltese Falcon,* is the best private-eye melodrama ever made. *San Pietro,* his microcosm of the meaning of war in terms of the fight for one hill town, is generally conceded to be the finest of war documentaries. *Treasure of the Sierra Madre,* which he developed from B. Traven's sardonic adventure-fable about the corrosive effect of gold on character, is the clearest proof in perhaps twenty years that first-rate work can come out of the big commercial studios.

Most of the really good popular art produced anywhere comes from Hollywood, and much of it bears Huston's name. To put it conservatively, there is nobody under fifty at work in movies, here or abroad, who can excel Huston in talent, inventiveness, intransigence, achievement or promise. Yet it is a fair bet that neither money, nor acclaim, nor a sense of dedication to the greatest art medium of his century have much to do with Huston's staying at his job: he stays at it because there is nothing else he enjoys so much. It is this tireless enjoyment that gives his work a unique vitality and makes every foot of film he works on unmistakably his.

Huston seems to have acquired this priceless quality many years ago at the time of what, in his opinion, was probably the most crucial incident in his life. When he was about twelve years old he was so delicate he was hardly expected to live. It was interminably dinned into him that he could never possibly be quite careful enough, and for even closer protection he was put into a sanitarium where every bite he ate and breath he drew could be professionally policed. As a result he became virtually paralyzed by timidity; "I haven't the slightest doubt." he still says, "that if things had gone on like that I'd have died inside a few more months." His only weapon was a blind desperation of instinct, and by day not even that was any use. Nights, however, when everyone was asleep, he used to sneak out, strip, dive into a stream which sped across the grounds and ride it down quite a steep and stony waterfall, over and over and over. "The first few times," he recalls, "it scared the living hell out of me, but I realized— instinctively anyhow—it was exactly fear I had to get over." He kept at it until it was the one joy in his life. When they first caught him at this primordial autotherapy the goons were of course aghast; but on maturer thought they decided he might live after all.

The traits revealed in this incident are central and permanent in Huston's character. Risk, not to say recklessness, are virtual reflexes in him. Action, and the most vivid possible use of the immediate present, were his personal salvation; they have remained lifelong habits. Because action also is the natural language of the screen and the instant present is its tense, Huston is a born popular artist. In his life, his dealings and his work as an artist he operates largely by instinct, unencumbered by much reflectiveness or abstract thinking, or any serious self-doubt. Incapable of yesing, apple-polishing or boot-licking, he instantly catches fire in resistance to authority.

Nobody in movies can beat Huston's record for trying to get away with more than the traffic will bear. *San Pietro* was regarded with horror by some gentlemen of the upper brass as "an antiwar picture" and was cut from five reels to three. *Treasure,* which broke practically every box-office law in the game and won three Oscars, was made over the virtually dead bodies of the top men at Warners' and was advertised as a Western. *The Asphalt Jungle* suggests that in some respects big-town crime operates remarkably like free enterprise. Huston seldom tries to "lick" the problem imposed by censorship, commercial queasiness or tradition; he has learned that nothing is so likely to settle an argument as to turn up with the accomplished fact, accomplished well, plus a bland lack of alternative film shots. And yet after innumerable large and small fights and a fair share of defeats he can still say of his movie career, "I've never had any trouble." Probably the whitest magic that protects him is that he really means it.

Nonetheless his life began with trouble—decorated with the best that his Irish imagination, and his father's, could add to it. He was born John Marcellus Huston on August 5, 1906, in Nevada, Missouri, a hamlet which his grandfather, a professional gambler, had by the most ambitious version of the family legend acquired in a poker game. John's father, a retired actor, was in charge of power and light and was learning his job, while he earned, via a correspondence course. Before the postman had taught him how to handle such a delicate situation, a fire broke out in town, Walter overstrained the valves in his effort to satisfy the fire department, and the Hustons decided it would be prudent to leave what was left of Nevada before morning. They did not let their shirttails touch their rumps until they hit Weatherford, Texas, another of Grandfather's jackpots. After a breather they moved on to St. Louis (without, however, re-peating the scorched-earth policy), and Walter settled down to engineering in dead earnest until a solid man clapped him on the shoulder and told him that with enough stick-to-itiveness he might well become a top-notch engi-neer, a regular crackerjack. Horrified, Walter instantly returned to the stage. A few years later he and his wife were divorced. From there on out the child's life lacked the stability of those early years.

John divided his time between his father and mother. With his father, who was still some years short of eminence or even solvency, he shared that bleakly glamorous continuum of three-a-days, scabrous fleabags and the cindery, ambling day coaches between, which used to be so much of the essence of the American theater. John's mother was a newspaper-woman with a mania for travel and horses (she was later to marry a vice-president of the Northern Pacific), and she and her son once pooled their last ten dollars on a 100-to-1 shot—which came in. Now and then she stuck the boy in one school or another, but mostly they traveled—well off the beaten paths.

After his defeat of death by sliding down the waterfall, there was no holding John. In his teens he became amateur lightweight boxing champi-on of California. A high-school marriage lasted only briefly. He won twen-ty-three out of twenty-five fights, many in the professional ring, but he abandoned this promise of a career to join another of his mother's eccen-tric grand tours. He spent two years in the Mexican cavalry, emerging at twenty-one as a lieutenant. In Mexico he wrote a book, a puppet play about Frankie and Johnny. Receiving, to his astonishment, a $500 advance from a publisher, he promptly entrained for the crap tables of Saratoga where, in one evening, he ran it up to $11,000, which he soon spent or gambled away.

After that Huston took quite a friendly interest in writing. He wrote a short story which his father showed to his friend Ring Lardner, who showed it to his friend H. L. Mencken, who ran it in the *Mercury.* He wrote several other stories about horses and boxers before the vein ran out. It was through these stories, with his father's help that he got his first job as a movie writer. He scripted *A House Divided,* starring his father, for William Wyler. But movies, at this extravagant stage of Huston's career, were just an incident. At other stages he worked for the New York *Graph-ic* ("I was the world's lousiest reporter"), broke ribs riding steeplechase, studied painting in Paris, knocked around with international Bohemians in

London and went on the bum in that city when his money ran out and he was too proud to wire his father. At length he beat his way back to New York where, for a time, he tried editing the *Midweek Pictorial*. He was playing Abraham Lincoln in a Chicago WPA production when he met an Irish girl named Leslie Black and within fifteen minutes after their meeting asked her to marry him. When she hesitated he hotfooted it to Hollywood and settled down to earn a solid living as fast as possible. Marrying Leslie was probably the best thing that ever happened to him, in the opinion of Huston's wise friend and studio protector during the years at Warner Brothers, the producer Henry Blanke. Blanke remembers him vividly during the bachelor interlude: "Just a drunken boy; hopelessly immature. You'd see him at every party, wearing bangs, with a monkey on his shoulder. Charming. Very talented but without an ounce of discipline in his make-up." Leslie Huston, Blanke is convinced, set her husband the standards and incentives which brought his abilities into focus. They were divorced in 1945, but in relation to his work he has never lost the stability she helped him gain.

At forty-four Huston still has a monkey and a chimpanzee as well, but he doesn't escort them to parties. His gray-sleeted hair still treats his scalp like Liberty Hall and occasionally slithers into bangs, but they can no longer be mistaken for a Bohemian compensation. He roughly suggests a jerked-venison version of his father, or a highly intelligent cowboy. A little over six foot tall, quite lean, he carries himself in a perpetual gangling-graceful slouch. The forehead is monkishly puckered, the ears look as clipped as a show dog's; the eyes, too, are curiously animal, an opaque red-brown. The nose was broken in the prize ring. The mouth is large, mobile and gap-toothed. The voice which comes out of this leatheriness is surprisingly rich, gentle and cultivated. The vocabulary ranges with the careless ease of a mountain goat between words of eight syllables and of four letters.

Some friends believe he is essentially a deep introvert using every outside means available as a form of flight from self-recognition—in other words, he is forever sliding down the waterfall and instinctively fears to stop. The same friends suspect his work is all that keeps him from flying apart. He is wonderful company, almost anytime, for those who can stand the pace. Loving completely unrestrained and fantastic play, he is particularly happy with animals, roughhousers and children; a friend who owns three of the latter describes him as "a blend of Santa Claus and the Pied

259

Piper." His friendships range from high in the Social Register to low in the animal kingdom, but pretty certainly the friend he liked best in the world was his father, and that was thoroughly reciprocated. It was a rare and heart-warming thing, in this Freud-ridden era, to see a father and son so irrepressibly pleased with each other's company and skill.

He has an indestructible kind of youthfulness, enjoys his enthusiasms with all his might and has the prompt appetite for new knowledge of a man whose intelligence has not been cloyed by much formal education. He regrets that nowadays he can read only two or three books a week. His favorite writers are Joyce, his friend Hemingway (perhaps his closest literary equivalent) and above all, O'Neill; it was one of the deepest disappointments of his career when movie commitments prevented his staging the new O'Neill's *The Iceman Cometh*. His other enjoyments take many forms. He still paints occasionally. He is a very good shot and a superlative horseman; he has some very promising runners of his own. He likes money for the fun it can bring him, is extremely generous with it and particularly loves to gamble. He generally does well at the races and siphons it off at the crap tables. He is a hard drinker (Scotch) but no lush, and a heavy smoker. Often as not he forgets to eat. He has a reputation for being attractive to women, and rough on them. His fourth wife is the dancer, Ricky Soma; their son Walter was born last spring. He makes most of his important decisions on impulse; it was thus he adopted his son Pablo in Mexico. The way he and his third wife, Evelyn Keyes, got married is a good example of Huston in action. He suggested they marry one evening in Romanoff's a week after they met, borrowed a pocketful of money from the prince, tore out to his house to pick up a wedding ring a guest had mislaid in the swimming pool and chartered Paul Mantz to fly them to Las Vegas where they were married that night.

Huston's courage verges on the absolute, or on simple obliviousness to danger. In Italy during the shooting of *San Pietro*, his simian curiosity about literally everything made him the beau ideal of the contrivers of booby traps; time and again he was spared an arm, leg or skull only by the grace of God and the horrified vigilance of his friend Lieutenant Jules Buck. He sauntered through mine fields where plain men feared to tread. He is quick to get mad and as quick to get over it. Once in Italy he sprinted up five flights of headquarters stairs in order to sock a frustrating superior officer; arriving at the top he was so winded he could hardly stand. Time enough to catch his breath was time enough to cool off: he just wobbled downstairs again.

Huston is swiftly stirred by anything which appeals to his sense of justice, magnanimity or courage; he was among the first men to stand up for Lew Ayres as a conscientious objector, he flew to the Washington hearings on Hollywood (which he refers to as "an obscenity") and sponsored Henry Wallace (though he voted for Truman) in the 1948 campaign. Some people think of him, accordingly, as a fellow traveler. Actually he is a political man chiefly in an emotional sense: "I'm against *anybody*," he says, "who tries to tell anybody else what to do." The mere sight or thought of a cop can get him sore. He is in short rather less of a Communist than the most ultramontane Republican, for like perhaps five out of seven good artists who ever lived he is—to lapse into technical jargon—a natural-born antiauthoritarian individualistic libertarian anarchist, without portfolio.

A very good screen writer, Huston is an even better director. He has a feeling about telling a story on a screen which sets him apart from most other movie artists and from all nonmovie writers and artists. "On paper," he says, "all you can do is say something happened, and if you say it well enough the reader believes you. In pictures, if you do it right, *the thing happens, right there on the screen.*"

This means more than it may seem to. Most movies are like predigested food because they are mere reenactment of something that happened (if ever) back in the scripting stage. At the time of shooting the sense of the present is not strong, and such creative energy as may be on hand is used to give the event finish, in every sense of the word, rather than beginning and life. Huston's work has a unique tension and vitality because the maximum of all contributing creative energies converge at the one moment that counts most in a movie—the continuing moment of committing the story to film. At his best he makes the story tell itself, makes it seem to happen for the first and last time at the moment of recording. It is almost magically hard to get this to happen. In the *Treasure* scene in which the bandits kill Bogart, Huston wanted it to be quiet and mockcasual up to its final burst of violence. He told two of his three killers—one a professional actor, the other two professional criminals—only to stay quiet and close to the ground, and always to move when Bogart moved, to keep him surrounded. Then he had everyone play it through, over and over, until they should get the feel of it. At length one of them did a quick scuttling slide down a bank, on his bottom and his busy little hands and feet. A motion as innocent as a child's and as frightening as a centipede's, it makes clear for the first time in the scene that death is absolutely inescapable, and very near. "When he did that slide," Huston says, "I knew they had the feel of it." He shot it accordingly.

Paradoxically in this hyperactive artist of action, the living, breathing texture of his best work is the result of a working method which relies on the utmost possible passiveness. Most serious-minded directors direct too much: "Now on this word," Huston has heard one tell an actor, "I want your voice to break." Actors accustomed to that kind of "help" are often uneasy when they start work with Huston. "Shall I sit down here?" one asked, interrupting a rehearsal. "*I* dunno," Huston replied. "You tired?" When Claire Trevor, starting work in *Key Largo,* asked for a few pointers, he told her, "You're the kind of drunken dame whose elbows are always a little too big, your voice is a little too loud, you're a little too polite. You're very sad, very resigned. Like this," he said, for short, and leaned against the bar with a peculiarly heavy, gentle disconsolateness. It was the leaning she caught onto (though she also used everything he said); without further instruction of any kind, she took an Oscar for her performance. His only advice to his father was a whispered, "Dad, that was a little too much like Walter Huston." Often he works with actors as if he were gentling animals; and although Bogart says without total injustice that "as an actor he stinks," he has more than enough mimetic ability to get his ideas across. Sometimes he discards instruction altogether; to get a desired expression from Lauren Bacall, he simply twisted her arm.

Even on disastrously thin ice Houston has the peculiar kind of well-learned luck which Heaven reserved exclusively for the intuitive and the intrepid. One of the most important roles in *Treasure* is that of the bandit leader, a primordial criminal psychopath about whom the most fascinating and terrifying thing is his unpredictability. It is impossible to know what he will do next because it is impossible to be sure what strange piece of glare-ice in his nature will cause a sudden skid. Too late for a change, it turned out that the man who played this role, though visually ideal for it, couldn't act for shucks. Worried as he was, Huston had a hunch it would turn out all right. It worked because this inadequate actor was trying so hard, was so unsure of what was he doing and was so painfully confused and angered by Huston's cryptic passivity. These several kinds of strain and uncertainty, sprung against the context of the story, made a living image of the almost unactable, real thing; and that had been Huston's hunch.

In placing and moving his characters within a shot Huston is nearly always concerned above all else to be simple and spontaneous rather than merely "dramatic" or visually effective. Just as he feels that the story belongs to the characters, he feels that the actors should as fully as possible belong to themselves. It is only because the actors are so free that their several individualities, converging in a scene, can so often knock the kinds of sparks off each other which cannot be asked for or invented or foreseen. All that can be foreseen is that this can happen only under favorable circumstances; Huston is a master at creating such circumstances.

Each of Huston's pictures has a visual tone and style of its own, dictated to his camera by the story's essential content and spirit. In *Treasure* the camera is generally static and at a middle distance from the action (as Huston says, "It's impersonal, it just looks on and lets them stew in their own juice"); the composition is—superficially—informal, the light cruel and clean, like noon sun on quartz and bone. Most of the action in *Key Largo* takes place inside a small Florida hotel. The problems are to convey heat, suspense, enclosedness, the illusion of some eighteen hours of continuous action in two hours' playing time, with only one time lapse. The lighting is stickily fungoid. The camera is sneakily "personal"; working close and in almost continuous motion, it enlarges the ambiguous suspensefulness of almost every human move. In *Strangers* the main pressures are inside a home and beneath it, where conspirators dig a tunnel. Here Huston's chief keys are lighting contrasts. Underground the players move in and out of shadow like trout; upstairs the light is mainly the luminous pallor of marble without sunlight: a cemetery, bank interior, a great outdoor staircase.

Much that is best in Huston's work comes of his sense of what is natural to the eye and his delicate, simple feeling for space relationships: his camera huddles close to those who huddle to talk, leans back a proportionate distance, relaxing, if they talk casually. He loathes camera rhetoric and the shot-for-shot's-sake; but because he takes each moment catch-as-catch-can and is so deeply absorbed in doing the best possible thing with it he has made any number of unforgettable shots. He can make an unexpected closeup reverberate like a gong. The first shot of Edward G. Robinson in *Key Largo*, mouthing a cigar and sweltering naked in a tub of cold water ("I wanted to get a look at the animal with its shell off") is one of the most powerful and efficient "first entrances" of a character on record.

Other great shots come through the kind of candor which causes some people to stare when others look away: the stripped, raw-sound scenes of psychiatric interviews in *Let There Be Light.* Others come through simple discretion in relating word and image. In *San Pietro,* as the camera starts moving along a line of children and babies, the commentator (Huston) remarks that in a few years they'll have forgotten there ever was a war; then he shuts up. As the camera continues in silence along the terrible frieze of shock and starvation, one realizes the remark was not the inane optimism it seemed: they, forgetting, are fodder for the next war.

Sometimes the shot is just a spark—a brief glint of extra imagination and perception. During the robbery sequence in *Asphalt Jungle* there is a quick glimpse of the downtown midnight street at the moment when people have just begun to hear the burglar alarms. Unsure, still, where the trouble is, the people merely hesitate a trifle in their ways of walking, and it is like the first stirrings of metal filings before the magnet beneath the paper pulls them into pattern. Very often the fine shot comes because Huston, working to please himself without fear of his audience, sharply condenses his storytelling. Early in *Strangers* a student is machinegunned on the steps of Havana's university. A scene follows which is breath-taking in its surprise and beauty, but storytelling, not beauty, brings it: what seems to be hundreds of young men and women, all in summery whites, throw themselves flat on the marble stairs in a wavelike motion as graceful as the sudden close swooping of so many doves. The shot is already off the screen before one can realize its full meaning. By their trained, quiet unison in falling, these students are used to this. They expect it any average morning. And that suffices, with great efficiency, to suggest the Cuban tyranny.

Within the prevailing style of a picture, Huston works many and extreme changes and conflicts between the "active" camera, which takes its moment of the story by the scruff of the neck and "tells" it, and the "passive" camera, whose business is transparency, to receive a moment of action purely and record it. But whether active or passive, each shot contains no more than is absolutely necessary to make its point and is cut off sharp at that instant. The shots are cantilevered, sprung together in electric arcs, rather than buttered together. A given scene is apt to be composed of highly unconventional alternations of rhythm and patterns of exchange between long and medium and close shots and the standing, swinging and dollying camera. The rhythm and contour are very powerful but very irregular, like the rhythm of good prose rather than of good verse; and it is this rangy, leaping, thrusting kind of nervous vitality which binds the whole picture together. Within this vitality he can bring about moments as thoroughly revealing as those in great writing. As an average sample of that, *Treasure*'s intruder is killed by bandits; the three prospectors come to identify the man they themselves were on the verge of shooting. Bogart, the would-be tough guy, cocks one foot up on a rock and tries to look at the corpse as casually as if it were fresh-killed game. Tim Holt, the essentially decent young man, comes past behind him and, innocent and unaware of it, clasps his hands as he looks down, in the respectful manner of a boy who used to go to church. Walter Huston, the experienced old man, steps quietly behind both, leans to the dead man as professionally as a doctor to a patient and gently rifles him for papers. By such simplicity Huston can draw the eye so deep into the screen that time and again he can make important points in medium shots, by motions as small as the twitching of an eyelid, for which most directors would require a close-up or even a line of dialogue.

Most movies are made in the evident assumption that the audience is passive and wants to remain passive; every effort is made to do all the work—the seeing, the explaining, the understanding, even the feeling. Huston is one of the few movies artists who, without thinking twice about it, honors his audience. His pictures are not acts of seduction or of benign enslavement but of liberation, and they require, of anyone who enjoys them, the responsibilities of liberty. They continually open the eye and require it to work vigorously; and through the eye they awaken curiosity and intelligence. That, by any virile standard, is essential to good entertainment. It is unquestionably essential to good art.

The most inventive director of his generation, Huston has done more to extend, invigorate and purify the essential idiom of American movies, the truly visual telling of stories, than anyone since the prime of D. W. Griffith. To date, however, his work as a whole is not on the level with the finest and most deeply imaginative work that has been done in movies— the work of Chaplin, Dovzhenko, Eisenstein, Griffith, the late Jean Vigo. For an artist of such conscience and caliber, his range is surprisingly narrow, both in subject matter and technique. In general he is leery of emotion—of the "feminine" aspects of art—and if he explored it with more assurance, with his taste and equipment, he might show himself to be a much more sensitive artist. With only one early exception, his movies have centered on men under pressure, have usually involved violence and have occasionally verged on a kind of romanticism about danger. Though he uses sound and dialogue more intelligently than most directors, he has not shown much interest in exploring the tremendous possibilities of the former or in solving the crippling problems of the latter. While his cutting is astute, terse, thoroughly appropriate to his kind of work, yet compared with that of Eisenstein, who regarded cutting as the essence of the art of movies, it seems distinctly unadventurous. In his studio pictures, Huston is apt to be tired and bored by the time the stages of ultrarefinement in cutting are reached, so that some of his scenes have been given perfection, others somewhat impaired, by film editors other than Huston. This is consistent with much that is free and improvisatory in his work and in his nature, but it is a startling irresponsibility in so good an artist.

During his past few pictures Huston does appear to have become more of a "camera" man, and not all of this has been to the good. The camera sometimes imposes on the story; the lighting sometimes becomes elaborately studioish or even verges on the arty; the screen at times becomes rigid, overstylized. This has been happening, moreover, at a time when another of Huston's liabilities has been growing: thanks to what Henry Blanke calls his "amazing capacity for belief," he can fall for, and lose himself in, relatively mediocre material. Sometimes—as in *Asphalt Jungle*—he makes a silk purse out of sow's ear, but sometimes—as in parts of *Strangers* and *Key Largo*—the result is neither silk nor sow.

Conceivably Huston lacks that deepest kind of creative impulse and that intense self-critical skepticism without which the stature of a great artist is rarely achieved. A brilliant adapter, he has yet to do a Huston "original," barring the war documentaries. He is probably too much at the mercy of his immediate surroundings. When the surroundings are right for him there is no need to talk about mercy: during the war and just after he was as hard as a rock and made his three finest pictures in a row. Since then the pictures, for all their excellence, are like the surroundings, relatively softened and blurred. Unfortunately no man in Hollywood can be sufficiently his own master or move in a direct line to personally selected goals. After *Treasure,* Huston was unable to proceed to *Moby Dick* as he wanted to; he still is awaiting the opportunity to make Dreiser's *Jennie Gerhardt* and Dostoevski's *The Idiot* although he is at last shooting Stephen Crane's *The Red Badge of Courage,* which he has wanted to make for years. "This has got to be a masterpiece," he recently told friends, "or it's nothing."

There is no reason to expect less of it than his finest picture yet, for the better his starting material, the better he functions as an artist: he is one of the very few men in the world of movies who has shown himself to be worthy of the best. He has, in abundance, many of the human qualities which most men of talent lack. He is magnanimous, disinterested and fearless. Whatever his job, he always makes a noble and rewarding fight of it. If it should occur to him to fight for his life—his life as the consistently great artist he evidently might become—he would stand a much better chance of winning than most people. For besides having talent and fighting ability, he has nothing to lose but his hide, and he has never set a very high value on that.

# John Huston

ANDREW SARRIS

The late James Agee canonized Huston prematurely in a *Life*-magazine auteur piece circa *Treasure of the Sierra Madre.* Agee was as wrong about Huston as Bazin was about Wyler, but Huston is still coasting on his reputation as a wronged individualist with an alibi for every bad movie. If it isn't Jack Warner, it's L. B. Mayer, and if it isn't L. B. Mayer, it's David O. Selznick, and if it isn't David O. Selznick it's Darryl F. Zanuck, and if it isn't any of these, it's the whole rotten system of making movies. But who except Huston himself is to blame for the middle-brow banality of *Freud,* a personal project with built-in compromises for the "mass" audience. Huston has confused indifference with integrity for such a long time that he is no longer even the competent craftsman of *The Asphalt Jungle, The Maltese Falcon,* and *The African Queen,* films that owe more to casting coups than to directorial acumen. *Falcon,* particularly, is an uncanny matchup of Dashiell Hammett's literary characters with their visual doubles: Mary

Astor, Humphrey Bogart, Sidney Greenstreet, Peter Lorre, and Elisha Cooke, Jr. Only Stendhal's Julien Sorel in search of Gérard Philipe can match *Falcon's* Pirandellian equation. Even in his palmier days, Huston displayed his material without projecting his personality. His technique has been evasive, his camera often pitched at a standoffish angle away from the heart of the action. *Treasure of the Sierra Madre* and *Beat the Devil,* his two most overrated films, end with howling laughter on the sound track, an echo perhaps of the director laughing at his own feeble jokes.

Huston's dismaying decline notwithstanding, his theme has been remarkably consistent from *The Maltese Falcon* to *Reflections in a Golden Eye.* His protagonists almost invariably fail at what they set out to do, generally through no fault or flaw of their own. Unfortunately, Huston is less a pessimist than a defeatist, and his characters manage to be unlucky without the world being particularly out of joint. Huston's best film, *The Asphalt Jungle,* deals fittingly enough with collective defeat, and even his cast represents an interesting gallery of talented players who did not reach the heights they deserved: Sterling Hayden, the sensitive giant who never made the Wayne-Mitchum-Heston bracket; James Whitmore, who never became the second Spencer Tracy; Jean Hagen, who never obtained the dramatic-pathetic roles her talents demanded; Sam Jaffe, who never won an Oscar; Louis Calhern, who never mounted an adequate Lear although he was tall enough for tragedy; and Marc Lawrence, who never found his niche as the all-purpose villain. Only Marilyn Monroe was sprinkled with stardust after *Asphalt,* and Huston nearly finished her with the casual cruelty of *The Misfits.* The turning point in Huston's career was probably *Moby Dick.* In retrospect, he should have acted Ahab himself and let Orson Welles direct. This was his one gamble with greatness, and he lost, and like the cagey poker player he is, he has been playing it cool and corrupt ever since. *The List of Adrian Messenger,* a case in point, is so corrupt that even a fox hunt is in drag, not to mention *Beat the Devil,* which was consciously (and Capotishly) campy long before camp was even a gleam in Susan Sontag's eye.

As a stylist, Huston has always overloaded the physical with the moral. He never cared for that sissy stuff in drawing rooms where people try to communicate with each other through dialogue. Indeed, Huston's intimate scenes are often staged as if he were playing croquet with a sledgehammer. His antics with the two ridiculously graceful beach boys in *Night of the Iguana* are as false as the breast-thrusting jitterbug routine of the teenager in *The Asphalt Jungle* and all the nonsense with the wild horses in *The Misfits*. Movies are still primarily a dramatic medium, and if you can't establish characters indoors, you're not going to illuminate them with any clarity outdoors. Unfortunately, Huston, unlike Hawks, does not believe sufficiently in the action ethos to enjoy action for its own sake. A director like Cukor may choose to make himself comfortable inside, a director like Hawks outside, a director like Huston nowhere. Ultimately, Huston mistrusts his own dramatic material to the point that he makes excessively meaningful flourishes with the smokily suffused color in *Moulin Rouge* and the severely subdued color in *Reflections in a Golden Eye*. It must have looked good on the drawing board with *Moulin Rouge* color equaling artistic expression and *Reflections in a Golden Eye* colorlessness equaling sexual repression. Very little of the intended effect came through on the screen. Mere technique can never transcend conviction.

# Johnny, We Finally Knew Ye

## ANDREW SARRIS

John Huston was honored by the Film Society of Lincoln Center on the evening of May 5 [1980] at a gala that was notable for the eloquence and dispatch with which it was conducted. The honor to Huston was long overdue, and I write this quite candidly as one of his erstwhile nonadmirers. Indeed, my own negative words on Huston in *The American Cinema* have come back to haunt me on many occasions. The real cutting edge of *The American Cinema* was that now notorious category entitled "Less Than Meets the Eye." The directors in this group were John Huston, Elia Kazan, David Lean, Rouben Mamoulian, Joseph L. Mankiewicz, Lewis Milestone, Carol Reed, William Wellman, Billy Wilder, William Wyler, and Fred Zinnemann.

I am often asked if I have changed my opinion on any of these directors. The answer is that I am always changing my opinions as I acquire more experience and perspective in relating one film to another, and one director to another, over the mobile canvas of cinema. The polemical period with its shock tactics is over. A reflective period of revision and recollection has led to my regrouping the directors into more precisely expressive categories.

Lean, Mamoulian, Milestone, Reed, Wyler, and Zinnemann seem to fit into an *objet d'art* category along with Rene Clair, Rene Clement, G. W. Pabst, Jack Clayton, Albert Lewin, and Louis Malle. These are directors who are more concerned with cultivating the unique qualities of each individual work rather than projecting their own personalities. There are no rivers of personal expressions in these careers, only archipelagoes of artistic achievements. The Politique des Auteurs has traditionally underestimated the *objet d'art* directors because of the auteurist emphasis on the stylistic unconscious.

Kazan's career is similar to Cukor's, Minnelli's, and Preminger's in that it eventually transcended its theatrical origins with epical aspirations. Wellman's gritty artistic personality places him somewhere between Hathaway and Hawks in the realm of the no-nonsense action directors. As for Billy Wilder, he has risen so far in my estimation as to be a prime candidate for the Pantheon.

Huston, however, is somewhat more difficult to define and categorize either positively or negatively. One notion I have is that of the deliberately dissonant director, the goer against the grain. Stroheim may be the prototype, Kubrick and Polanski the spiritual descendants, Buñuel the apotheosis of this innately rebellious impulse.

But these are merely thematic and stylistic approximations. Huston has been in the cinema for over half a century during which time he has been involved in close to seventy movies in his various capacities of writer, director, and actor. Yet, if you ask most people for their favorite Huston film, their choices will run within remarkably narrow range: *The Maltese Falcon, Treasure of the Sierra Madre, The Asphalt Jungle,* and *The African Queen.* Serious documentarians will hail the widely unseen *Report from the Aleutians. The Battle of San Pietro, Let There Be Light,* and *Fat City* have acquired reputations as flawed but courageous projects, *Moulin Rouge* and *Reflections in a Golden Eye* as fascinating aesthetic experiments, *Beat the Devil* and *Casino Royale* as unusually playful exercises, *Across the Pacific, Key Largo,* and *We Were Strangers* as entertaining but ultimately overblown melodramas, and *The Man Who Would Be King* and *Wise Blood* as unexpectedly vigorous and satisfying vindications of his later career.

Overall, however, the impression of decline and waste in Huston's career has been widely accepted ever since the early 1950s. He was the charming villain of Lillian Ross's satiric account of the misadventures of *The Red Badge of Courage* at Metro, and he was the chillingly charming protagonist of Peter Viertel's extraordinarily illuminating novel of clef *White Hunter, Black Heart.* The irrepressible Leslie Fiedler once declared flatly on a panel that the late James Agee went to Hollywood to commit suicide, and that in Huston he found a director who could accommodate him.

It seemed only fitting that in his later years Huston should be cast in roles of imaginatively monstrous evil in *Chinatown* and *Winter Kills.* There was all around him an aura of danger and recklessness and ruthlessness and irresponsibility. His riding, his drinking, his womanizing were given an added dimension by his impenetrable armor of despair and defeatism.

For those of us with any historical perspective on the cinema John Huston's was clearly an ancestral curse: His famous father Walter Huston was notoriously restless and unstable in his own lifelong flight from any kind of existence that promised security. What else is *Treasure of the Sierra Madre,* but an account of a life's work being blown away in the dust. What I have always tended to underestimate in Huston was how deep in his guts he could feel the universal experience of pointlessness and failure. Hence, I have begun to revise upwards my judgment of such hitherto neglected Huston works as *Heaven Knows, Mr. Allison* with its marvelously restrained, truly gentlemanly characterization of the marine by Robert Mitchum, in the company of the womanly, dignified nun played by Deborah Kerr; *The Unforgiven,* with the racist intensity of *The Searcher* and a fiery performance by Audrey Hepburn; *The Kremlin Letter,* with its remarkably sophisticated awareness of evil in every facet of life; *The Life and Times of Judge Roy Bean,* which mellowed John Milius's downbeat epic without reducing its physical ferocity, and *The Mackintosh Man,* a work of pitiless nihilism such as the scenarist Walter Hill has never been able to achieve in his own directed films.

One of the most fascinating works in the Huston oeuvre is *In This Our Life,* made in 1942. When Huston was still in critical vogue in the mid-1950s his admirers tended to dismiss the film as a Bette Davis vehicle for which Huston has been routinely commissioned. (Actually, Bette Davis was miscast as the man-stealing sister to Olivia de Havilland's nobly suffering sister. Warners would have been better advised to follow the casting of *Strawberry Blonde* with Rita Hayworth in the Davis role, and Davis—or de Havilland—in the de Havilland role.) I had not read the Ellen Glasgow novel until then, hadn't the slightest inkling how depressing it was in its being told from the point of view of the father (Frank Craven), a complete failure in life. Back in the early 1940s, however, even Huston and his scenarist, Howard Koch, two of the most enlightened artists in Hollywood, could not render Glasgow's grim vision of thinly disguised Richmond society. It was not until the late 1970s that Huston was able to pour out the pessimism full blast in *Wise Blood.*

Yet, I am not sure that I can ever completely embrace Huston's art emotionally as much as I may come to terms with it intellectually. Huston's laughter is much too sour for my taste, and his characters seem to indulge too freely in the sin of despair. If, as Brendan Gill so candidly observed in his enthusiastic tribute to the director, Huston's talent, like Oscar Wilde's, was in his work, and his genius was in his life, then some of the short-changing of audiences before the final cut can be rationalized.

Huston at seventy-three is clearly some kind of *hombre.* Of that there can be no doubt. As he sat in patriarchal splendor in his box on the evening of the gala, I could not help wondering whether he was the god of light or the god of darkness. Probably, he was a tantalizing mixture of both, capable of both tenderness and cruelty in equal measure. Even the eloquent tributes by Lauren Bacall and Richard Burton contained within them the suggestion that the culture hero of the evening could be a bit of a rascal if not an outright scoundrel. Bill Mauldin was on hand from another age to remind us of Huston, the man's man and the dogface as champion in the good old days during and after World War II when James Agee could see in Huston the brightest and most honest directorial hope of that generation. When Huston himself finally appeared on the stage he was brief, vital and overwhelmingly charming. I admit that I was beguiled by some dark magic in the man. But afterward I did not feel much like celebrating. The film clips, sketchy and star-oriented, left an aftertaste of acute, lifelong depression. There can be no doubt that Huston has translated his feelings into film, but I am still not sure that his films have succeeded in transcending his feelings. I could be wrong. Only more time will tell.

# Filmography
# Selected Bibliography
# Photo Credits
# Contributors

# Filmography

FILMS SCRIPTED BY JOHN HUSTON BUT DIRECTED BY OTHERS

*A House Divided* (1931)

**Studio:** Universal
**Producer:** Carl Laemmle, Jr., Paul Kohner (associate)
**Director:** William Wyler
**Screenplay:** John B. Clymer and Dale Van Every, from the novel *Hearts and Hands,* by Olive Edens; additional dialogue by John Huston
**Cinematographer:** Charles Stumar
**Editor:** Ted Kent, Maurice Pivar (supervising)
**Art Director:** John Hughes
**Cast:** Walter Huston (Seth Law), Kent Douglass (Matt Law), Helen Chandler (Ruth Evans), Vivian Oakland (Bess), Marjorie Main (woman), Charles Middleton (minister), Lloyd Ingraham (Doc), Walter Brennan (musician)

## Murders in the Rue Morgue (1932)

**Studio:** Universal
**Producer:** Carl Laemmle, Jr., E. M. Asher (associate)
**Director:** Robert Florey
**Screenplay:** Robert Florey, Tom Reed, and Dale Van Every, from the short story by Edgar Allan Poe; additional dialogue by John Huston
**Cinematographer:** Karl Freund
**Editor:** Milton Carruth, Maurice Pivar (supervising)
**Art Director:** Charles D. Hall
**Cast:** Bela Lugosi (Dr. Mirakle), Sidney Fox (Camille L'Espanaye), Leon Way-coff (Pierre Dupin), Brandon Hurst (prefect of police), Noble Johnson (Janos the Black One), Arlene Francis (Monette), Bert Roach (Paul), D'Arcy Corrigan (morgue keeper)

## Law and Order (1932)

**Studio:** Universal
**Producer:** Carl Laemmle, Jr.
**Director:** Edward L. Cahn
**Screenplay:** Tom Reed, from the novel *Saint Johnson,* by W. R. Burnett; additional dialogue by John Huston
**Cinematographer:** Jackson Rose
**Cast:** Walter Huston (Frame Johnson), Harry Carey (Ed Brandt), Raymond Hatton (Deadwood), Andy Devine (Johnny Kinsman), Walter Brennan (Lanky Smith), Ralph Ince (Poe Northrup), Harry Woods (Walt Northrup), Richard Alexander (Kurt Northrup), Alphonz Ethier (Fin Elder), Dewey Robinson (Ed Deal), Russell Simpson (Judge Williams)

## Jezebel (1938)

**Studio:** Warner Brothers
**Producer:** Henry Blanke, Hal B. Wallis (executive)
**Director:** William Wyler
**Screenplay:** Clements Ripley, Abem Finkel, and John Huston, from the play by Owen Davis
**Cinematographer:** Ernest Haller
**Editor:** Warren Low
**Music:** Max Steiner
**Art Director:** Robert Haas
**Cast:** Bette Davis (Julie Morrison), Henry Fonda (Preston Dillard), George Brent (Buck Cantrell), Margaret Lindsay (Amy Bradford Dillard), Fay Bainter (Aunt Belle Massey), Richard Cromwell (Ted Dillard), Donald Crisp (Dr. Livingstone),

Henry O'Neill (General Bogardus), John Litel (Jean La Cour), Gordon Oliver
(Dick Allen), Janet Shaw (Molly Allen), Theresa Harris (Zette)

## The Amazing Dr. Clitterhouse (1938)
**Studio:** Warner Brothers
**Producer:** Anatole Litvak, Robert Lord (associate)
**Director:** Anatole Litvak
**Screenplay:** John Huston and John Wexley, from the play by Barré Lyndon
**Cinematographer:** Tony Gaudio
**Editor:** Warren Low
**Cast:** Edward G. Robinson (Dr. Clitterhouse), Claire Trevor (Jo Keller),
Humphrey Bogart (Rocks Valentine), Allen Jenkins (Okay), Donald Crisp (Inspec-
tor Lane), Gale Page (Nurse Randolph), Henry O'Neill (judge), Thurston Hall
(Grant), Maxie Rosenbloom (Butch), Burt Hanlon (pal), Curt Bois (Rabbit),
Vladimir Sokoloff (Popus), Billy Wayne (Candy), Robert Homans (Lt. Johnston),
Irving Bacon (jury foreman)

## Juarez (1939)
**Studio:** Warner Brothers
**Producer:** Hal Wallis
**Director:** William Dieterle
**Screenplay:** John Huston, Wolfgang Reinhardt, Aeneas Mackenzie, based on
*Maximilian and Carlotta,* by Franz Werfel, and *The Phantom Crown,* by Bertita
Harding
**Cinematographer:** Tony Gaudio
**Editor:** Warren Low
**Music:** Erich Wolfgang Korngold
**Art Director:** Anton Grot
**Cast:** Paul Muni (Benito Pablo Juarez), Bette Davis (Empress Carlotta von Haps-
burg), Brian Aherne (Emperor Maximilian von Hapsburg), Claude Rains (Louis
Napoleon), John Garfield (Porfirio Diaz), Donald Crisp (Marechale Bazaine), Gale
Sondergaard (Empress Eugenie), Joseph Calleia (Alejandro Uradi), Gilbert Roland
(Col. Miguel Lopez), Henry O'Neill (Miguel de Miramon)

## Dr. Ehrlich's Magic Bullet (1940)
**Studio:** Warner Brothers
**Producer:** Hal Wallis
**Director:** William Dieterle
**Screenplay:** John Huston, Heinz Herald, Norman Burnside, from an idea by
Burnside, developed from letters and notes held by Mrs. Ehrlich

**Cinematographer:** James Wong Howe
**Editor:** Warren Low
**Music:** Max Steiner
**Art Director:** Carl Jules Weyl
**Cast:** Edward G. Robinson (Dr. Paul Ehrlich), Ruth Gordon (Mrs. Ehrlich), Otto Kruger (Dr. Emil von Behring), Donald Crisp (Minister Althoff), Maria Ouspenskaya (Franziska Speyer), Montagu Love (Professor Hartmann), Sig Rumann (Dr. Hans Wolfert), Donald Meek (Mittelmeyer), Henry O'Neill (Dr. Lentz), Albert Bassermann (Dr. Robert Koch), Edward Norris (Dr. Morgenroth), Louis Calhern (Dr. Brockdorf), Louis Jean Heydt (Dr. Kunze)

## *High Sierra* (1941)

**Studio:** Warner Brothers
**Producer:** Jack Warner, Hal Wallis
**Director:** Raoul Walsh
**Screenplay:** John Huston and W. R. Burnett, from the novel by Burnett
**Cinematographer:** Tony Gaudio
**Editor:** Jack Killifer
**Music:** Adolph Deutsch
**Art Director:** Ted Smith
**Cast:** Humphrey Bogart (Roy "Mad Dog" Earle), Ida Lupino (Marie Garson), Alan Curtis (Babe), Arthur Kennedy (Red Hattery), Joan Leslie (Velma), Henry Hull ("Doc" Banton), Elizabeth Risdon (Ma), Cornell Wilde (Louis Mendoza), Minna Gombel (Mrs. Baugham), Paul Harvey (Mr. Baugham), Henry Travers (Pa), Barton MacLane (Jake Kranmer)

## *Sergeant York* (1941)

**Studio:** Warner Brothers
**Producer:** Jesse Lasky, Hal Wallis
**Director:** Howard Hawks
**Screenplay:** Abem Finkel, Harry Chandler, John Huston, and Howard Koch, from *War Diary of Sergeant York,* by Sam K. Cowan; *Sergeant York and his People,* by Sam K. Cowan; *Sergeant York: Last of the Long Hunters,* by Tom Skeyhill
**Cinematographer:** Sol Polito (Arthur Edeson, battle sequences)
**Editor:** William Holmes
**Music:** Max Steiner
**Art Director:** John Hughes
**Cast:** Gary Cooper (Alvin York), Walter Brennan (Pastor Rosier Pile), Joan Leslie (Gracie Williams), George Tobias ("Pusher" Ross), David Bruce (Bert Thomas), Stanley Ridges (Major Buxton), Margaret Wycherly (Ma York), Dickie Moore (George York), Ward Bond (Ike Botkin), Noah Beery, Jr. (Buck Lipscomb),

Harvey Stephens (Captain Danforth), Charles Trowbridge (Cordell Hull), Howard da Silva (Lem), June Lockhart (Rosie York), Elisha Cook, Jr. (the pianist)

## The Killers (1946)

**Studio:** Universal
**Producer:** Mark Hellinger
**Director:** Robert Siodmak
**Screenplay:** Anthony Veiller and John Huston (Huston was not credited; see "Encounter with Rui Nogueira and Bertrand Tavernier," this volume.)
**Editor:** Arthur Hilton
**Music:** Miklos Rozsa
**Art Director:** Jack Otterson, Martin Obzina
**Cast:** Burt Lancaster (Swede Lunn), Edmund O'Brien (James Reardon), Ava Gardner (Kitty Collins), Albert Dekker (Jim Colfax), Sam Levene (Sam Lubinsky), Charles McGraw, William Conrad (the killers)

## The Stranger (1946)

**Studio:** RKO, International Pictures
**Producer:** S. P. Eagle (pseudonym for Sam Spiegel), William Goetz (executive)
**Director:** Orson Welles
**Screenplay:** Anthony Veiller, from a story by Victor Trivas and Decla Dunning; John Huston and Orson Welles (uncredited)
**Cinematographer:** Russell Metty
**Editor:** Ernest Nims
**Music:** Bronislau Kaper
**Art Director:** Perry Ferguson
**Cast:** Orson Welles (Franz Kindler, alias Professor Charles Rankin), Edward G. Robinson (Inspector Wilson), Loretta Young (Mary Longstreet), Philip Merivale (Judge Longstreet), Richard Long (Noah Longstreet), Byron Keith (Dr. Lawrence), Billy House (Mr. Potter), Martha Wentworth (Sarah)

## Three Strangers (1946)

**Studio:** Warner Brothers
**Producer:** Jean Negulesco
**Director:** Jean Negulesco
**Screenplay:** John Huston, Howard Koch, from a 1936 story by Huston
**Cinematographer:** Arthur Edeson
**Editor:** George Amy
**Music:** Adolphe Deutsch
**Art Director:** Ted Smith
**Cast:** Geraldine Fitzgerald (Crystal), Sydney Greenstreet (Arbutny), Peter Lorre

(Johnny West), Peter Whitney (Gabby), Rosalind Ivan (Lady Rhae), Robert Shayne (Fallon), Clifford Brooke (senior clerk), John Alvin (junior clerk), Arthur Shields (prosecutor), Marjorie Riordan (Janet), Stanley Logan (Major Beach), Alan Napier (Shackleford), Joan Loring (Icy)

## FILMS DIRECTED BY JOHN HUSTON

### The Maltese Falcon (1941)

**Studio:** Warner Brothers
**Producer:** Hal Wallis
**Director:** John Huston
**Screenplay:** John Huston, from the novel by Dashiell Hammett
**Cinematographer:** Arthur Edeson
**Editor:** Thomas Richards
**Music:** Adolph Deutsch
**Art Director:** Robert Haas
**Cast:** Humphrey Bogart (Sam Spade), Mary Astor (Brigid O'Shaughnessy), Sidney Greenstreet (Kasper Gutman), Gladys George (Iva Archer), Peter Lorre (Joel Cairo), Barton MacLane (Lieutenant Dundy), Ward Bond (Det. Tom Polhaus), Jerome Cowan (Miles Archer), Lee Patrick (Effie Perine), Elisha Cook, Jr. (Wilmer Cook), Murray Alper (Frank Richman), John Hamilton (Bryan), James Burke (Luke), Walter Huston (Captain Jacobi)

### In This Our Life (1942)

**Studio:** Warner Brothers
**Producer:** Hal Wallis
**Director:** John Huston
**Screenplay:** Howard Koch (and John Huston, uncredited), from the novel by Ellen Glasgow
**Cinematographer:** Ernest Haller
**Editor:** William Holmes
**Music:** Max Steiner
**Art Director:** Robert Haas
**Cast:** Bette Davis (Stanley Timberlake), Olivia de Havilland (Roy Timberlake), George Brent (Craig Fleming), Dennis Morgan (Peter Kingsmill), Charles Coburn (William Fitzroy), Frank Craven (Asa Timberlake), Billie Burke (Lavinia Timberlake), Hattie McDaniel (Minerva Clay), Ernest Anderson (Passy Clay), Walter Huston (bartender)

## Across the Pacific (1942)

**Studio:** Warner Brothers
**Producer:** Jerry Wald, Jack Saper
**Director:** John Huston (finished by Vincent Sherman)
**Screenplay:** Richard Macaulay, from the *Saturday Evening Post* serial "Aloha Means Goodbye," by Robert Carson
**Cinematographer:** Arthur Edeson
**Editor:** Frank Magee (montage sequences by Don Seigel)
**Music:** Adolph Deutsch
**Art Director:** Robert Haas
**Cast:** Humphrey Bogart (Rick Leland), Mary Astor (Alberta Marlow), Sydney Greenstreet (Dr. Lorenz), Charles Halton (A. V. Smith), Victor Sen Yung (Joe Totsuiko), Roland Got (Sugi), Lee Tung Foo (Sam Wing)

## Report from the Aleutians (documentary) (1943)

**Producer:** Army Pictorial Service, Signal Corps, U.S. War Department
**Director:** (Capt.) John Huston
**Screenplay:** John Huston
**Narrator:** Walter Huston and John Huston
**Cinematographer:** Jules Buck, Rey Scott, Freeman Collins, Herman Crabtree, Buzz Ellsworth
**Music:** Dmitri Tiomkin

## (The Battle of) San Pietro (documentary) (1945)

**Producer:** Army Pictorial Service, Signal Corps, U.S. War Department
**Director:** (Maj.) John Huston
**Screenplay:** John Huston
**Narrator:** John Huston
**Cinematographer:** John Huston, Jules Buck, and other Signal Corps members
**Music:** Dmitri Tiomkin

## Let There Be Light (documentary) (1946)

**Producer:** Army Pictorial Service, Signal Corps, U.S. War Department
**Director:** John Huston
**Screenplay:** Charles Kaufman, John Huston
**Narrator:** Walter Huston
**Cinematographer:** Stanley Cortez, John Huston, John Doran, Lloyd Fromm, Joseph Jackman, George Smith
**Editor:** Gene Fowler, Jr.
**Music:** Dimitri Tiomkin

### The Treasure of the Sierra Madre (1948)

**Studio:** Warner Brothers
**Producer:** Henry Blanke
**Director:** John Huston
**Screenplay:** John Huston, from the novel by B. Traven
**Cinematographer:** Ted McCord
**Editor:** Owen Marks
**Music:** Max Steiner
**Music Director:** Leo Forbstein
**Art Director:** John Hughes
**Cast:** Humphrey Bogart (Fred C. Dobbs), Walter Huston (Howard), Tim Holt (Curtin), Bruce Bennett (Cody), Barton MacLane (Pat McCormick), Alfonso Bedoya (Gold Hat), Arthur Soto Rangel (Presidente), Manuel Donde (El Jefe), Jose Torvay (Pablo), Margarito Luna (Panch), Robert (Bobby) Blake (Mexican lottery boy), Jacqueline Dalya ("Chiquita" Lopez), John Huston (American in the white suit)

### Key Largo (1948)

**Studio:** Warner Brothers
**Producer:** Jerry Wald
**Director:** John Huston
**Screenplay:** John Huston and Richard Brooks, from the play by Maxwell Anderson
**Cinematographer:** Karl Freund
**Editor:** Rudi Fuhr
**Music:** Max Steiner
**Art Director:** Leo Kuter
**Cast:** Humphrey Bogart (Frank McCloud), Lauren Bacall (Nora Temple), Lionel Barrymore (James Temple), Edward G. Robinson (Johnny Rocco), Claire Trevor (Gaye Dawn), Thomas Gomez (Curly), Harry Lewis ("Toots" Bass), John Rodney (Clyde Sawyer), Marc Lawrence (Ziggy), Monte Blue (Ben Wade), Dan Seymour ("Angel" Garcia), Jay Silverheels (Johnny Osceola), Rodric Redwing (Tom Osceola)

### We Were Strangers (1949)

**Producer:** S. P. Eagle (pseudonym for Sam Spiegel); a Horizon Production released by Columbia Pictures
**Director:** John Huston
**Screenplay:** John Huston, Peter Viertel, from a segment in *Rough Sketch,* by Robert Sylvester

**Cinematographer:** Russell Metty
**Editor:** Al Clark
**Music:** George Antheil
**Art Director:** Gary Odell
**Cast:** John Garfield (Tony Fenner), Jennifer Jones (China Valdes), Pedro Armendariz (Armando Ariete), Gilbert Roland (Guillermo), Wally Cassel (Miguel), Ramon Navarro (leader of the revolutionaries), David Bond (Ramon), John Huston (no credit)

## The Asphalt Jungle (1950)

**Studio:** Metro-Goldwyn-Mayer
**Producer:** Arthur Hornblow, Jr.
**Director:** John Huston
**Screenplay:** John Huston and Ben Maddow, from the novel by W. R. Burnett
**Cinematographer:** Harold Rosson
**Editor:** George Boemler
**Music:** Miklos Rozsa
**Art Director:** Cedric Gibbons
**Cast:** Sterling Hayden (Dix Handley), Louis Calhern (Alonzo D. Emmerich), Jean Hagen (Doll Conovan), Sam Jaffe ("Doc" Erwin Riedenschneider), James Whitmore (Gus Minissi), Marc Lawrence (Cobby), John McIntire (Hardy), Anthony Caruso (Louis Ciavelli), Teresa Celli (Maria Ciavelli), Marilyn Monroe (Angela Phinlay), Barry Kelley (Dietrich), William Davis (Timmons), Dorothy Tree (May Emmerich), Brad Dexter (Bob Brannen), John Maxwell (Swanson)

## The Red Badge of Courage (1951)

**Studio:** Metro-Goldwyn-Mayer
**Producer:** Gottfried Reinhardt
**Director:** John Huston
**Screenplay:** John Huston, from the novel by Stephen Crane
**Cinematographer:** Harold Rosson
**Editor:** Ben Lewis, supervised by Marguerite Booth
**Music:** Bronislau Kaper
**Art Director:** Cedric Gibbons
**Cast:** Audie Murphy (Henry Fleming, "The Youth"), Bill Mauldin (Tom Wilson, "The Loud Soldier"), John Dierkes (Jim Mauldin, "The Tall Soldier"), Royal Dano ("The Tattered Soldier"), Arthur Hunnicutt (Bill Porter), Tim Durant (the general), Douglas Dick (the lieutenant), Robert Easton Burke (Thompson), Andy Devine ("The Fat Soldier"), Smith Bellow (the captain), Dixon Porter (a veteran). Added voice-over commentary spoken by James Whitmore.

### The African Queen (1951)

**Producer:** Horizon-Romulus in association with S. P. Eagle (pseudonym for Sam Spiegel) for United Artists release
**Director:** John Huston
**Screenplay:** John Huston and James Agee, from the novel by C. S. Forester; additional dialogue by Peter Viertel
**Cinematographer:** Jack Cardiff
**Editor:** Ralph Kemplen
**Music:** Allan Gray
**Art Director:** Wilfred Shingleton
**Costumes:** Doris Langley Moore
**Cast:** Humphrey Bogart (Charlie Allnutt), Katharine Hepburn (Rose Sayer), Robert Morley (Samuel Sayer), Peter Bull (captain of the *Luisa*)

### Moulin Rouge (1952)

**Producer:** John Huston; a Romulus Production for United Artists release
**Director:** John Huston
**Screenplay:** Anthony Veiller, John Huston, from the book by Pierre de La Mure
**Cinematographer:** Oswald Morris
**Editor:** Ralph Kemplen
**Music:** Georges Auric
**Art Director:** Paul Sheriff, Maracel Vertés
**Cast:** José Ferrer (Toulouse-Lautrec), Colette Marchand (Marie Charlet), Suzanne Flon (Myriamme Hayen), Zsa Zsa Gabor (Jane Avril), Katherine Kath (La Goulue), Claude Nollier (Countess Toulouse-Lautrec), Muriel Smith (Aicha), George Lannes (Patov), Rupert John (Chocolate), Tutti Lemkov (Aicha's partner), Eric Pohlmann (bar owner), Walter Crisham (Valentin le Desosse), Mary Clare (Mme Loubet), Lee Montague (Maurice Joyant), Christopher Lee (Paul Gaugin)

### Beat the Devil (1954)

**Producer:** John Huston (with Humphrey Bogart); a Romulus-Santana Production for United Artists release
**Director:** John Huston
**Screenplay:** John Huston, Truman Capote, from the novel by James Helvick; Anthony Veiller, Peter Viertel (uncredited)
**Cinematographer:** Oswald Morris
**Editor:** Ralph Kemplen
**Music:** Franco Mannino
**Art Director:** Wilfred Shingleton
**Cast:** Humphrey Bogart (Billy Dannreuther), Gina Lollobrigida (Maria Dann-reuther), Jennifer Jones (Gwendolyn Chelm), Robert Morley (Peterson), Peter

Lorre (O'Hara), Edward Underdown (Harry Chelm), Ivor Barnard (Major Ross), Marco Tulli (Ravello)

## Moby Dick (1956)

**Producer:** John Huston, Vaughan Dean; a Moulin Picture released by Warner Brothers
**Director:** John Huston
**Screenplay:** John Huston, Ray Bradbury, from the novel by Herman Melville
**Cinematographer:** Oswald Morris
**Editor:** Russell Lloyd
**Music:** Philip Stanton
**Art Director:** Ralph Brinton
**Cast:** Gregory Peck (Ahab), Richard Basehart (Ishmael), Orson Welles (Father Mapple), Leo Genn (Starbuck), Harry Andrews (Stubb), Bernard Miles (Manxman), Mervyn Johns (Peleg), Noel Purcell (Carpenter), Friedrich Ledebur (Queequeg), James Robertson Justice (Captain Boomer), Edric Conner (Daggoo), Seamus Kelly (Flask), Royal Dano (Elijah), Francis de Wolff (Captain Gardiner), Philip Stainton (Bildad), Joseph Tornelty (Peter Coffin), Tamba Alleney (Pip), Ted Howard (blacksmith), Tom Clegg (Tashtego)

## Heaven Knows, Mr. Allison (1957)

**Producer:** Buddy Adler, Eugene Frenke for Twentieth Century-Fox Film Corp.
**Director:** John Huston
**Screenplay:** John Huston, John Lee Mahin, from the novel by Charles Shaw
**Cinematographer:** Oswald Morris
**Editor:** Russell Lloyd
**Music:** Georges Auric
**Art Director:** Stephen Grimes
**Cast:** Robert Mitchum (Marine Corporal Allison), Deborah Kerr (Sister Angela)

## The Barbarian and the Geisha (1958)

**Producer:** Eugene Frenke for Twentieth Century-Fox Film Corp.
**Director:** John Huston
**Screenplay:** Charles Grayson, story by Ellis St. Joseph
**Cinematographer:** Charles G. Clarke
**Editor:** Stuart Gilmore
**Music:** Hugo Friedhofer
**Art Director:** Lyle Wheeler, Jack Martin Smith, and Walter M. Scott
**Cast:** John Wayne (Townsend Harris), Eiko Ando (Okichi), Sam Jaffe (Henry Heusken), So Yamamamura (Tamura), Norman Thomson (captain), James Robbins (Lieutenant Fisher), Morika (prime minister), Kodaya Ichikawa (Daimyo), Hiroshi

Yamato (the shogun), Tokujiro Ichikawa (Harusha), Fuji Kasai (Lord Hotta), Takeshi Kumagai (chamberlain)

### The Roots of Heaven (1958)

**Producer:** Darryl F. Zanuck for Twentieth Century-Fox Film Corp.
**Director:** John Huston
**Screenplay:** Romain Gary, Patrick Leigh-Fermor, from the novel by Romain Gary
**Cinematographer:** Oswald Morris
**Editor:** Russell Lloyd
**Music:** Malcolm Arnold
**Art Director:** Stephen Grimes
**Cast:** Errol Flynn (Forsythe), Trevor Howard (Morel), Juliette Greco (Minna), Eddie Albert (Abe Fields), Orson Welles (Cy Sedgewick), Paul Lukas (Saint Denis), Herbert Lom (Orsini), Gregoire Aslan (Habib), Friedrich Ledebur (Peter Qvist), Edric Connor (Waitari), André Luguet (governor), Olivier Hussenot (the Baron), Pierre Dudan (Major Aholscher), Marc Doelnitz (De Vries), Dan Jackson (Madjumba), Maurice Cannon (Haas), Jacques Marin (Cerisot), Bachir Touré (Yussef)

### The Unforgiven (1960)

**Producer:** James Hill for Continental Hecht/Hill/Lancaster; released by United Artists
**Director:** John Huston
**Screenplay:** Ben Maddow, from the novel by Alan LeMay
**Cinematographer:** Franz Planer
**Editor:** Hugh Russell Lloyd
**Music:** Dimitri Tiomkin
**Art Director:** Stephen Grimes
**Cast:** Burt Lancaster (Ben Zachary), Audrey Hepburn (Rachel Zachary), Lillian Gish (Mattilda Zachary), John Saxon (Johnny Portugal), Charles Bickford (Zeb Rawlins), Albert Salmi (Charlie Rawlins), Audie Murphy (Cash Zachary), Joseph Wiseman (Abe Kelsey), Doug McClure (Andy Zachary), Kipp Hamilton (Georgia Rawlins), Carlos Rivas (Lost Bird)

### The Misfits (1961)

**Producer:** Frank E. Taylor for Seven Arts Productions; distributed by United Artists
**Director:** John Huston
**Screenplay:** Arthur Miller, from his novella published in *Esquire* in 1957
**Cinematographer:** Russell Metty
**Editor:** George Tomasini
**Music:** Alex North

**Art Director:** William Newberry, Stephen Grimes
**Costumes:** Jesse Munden
**Cast:** Marilyn Monroe (Roslyn Taber), Clark Gable (Gay Langland), Montgomery Clift (Perce Howland), Eli Wallach (Guido Dellini), Thelma Ritter (Isabelle Steers), James Barton (old man in bar), Kevin McCarthy (Roslyn's husband), Dennis Shaw (boy in bar), Philip Mitchell (Charles Steers), Walter Ramage (aged groom), Peggy Barton (young bride), Estelle Winwood (woman collecting money), Marietta Tree (Susan), Bobby Lasalle (bartender)

### Freud (The Secret Passion) (1962)

**Producer:** Wolfgang Reinhardt; a John Huston Production for Universal International Pictures
**Director:** John Huston
**Screenplay:** Wolfgang Reinhardt, Charles Kaufman
**Cinematographer:** Douglas Slocombe
**Editor:** Ralph Kemplen
**Music:** Jerry Goldsmith, with electronic music sequence by Henk Badings
**Art Director:** Stephen Grimes
**Cast:** Montgomery Clift (Sigmund Freud), Susannah York (Cecily Koertner), Larry Parks (Dr. Joseph Breuer), Susan Kohner (Martha Freud), Eileen Herlie (Frau Ida Koertner), Fernand Ledoux (Professor Charcot), David McCallum (Carl von Schlosser), Rosalie Crutchley (Frau Freud), David Kossoff (Jacob Freud), Joseph Furst (Herr Jacob Koertner), Eric Portman (Dr. Theodore Meynert), Alexander Mango (Babinsky), Leonard Sachs (Brouhardier), Allan Cuthbertson (Wilkie), Moira Redmond (Nora Wimmer)

### The List of Adrian Messenger (1963)

**Producer:** Edward Lewis, Edward Muhl (in charge of production) for Joel Productions-Universal Pictures; distributed by Universal Pictures
**Director:** John Huston
**Screenplay:** Anthony Veiller, from the novel by Phillip MacDonald
**Cinematographer:** Joseph McDonald, Ted Scaife
**Editor:** Terry Morse, Hugh S. Fowler
**Music:** Jerry Goldsmith
**Art Director:** Alexander Golitzen, Stephen Grimes, George Webb
**Makeup Creator:** Bud Westmore
**Cast:** Kirk Douglas (George Bruttenholm), George C. Scott (Anthony Gethryn), Clive Brook (Marquis of Gleneyre), Dana Wynter (Lady Jocelyn Bruttenholm), Gladys Cooper (Mrs. Karoudjian), Herbert Marshall (Sir Wilfred Lucas), Jacques Roux (Raoul LeBorg), John Merivale (Adrian Messenger), Marcel Dalio (Max Karoudjian), Walter Anthony Huston (Derek Bruttenholm), Bernard Archard

(Inspector Pike), Roland D. Long (Carstairs), John Huston (Lord Acton), Tony Curtis (organ grinder), Burt Lancaster (protesting woman), Frank Sinatra (gypsy with a horse), Robert Mitchum (Jim Slattery)

## The Night of the Iguana (1964)

**Producer:** Ray Stark; a John Huston-Ray Stark Production for Seven Arts; released through Metro-Goldwyn-Mayer
**Screenplay:** John Huston, Anthony Veiller, from the play by Tennessee Williams
**Cinematographer:** Gabriel Figueroa
**Editor:** Ralph Kemplen
**Music:** Benjamin Frankel
**Art Director:** Stephen Grimes
**Costumes:** Dorothy Jeakins
**Cast:** Richard Burton (Rev. T. Lawrence Shannon), Ava Gardner (Maxine Faulk), Deborah Kerr (Hannah Jelkes), Sue Lyon (Charlotte Goodall), James Ward (Hank Prosner), Grayson Hall (Judith Fellowes), Cyril Delevanti (Nonno), Mary Boylan (Miss Peebles), Gladys Hill (Miss Dexter), Billie Matticks (Miss Throxton), Emilio Fernandes (barkeeper), Fidelmar Duran (Pepe), Roberto Leyra (Pedro), C. G. Kim (Chang), Eloise Hardt, Thelda Victor, Betty Proctor, Dorthy Vance, Liz Rubey, Bernice Starr, Barbara Joyce (teachers)

## The Bible . . . In the Beginning (1966)

**Producer:** Dino De Laurentiis for De Laurentiis Cinematografica; distributed by Twentieth Century-Fox Film Corp., Seven Arts Pictures
**Director:** John Huston
**Screenplay:** Christopher Fry
**Cinematographer:** Giuseppe Rottunno
**Editor:** Alberto Galliti
**Music:** Toshiro Mayuzumi
**Art Director:** Stephen Grimes
**Cast:** Michael Parks (Adam), Ulla Bergryd (Eve), Richard Harris (Cain), Franco Nero (Abel), Stephen Boyd (Nimrod), John Huston (Noah), George C. Scott (Abraham), Ava Gardner (Sarah), Peter O'Toole (the angel messenger), Gabriele Ferzetti (Lot), Eleonara Rossi Drago (Lot's wife), Pupella Maggio (Noah's wife), Grazia Maria Spina and Adriana Ambesi (Lot's daughters), Zoe Sallis (Hagar)

## Casino Royale (1967)

**Producer:** Charles K. Feldman, Jerry Bresler for Famous Artists Productions; a Columbia Pictures release
**Director:** John Huston, Ken Hughes, Val Guest, Robert Parrish, Joseph McGrath
**Screenplay:** Wolf Mankowitz, John Law, Michael Sayers, suggested by the novel

by Ian Fleming; additional writing by Billy Wilder, Ben Hecht, John Huston, Val Guest, Joseph Heller, Terry Southern
**Cinematographer:** Jack Hildyard; additional photography by John Wilcox, Nicholas Roeg
**Editor:** Bill Lenny
**Music:** Burt Bacharach
**Production Designer:** Michael Stringer
**Art Director:** John Howell, Ivor Beddoes, Lionel Couch
**Cast:** Peter Sellers (Evelyn Tremble, 007), Ursula Andress (Vesper Lynd), David Niven (Sir James Bond), Orson Welles (Le Chiffre), Joanna Pettit (Mata Bond), Daliah Lavi (the detainer), Woody Allen (Jimmy Bond/Dr. Nash), Deborah Kerr (Agent Mimi/Lady Fiona), William Holden (Ransome), Charles Boyer (Le Grand), John Huston (McTarry/M), Kurt Kasznar (Smernov), George Raft (himself), Jean-Paul Belmondo (French legionnaire), Terence Cooper (Cooper), Barbara Bouchet (Moneypenny), Angela Scoular (Buttercup), Gabriella Licudi (Eliza), Tracy Crisp (Heather), Elaine Taylor (Peg), Jacqueline Bisset (Miss Goodthighs)

### Reflections in a Golden Eye (1967)
**Producer:** Ray Stark for the John Huston-Ray Stark Production; a Warner Brothers-Seven Arts International release
**Director:** John Huston
**Screenplay:** Chapman Mortimer, Gladys Hill, based on the novel by Carson McCullers
**Cinematographer:** Aldo Tonti
**Editor:** Russell Lloyd
**Music:** Toshiro Mayuzumi
**Production Designer:** Stephen Grimes
**Art Director:** Bruno Avesani
**Cast:** Elizabeth Taylor (Leonora Pemberton), Marlon Brando (Maj. Weldon Pemberton), Brian Keith (Lt. Col. Morris Langdon), Julie Harris (Alison Langdon), Robert Forster (Private Williams), Zorro David (Anacleto), Gordon Mitchell (stables sergeant), Irvin Dugan (Captain Weincheck), Fay Sparks (Susie), Douglas Stark (Dr. Burgess), Al Mullock (old soldier), Ted Beniades (sergeant)

### Sinful Davey (1969)
**Producer:** William N. Grof, Walter Mirisch (executive producer) for the John Huston-Walter Mirisch Production; distributed by United Artists
**Director:** John Huston
**Screenplay:** James R. Webb, based on the book *The Life of David Haggart,* by David Haggart
**Cinematographer:** Freddie Young, Edward (Ted) Scaife

**Editor:** Russell Lloyd
**Music:** Ken Thorne
**Production Designer:** Stephen Grimes
**Art Director:** Carmen Dillon
**Costumes:** Margaret Furse
**Cast:** John Hurt (Davey Haggart), Pamela Franklin (Annie), Nigel Davenport (Constable Richardson), Ronald Fraser (McNab), Robert Morley (Duke of Argyll), Fidelma Murphy (Jean Carlisle), Maxine Audley (Duchess of Argyll), Fionnuala Flanagan (Penelope), Donal McCann (Sir James Graham), Allan Cuthbertson (Captain Douglas), Eddie Byrne (Yorkshire Bill), Niall MacGinnis (Boots Simpson), Noel Purcell (Jock), Judith Furse (Mary), Francis De Wolff (Andrew), Paul Farell (bailiff of Stirling), Geoffrey Golden (Warden McEwan), Leo Collins (Dr. Gresham), Mickster Reid (Billy the Goat), Derek Young (Bobby Rae), John Franklin (George Bagrie), Eileen Murphy (Mary Kidd)

### A Walk with Love and Death (1969)

**Producer:** Carter De Haven III for a John Huston-Carter DeHaven III Production; Twentieth Century-Fox Film Corp.
**Director:** John Huston
**Screenplay:** Dale Wasserman; adapted by Hans Koningsberger from his novel
**Cinematographer:** Ted Scaife
**Editor:** Russell Lloyd
**Music:** Georges Delerue
**Production Designer:** Stephen Grimes
**Art Director:** Wolf Witzemann
**Costumes:** Leonor Fini
**Cast:** Anjelica Huston (Lady Claudia), Assaf Dayan (Heron of Foix), Anthony Corlan (Robert), John Hallam (Sir Meles), Robert Lang (pilgrim leader), Guy Deghy (priest), Michael Gough (mad monk), George Murcell (captain), Eileen Murphy (gypsy), Anthony Nicholls (father superior), Joseph O'Connor (St. Jean), John Huston (Robert the Elder), John Franklin (whoremaster), Francis Heim (knight lieutenant)

### The Kremlin Letter (1970)

**Producer:** Carter De Haven III, Sam Wiesenthal (executive producer); a John Huston-Carter De Haven III Production; Twentieth Century-Fox Film Corp.
**Director:** John Huston
**Screenplay:** John Huston, Gladys Hill, from the novel by Noel Behn
**Cinematographer:** Ted Scaife
**Editor:** Russell Lloyd
**Music:** Robert Drasnin, composed by Toshiro Mayuzumi

**Art Director:** Elven Webb
**Costumes:** John Furness
**Cast:** Bibi Andersson (Erika), Richard Boone (Ward), Nigel Green (Janis, alias "the Whore"), Dean Jagger (Highwayman), Lila Kedrova (Sophie), Michael MacLiammoir (Sweet Alice), Patrick O'Neal (Rone), Barbara Parkins (B. A.), Ronald Radd (Potkin), George Sanders (Warlock), Raf Vallone (Puppet Maker), Max Von Sydow (Kosnov), Orson Welles (Bresnavitch), Sandor Eles (Grodin), Niall MacGinnis (Erector Set), Anthony Chinn (Kitai), Guy Degny (professor), John Huston (Admiral), Fulvia Ketoff (Sonia), Vonetta McGee (Negress), Marc Lawrence (priest), Cyril Shaps (police doctor), Christopher Sanford (Rudolph), Anna-Maria Pravda (Mrs. Kazar), George Pravda (Kazar), Ludmilla Dutarova (Mrs. Potkin), Dimitri Tamarov (Ilya), Pehr-Olof Siren (receptionist), Daniel Smid (waiter)

### Fat City (1972)

**Producer:** Ray Stark; a John Huston-Rastar Production; Columbia Pictures release
**Director:** John Huston
**Screenplay:** Leonard Gardner, from his novel
**Cinematographer:** Conrad Hall
**Editor:** Marguerite Booth
**Music:** Marvin Hamlisch (supervision)
**Production Designer:** Richard Sylbert
**Cast:** Stacy Keach (Billy Tully), Jeff Bridges (Ernie Munger), Candy Clark (Faye), Susan Tyrell (Oma), Nicholas Colosanto (Ruben), Art Aragon (Babe), Curtis Cokes (Earl), Sixto Rodriguez (Lucero), Billy Walker (Wes), Wayne Mahan (Buford), Ruben Navarro (Fuentes)

### The Life and Times of Judge Roy Bean (1972)

**Producer:** John Foreman for National General
**Director:** John Huston
**Screenplay:** John Milius
**Cinematographer:** Richard Moore
**Editor:** Hugh S. Fowler
**Music:** Maurice Jarre
**Art Director:** Tambi Larsen
**Cast:** Paul Newman (Judge Roy Bean), Ava Gardner (Lillie Langtry), Victoria Principal (Marie Elena), Anthony Perkins (Reverend LaSalle), Tab Hunter (Sam Dodd), John Huston (Grizzly Adams), Stacy Keach (Bad Bob), Roddy McDowell (Frank Gass), Jacqueline Bisset (Rose Bean), Ned Beatty (Tector Crites), Jim Buck (Bart Jackson), Matt Clark (Nick the Grub), Steve Kanaly (Whorehouse Lucky Jim), Bill McKinney (Fermil Parlee)

## The Mackintosh Man (1973)

**Producer:** John Foreman, William Hill (associate) for Warner Brothers
**Director:** John Huston
**Screenplay:** Walter Hill, from *The Freedom Trap,* by Desmond Bagley
**Cinematographer:** Oswald Morris
**Editor:** Russell Lloyd
**Music:** Maurice Jarre
**Art Director:** Alan Tomkins
**Production Designer:** Terry Marsh
**Cast:** Paul Newman (Reardon), Dominique Sanda (Mrs. Smith), James Mason (Sir George Wheeler), Harry Andrews (Mackintosh), Ian Bannen (Slade), Michael Hordern (Brown), Nigel Patrick (Soames/Trevelan), Peter Vaughan (Brunskill), Roland Culver (judge), Percy Herbert (Taafe), Robert Lang (Jack Summers), Jenny Runacre (Gerda), John Bindon (Buster), Hugh Manning (prosecutor), Wolfe Morris (Malta police commissioner), Noel Purcell (O'Donovan), Donald Webster (Trevis), Keith Bell (Palmer), Niall MacGinnis (Warder)

## The Man Who Would Be King (1975)

**Producer:** John Foreman, James Arnett (associate) for Associated Artists; released by Columbia Pictures
**Director:** John Huston
**Screenplay:** Gladys Hill, John Huston, from the story by Rudyard Kipling
**Cinematographer:** Oswald Morris
**Editor:** Russell Lloyd
**Music:** Maurice Jarre
**Production Designer:** Alex Trainer
**Art Director:** Tony Inglis
**Costumes:** Edith Head
**Cast:** Sean Connery (Daniel Dravot), Michael Caine (Peachy Carnehan), Christopher Plummer (Rudyard Kipling), Saeed Joffrey (Billy Fish), Karrovin Ben Bouih (Kafu-Selim), Jack May (district commissioner), Doghmi Larbi (Ootah), Shakira Caine (Roxanne), Mohammed Shamsi (Babu), Paul Antrim (Mulvaney), Albert Moses (Ghulam)

## Independence (1976)

**Producers:** Joyce Ritter, Lloyd Ritter for National Park Service and Twentieth Century-Fox
**Director:** John Huston
**Screenplay:** Joyce Ritter, Lloyd Ritter, Thomas McGrath
**Cinematographer:** Owen Roizman
**Cast:** Ken Howard (Thomas Jefferson), Patrick O'Neal (George Washington),

William Atherton (Benjamin Rush), Eli Wallach (Benjamin Franklin), Anne Jackson (Abigail Adams), Pat Hingle (John Adams), Paul Sparer (John Hancock)

## *Wiseblood* (1979)

**Producer:** Michael Fitzgerald, Kathy Fitzgerald for Ithaca-Anthea; released through New Line Cinema
**Director:** John Huston
**Screenplay:** Benedict Fitzgerald, from the novel by Flannery O'Connor
**Cinematographer:** Gerry Fisher
**Editor:** Roberto Silvi
**Music:** Alex North (composition and adaptation)
**Set and Costume Design:** Sally Fitzgerald
**Cast:** Brad Dourif (Hazel Motes), Ned Beatty (Hoover Shoates), Harry Dean Stanton (Asa Hawks), Amy Wright (Sabbath Lily), Mary Nell Santacroce (landlady), John Huston (Hazel's grandfather), Daniel Shor (Enoch Emery), William Hickey (preacher)

## *Phobia* (1980)

**Producer:** Larry Spiegel for Spiegel-Bergman Films
**Director:** John Huston
**Screenplay:** Ronald Shusett, Gary Sherman, Lew Lehman, James Sangster, Peter Bellwood
**Cinematographer:** Reginald Morris
**Editor:** Stan Cole
**Music:** Andre Gagnon
**Production Designer:** Ben Edwards
**Cast:** Paul Michael Glaser (Dr. Peter Ross), John Colicos (Inspector Barnes), Susan Hogan (Jenny St. Clair), Alexandra Stewart (Barbara Grey), Robert O'Ree (Bubba King), David Bolt (Henry Owen), David Eisner (Johnny Venuti), Lisa Langlois (Laura Adams), Kenneth Walsh (Sergeant Wheeler), Neil Vipond (Dr. Clegg), Patricia Collins (Dr. Alice Toland)

## *Victory* (1981)

**Producer:** Freddie Fields for Lorimar; a Paramount release
**Director:** John Huston
**Screenplay:** Evan Jones, Yabo Yablonsky, from a story by Yablonsky, Djordje Milicevic, Jeff Macquire
**Cinematographer:** Gerry Fisher
**Editor:** Roberto Silvi
**Music:** Bill Conti
**Art Director:** J. Dennis Washington

**Cast:** Sylvester Stallone (Robert Hatach), Michael Caine (John Colby), Pélé (Luis Fernandez), Max Von Sydow (Maj. Karl von Steiner), Anton Diffring (chief commentator), Tom Pigott-Smith (Rose), Daniel Massey (Colonel Waldron), Gary Waldhorn (Coach Mueller), Carole Laure (Renee), Julian Curry (Shurlock), Bobby Moore (Terry Brady)

## *Annie* (1982)

**Producer:** Ray Stark for Rastar; a Columbia Pictures release
**Director:** John Huston
**Screenplay:** Carol Sobieski, from the stage play by Thomas Meehan, based on the comic strip created by Harold Gray
**Cinematography:** Richard Moore
**Editor:** Margaret Booth (supervising), Michael A. Stevenson
**Music:** Ralph Burns; songs by Charles Strouse, Martin Charnin
**Costumes:** Theoni Aldredge
**Cast:** Aileen Quinn (Annie), Carol Burnett (Miss Hannigan), Albert Finney ("Daddy" Warbucks), Ann Reinking (Grace Farrell), Bernadette Peters (Lily), Tim Curry (Rooster), Geoffrey Holder (Punjab), Edward Herrmann (FDR), Sandy (himself).

## *Under the Volcano* (1984)

**Producer:** Moritz Borman and Wieland Schulz-Kiel in association with Ithaca-Conacine; a Universal release
**Screenplay:** Guy Gallo, based on the novel by Malcolm Lowry
**Cinematographer:** Gabriel Figueroa
**Editor:** Roberto Silvi
**Music:** Alex North
**Production Designer:** Gunther Gerzso
**Cast:** Albert Finney (Geoffrey Firmin), Jacqueline Bisset (Yvonne Firmin), Anthony Andrews (Hugh Firmin), Katy Jurado (Señora Gregoria) James Villiers (Brit), Ignacio Lopez-Tarzo (Dr. Vigil), Dawson Bray (Quincey), Jim McCarthy (Gringo), Rene Ruiz (Dwarf), Emilio Fernandez (Diosdado), Carlos Requelme (Bustamante)

## *Prizzi's Honor* (1985)

**Producer:** John Foreman; an ABC Motion Pictures Presentation; released by Twentieth Century-Fox Film Corp.
**Director:** John Huston
**Screenplay:** Richard Condon, Janet Roach, based on the novel by Richard Condon
**Cinematographer:** Andre Barthowiak
**Editor:** Rudi and Kaja Fehr

**Music:** Alex North
**Production Designer:** Dennis Washington
**Cast:** Jack Nicholson (Charlie Partanna), Kathleen Turner (Irene Walker), Robert Loggia (Eduardo Prizzi), John Rudolph (Angelo "Pop" Partanna), William Hickey (Don Carrado Prizzi), Lee Richardson (Dominic Prizzi), Anjelica Huston (Maerose Prizzi), Michael Lombard (Filargi "Finlay"), Lawrence Tierney (Lieutenant Hanley), Joseph Ruskin (Marxie Heller)

### The Dead (1987)

**Producer:** Wieland Schulz-Keil and Chris Sievernich for Liffey Films; released by Vestron Pictures
**Director:** John Huston
**Screenplay:** Tony Huston, based on the short story from *Dubliners,* by James Joyce
**Cinematographer:** Fred Murphy
**Editor:** Roberto Silvi
**Music:** Alex North
**Production Designer:** Stephen Grimes, Dennis Washington; Josie MacAvin (set decoration)
**Costumes:** Dorothy Jeakins
**Cast:** Donal McCann (Gabriel Conroy), Anjelica Huston (Gretta Conroy), Helena Carroll (Aunt Kate), Cathleen Delaney (Aunt Julia), Frank Patterson (Bartell D'Arcy), Rachael Dowling (Lily), Katherine O'Toole (Miss Furlong), Bairbre Dowling (Miss Higgins), Maria Hayden (Miss O'Callaghan), Cormac O'Herlihy (Mr. Kerrigan), Colm Meaney (Mr. Bergin), Ingrid Craigie (Mary Jane), Dan O'Herlihy (Mr. Brown), Marie Kean (Mrs. Malins), Donal Donnelly (Freddy Malins), Sean McClory (Mr. Grace), Maria McDermottroe (Molly Ivors), Lyda Anderson (Miss Daly)

## FILMS IN WHICH JOHN HUSTON APPEARED AS AN ACTOR OR WHICH HE NARRATED

### Report from the Aleutians (1943)

**Producer:** U.S. Army Pictorial Service
**Director:** John Huston
**Narrator:** John Huston

### The Battle of San Pietro (documentary) (1945)

**Producer:** U.S. Army Pictorial Service
**Director:** (Maj.) John Huston
**Narrator:** John Huston

## We Were Strangers (1949)

**Producer:** S. P. Eagle (pseudonym for Sam Spiegel)
**Director:** John Huston
**Cast:** John Garfield, Jennifer Jones, Pedro Armendariz, Gilbert Roland, Wally Cassel, Ramon Novarro, David Bond, John Huston

## Freud (The Secret Passion) (1962)

**Producer:** Wolfgang Reinhardt for Universal International Pictures
**Director:** John Huston
**Cast:** Montgomery Clift, Larry Parks, Susannah York, Susan Kohner. Huston provided the voice-over narration.

## The List of Adrian Messenger (1962)

**Producer:** Edward Lewis
**Director:** John Huston
**Cast:** Kirk Douglas, George C. Scott, Dana Wynter, Clive Brook, Herbert Marshall, Gladys Cooper, John Merivale, Maracel Dalio, Walter Anthony (Tony) Huston, Bernard Arachard, Roland D. Long, Tony Curtis, Burt Lancaster, Frank Sinatra, Robert Mitchum. Huston appeared in the climactic hunt scene as Lord Acton.

## The Cardinal (1963)

**Producer:** Otto Preminger for Gamma Productions; distributed by Columbia Pictures
**Director:** Otto Preminger
**Cast:** Tom Tryon, Romy Schneider, John Saxon, Carol Lynley, Raf Vallone, Burgess Meredith. Huston essayed the role of Cardinal Glennon.

## The Bible . . . In the Beginning (1966)

**Producer:** Dino De Laurentiis
**Director:** John Huston
**Cast:** Michael Parks, Ulla Bergryd, Richard Harris, John Huston, Stephen Boyd, George C. Scott, Ava Gardner, Peter O'Toole. Huston played the role of Noah and narrated the film.

## The Life and Times of John Huston (1966)

**Producer:** Roger Graef for Allan King and Associates/NET/BBC/CBC
**Director:** Roger Graef
**Screenwriter:** Roger Graef
**Cinematographer:** Charles Stewart
**Cast:** John Huston, Anjelica Huston, Tony Huston, Gladys Hill, Evelyn Keyes, Elizabeth Taylor, Marlon Brando, Burl Ives

## Casino Royale (1967)

**Producer:** Charles K. Feldman, Jerry Bresler
**Director:** John Huston, Ken Hughes, Val Guest, Robert Parrish, Joseph McGrath
**Cast:** Peter Sellers, Ursula Andress, David Niven, Orson Welles, Joanna Pettit, Daliah Lavi, Woody Allen, Deborah Kerr, William Holden, Charles Boyer, John Huston, Kurt Kasznar, George Raft, Jean-Paul Belmondo, Terence Cooper, Barbara Bouchet, Angela Scoular, Gabriella Licudi, Tracy Crisp, Elaine Taylor, Jacqueline Bisset. Huston played McTarry (also known as "M").

## Candy (1968)

**Producer:** Robert Haggiag, Selig J. Seligman (executive producer) for Selmur Pictures-Dear Film-Les Films Corona; distributed by Cinerama Releasing Corp.
**Director:** Christian Marquand
**Cast:** Ewa Aulin, Marlon Brando, Ringo Starr, Charles Aznavour, Richard Burton, James Coburn, Walter Matthau, John Astin, Elsa Martinelli. Huston played Dr. Dunlap.

## De Sade (1969)

**Producer:** Samuel Z. Arkoff, James H. Nicholson, Louis M. Heyward (executive producer) for American International Productions-Trans-Continental Film-CCC-Filmkunst
**Director:** Cy Enfield
**Cast:** Keir Dullea, Senta Berger, Lilli Palmer. Huston played Abbé de Sade.

## A Walk with Love and Death (1969)

**Producer:** Carter De Haven III for a John Huston-Carter De Haven III Production; released by Twentieth Century-Fox Film Corp.
**Director:** John Huston
**Cast:** Anjelica Huston, Assaf Dayan, Anthony Corlan, John Hallam, Robert Lang, Guy Deghy, Michael Gough, George Murcell, Eileen Murphy, Anthony Nicholls, Joseph O'Connor, John Franklin, Francis Heim, Melvin Hayes, Barry Keegan, Nicholas Smith. Huston played Robert the Elder.

## The Kremlin Letter (1970)

**Producer:** Carter De Haven III, Sam Wiesenthal
**Cast:** Bibi Andersson, Richard Boone, Nigel Green, Dan Jagger, Lila Kedrova, Michael MacLiammoir, Patrick O'Neal, Barbara Parkins, Ronald Radd, George Sanders, Raf Vallone, Max Von Sydow, Orson Welles, Sandor Eles, Niall MacGinnis, Anthony Chinn, Guy Degny. Huston played Admiral.

*The Other Side of the Wind (never completed production)* (1970)
**Producer:** Orson Welles
**Director:** Orson Welles
**Cast:** John Huston, Peter Bogdanovich, Lilli Palmer, Bob Ransom, Howard Grossman, Dennis Hopper. Huston played Jake Hannaford.

*Myra Breckenridge* (1970)
**Producer:** Robert Fryer for Twentieth Century-Fox Film Corp.
**Director:** Michael Sarne
**Cast:** Raquel Welch, Mae West, Rex Reed, Farrah Fawcett, Roger C. Carmel, Jim Backus. Huston played Buck Loner.

*The Bridge in the Jungle* (1971)
**Producer:** Pancho Kohner; released through United Artists
**Director:** Pancho Kohner
**Cast:** Charles Robinson, Katy Jurado. Huston played Sleigh.

*The Deserter* (1971)
**Producer:** Norman Baer, Ralph Serpe; released through Paramount
**Director:** Burt Kennedy
**Cast:** Bekim Fehmiu, Richard Crenna, Chuck Connors, Ricardo Montalban, Ian Bannen, Brandon de Wilde, Slim Pickens. Huston played General Miles.

*Man in the Wilderness* (1971)
**Producer:** Sanford Howard
**Director:** Richard Sarafin
**Cast:** Richard Harris, John Bindon, Ben Carruthers, Percy Herbert, Henry Wilcoxon. Huston played Captain Hendry.

*The Life and Times of Judge Roy Bean* (1972)
**Producer:** John Foreman
**Director:** John Huston
**Cast:** Paul Newman, Ava Gardner, Victoria Principal, Anthony Perkins. Huston played the role of Grizzly Adams.

*Battle for the Planet of the Apes* (1974)
**Producer:** Arthur P. Jacobs; released through Twentieth Century-Fox Film Corp.
**Director:** J. Lee Thompson
**Cast:** Roddy McDowell, Claude Atkins, Natalie Trundy. Huston played Lawgiver.

## Chinatown (1974)

**Producer:** Robert Evans; released through Paramount
**Director:** Roman Polanski
**Cast:** Jack Nicholson, Faye Dunaway. Huston played Noah Cross.

## Breakout (1975)

**Producer:** Robert Chartoff, Irwin Winkler; released through Columbia Pictures
**Director:** Tom Gries
**Cast:** Charles Bronson, Robert Duvall, Jill Ireland, Randy Quaid. Huston played Harris.

## The Wind and the Lion (1975)

**Producer:** Herb Jaffe; released through United Artists
**Director:** John Milius
**Cast:** Sean Connery, Candice Bergen, Brian Keith. Huston played John Hay.

## Sherlock Holmes in New York (1976)

**Producer:** John Cutts for Twentieth Century-Fox Television/NBC-TV
**Director:** Boris Sagal
**Cast:** Roger Moore, Charlotte Rampling, Gig Young. Huston played Professor Moriarty.

## Tentacles (1977)

**Producer:** E. F. Doria; released through American International Pictures
**Director:** Oliver Hellman (Ouido Assonitis)
**Cast:** Shelley Winters, Henry Fonda, Bo Hopkins. Huston played Ned Turner.

## The Rhinemann Exchange (1977)

**Producer:** Richard Collins for NBC-TV
**Director:** Burt Kennedy
**Cast:** Stephen Collins, Larry Hagman, Lauren Hutton, José Ferrer. Huston played an American ambassador.

## Hollywood on Trial (documentary) (1977)

**Producer:** James C. Gutman
**Director:** David Helpern, Jr.
**Narrator:** John Huston

## The Hobbit (animated) (1977)

**Producer:** Arthur Rankin, Jr., Jules Bass for NBC-TV and Rankin-Bass Productions

**Director:** Arthur Rankin, Jr.
**Voices:** Orson Bean, John Huston, Richard Boone, Otto Preminger, Hans Conreid

## *The Word* (1978)
**Producer:** David Manson for CBS-TV and Charles Fries Productions
**Director:** Richard Lang
**Cast:** David Janssen, James Whitmore, Florinda Bolkan, Eddie Albert, John Huston

## *The Bermuda Triangle* (1978)
**Producer:** Rene Cardona, Jr., for Concacine/Nucleo
**Director:** Rene Cardona, Jr.
**Cast:** John Huston, Gloris Guida, Marina Vlady, Claudine Auger, Hugo Stiglitz

## *Angela* (1978)
**Producer:** Zev Braun, Leland Nolan for Zev Braun Productions
**Director:** Boris Sagal
**Cast:** Sophia Loren, Steve Railsback, John Huston, John Vernon

## *Jaguar Lives!* (1979)
**Producer:** Derek Gibson; released through American International Pictures
**Director:** Ernest Pintoff
**Cast:** Joe Lewis, Christopher Lee, Donald Pleasance, Barbara Bach, John Huston

## *Winter Kills* (1979)
**Producer:** Fred Caruso; an Avco Embassy Pictures/Richert International release
**Director:** William Richert
**Cast:** Jeff Bridges, John Huston, Anthony Perkins, Sterling Hayden, Dorothy Malone, Elizabeth Taylor

## *The Battle of Mareth/The Greatest Battle* (1979)
**Producer:** Titanus/Dimension Pictures
**Director:** Hank Milestone (Umberto Lenzi)
**Cast:** John Huston, Henry Fonda, Stacy Keach, Samantha Eggar, Helmut Berger, Orson Welles (narrator)

## *Head On* (1979)
**Producer:** Alan Simmonds for Michael Grant Productions
**Director:** Michael Grant
**Cast:** Sally Kellerman, Stephen Lack, John Huston, Larry Dane

### John Huston's Dublin (documentary) (1980)
**Producer:** John McGreevy, Pat Ferns
**Director:** John McGreevy
**Writer:** James Plunkett
**Cinematographer:** Ron Stannett
**Cast:** John Huston, Niall Tobin, Gerard Gillen, Jos Begley

### Agee (documentary) (1980)
**Producer:** Ross Spears
**Director:** Ross Spears
**Appearing as Themselves:** John Huston, Jimmy Carter, Father James Flye, Mia Agee, Olivia Wood, Dwight Macdonald, Robert Fitzgerald

### The Visitor (1980)
**Producer:** Ovidio Assonitis for the International Picture Show Co.
**Director:** Michael J. Paradise
**Cast:** Mel Ferrer, Glenn Ford, John Huston, Sam Peckinpah, Shelley Winters

### John Huston: A War Remembered (1981)
**Producer:** Jim Washburn for KCET-TV, Los Angeles/Rastar Televison
**Director:** Jim Washburn
**Cast:** John Huston, Clete Roberts. Huston and Roberts discuss *Report from the Aleutians, The Battle of San Pietro,* and *Let There Be Light,* which are shown in their entirety.

### Cannery Row (1982)
**Producer:** Michael Phillips for Metro-Goldwyn-Mayer/United Artists)
**Director:** David S. Ward
**Cast:** Nick Nolte, Deborah Winger, Audra Lindley, Frank McRae, M. Emmet Walsh, John Huston (narrator)

### Lights! Camera! Annie! (documentary) (1982)
**Producer:** Margery Doppelt, Gregory McClatchey for KCET-TV, Los Angeles/Kaleidoscope Films/Columbia/Rastar
**Director:** Andrew J. Kuehn
**Cast:** John Huston, Ray Stark, Aileen Quinn, Albert Finney, Carol Burnett, Tim Curry, Bernadette Peters

### The Directors Guild Series: John Huston (documentary) (1982)
**Producer:** Randolph Turrow for Maddox-Turrow Productions/DGA Educational and Benevolent Foundation

**Director:** William Crain
**Cast:** John Huston, Phillip Dunne

Lovesick (1983)

**Producer:** Charles Okun for Ladd Pictures; released through Warner Brothers
**Director:** Marshall Brickman
**Cast:** Dudley Moore, Elizabeth McGovern, Alec Guinness, Alan King. Huston played a psychiatrist.

A Minor Miracle/Young Giants (independent) (1983)

**Producer:** Tom Moyer
**Director:** Terry Tanen
**Cast:** David Ruprecht, Pélé, John Huston

John Huston and the Dubliners<br>(documentary; no information available) (1987)

Momo (independent) (1986)

**Producer:** Horst Wendlandt
**Director:** Johannes Schaaf
**Cast:** Radost Bokel, Leopoldo Trieste, Bruno Stori, Ninetto Davoli, Mario Adorf, John Huston

# Bibliography

Goode, James. *The Making of the "The Misfits."* New York: Bobbs-Merrill, 1963.

Grobel, Lawrence. *The Hustons.* New York: Charles Scribner's Sons, 1989.

Hammen, Scott. *John Huston.* Boston: Twayne, 1985.

Hepburn, Katharine. *The Making of The African Queen: Or, How I Went to Africa with Bogart, Bacall and Huston and Almost Lost My Mind.* New York: Alfred A. Knopf, 1987.

Huston, John. *An Open Book.* New York: Alfred A. Knopf, 1980.

Kaminsky, Stuart. *John Huston: Maker of Magic.* Boston: Houghton Mifflin, 1978.

McCarthy, John. *The Films of John Huston.* Secaucus, N.J.: Citadel, 1987.

Nolan, William F. *John Huston: King Rebel.* Los Angeles: Sherbourne, 1965.

Pratley, Gerald. *The Cinema of John Huston.* South Brunswick, N.J.: A. S. Barnes, 1977.

Ross, Lillian. *Picture.* New York: Rinehart and Co., 1952.

Viertel, Peter. *White Hunter, Black Heart.* New York: Doubleday, 1953.

# Photo Credits

# Contributors

STEPHEN COOPER earned his Ph.D. at the University of Southern California, where he now teaches. His work has appeared in *Film Quarterly, American Film,* and numerous literary journals. Winner of a 1991 National Endowment for the Arts Fellowship for his fiction, Cooper is preparing *Toward a Theory of Adaptation: John Huston and the Interlocutive* for publication.

DAVID DESSER teaches film at the University of Illinois, Urbana-Champaign. He is the author of *The Samurai Films of Akira Kurosawa* and *Eros plus Massacre: An Introduction to the Japanese New Wave Cinema;* the coeditor of *Reframing Japanese Cinema: Authorship, Genre, History* and *Cinematic Landscapes: The Visual Arts and the Cinema in China and Japan;* and the coauthor of *American-Jewish Filmmakers: Traditions and Trends.*

GARY EDGERTON is the chairperson of the Communication Department at Goucher College in Baltimore. He has written extensively on aspects of the media and cultural history, theory, and criticism in a number of books and journals, including the *Journal of Popular Film and Television,* of which he is now senior associate editor. In 1990–1991 he was visiting professor of American and Commonwealth arts at the University of Exeter, United Kingdom.

JOHN ENGELL teaches American literature at San Jose State University. His essays have appeared in *Early American Literature, Walt Whitman Quarterly Review, Studies in American Fiction, South Atlantic Review,* and other journals. He has also published short stories, poems, and a play.

RUTH A. HOTTELL holds a Ph.D. from the University of Illinois at Urbana-Champaign in expanded French studies and is assistant professor of French at the University of Toledo. Her primary areas of research are feminist film and literary theory, French film, and *ecriture feminine.*

JAMES NAREMORE is professor of English and comparative literature and director of film studies at Indiana University. His writings on film include *The Filmguide to "Psycho," The Magic World of Orson Welles,* and *Acting in the Cinema.* He also edited the published screenplay of Huston's *The Treasure of the Sierra Madre.*

MARTIN RUBIN received his Ph.D. at Columbia University and has taught film studies at Wright State University, University of California at Santa Barbara, and SUNY College at Purchase. He has contributed articles to *Film Comment, Village Voice, Persistence of Vision,* and several anthologies. He is currently completing a book on Busby Berkeley.

ROBERT SKLAR is a professor of cinema at New York University. His most recent book is *City Boys: Cagney, Bogart, Garfield* (Princeton University Press, 1992). He is also author of *Movie-Made America: A Cultural History of American Movies* (1975), and *Prime-Time America: Life on and behind the Television Screen* (1980), among other books.

GAYLYN STUDLAR is associate professor of film studies at Emory University. The author of *In the Realm of Pleasure: Von Sternberg, Dietrich, and the Masochistic Aesthetic* (1988/1992 Morningside ed.), she has also published essays in numerous film journals and many anthologies, including *Film Theory and Criticism, Screening the Male, Movies and Methods II, Fabrications,* and *The Cult Film Experience.*

She is completing her latest book, a cultural study of male film stardom in post-World War I America.

VIRGINIA WRIGHT WEXMAN teaches film and cultural studies at the University of Illinois at Chicago. Her book *Creating the Couple: Love, Marriage, and Hollywood Performance* is forthcoming from Princeton University Press. She is president-elect of the Society for Cinema Studies and former editor of *Cinema Journal.*